To Chantal
With love *of*

FROM TY.   .ES
VIA 'THE USι   .ANNELS'

Love Ted *of* Ed

~~23/9/14~~
11/2/15

From Tyne to Thames Via 'The Usual Channels'

by

Lord Graham

The Memoir Club

© Lord Graham 2005

First Edition 2005
Reprinted 2010

The Memoir Club
Dartmoor Suite
Arya House
Langley Park
Durham
DH7 9XE

Tel: 0191 373 5660
Email: memoirclub@msn.com

British Library Cataloguing in
Publication Data.
A catalogue record for this book
is available from the
British Library

ISBN: 9781841041230

Typeset by TW Typesetting, Plymouth, Devon
Printed by The Amadeus Press, Ezra House, Cleckheaton, BD19 4TQ

This book is dedicated to all those members of the Labour Peers Group in the House of Lords who fought the good fight during the wilderness years of 1979–1997 – and helped to ensure the great Labour victory of 1997.

Contents

List of Illustrations

Preface
From Tyne to Thames via the usual channels

'WHAT SHOULD WE call you now that you are a member of the House of Lords?' I was often asked. I crack the old one that when the Garter King of Arms asked me almost the very same question ('My Lord, what should be your title?') I had replied that I would like to be called Lord Helpus, but had settled for Edmonton, the name of the constituency I had happily represented in the Commons. Locally everyone had called me Ted, so that had to be in the local title and for now more than 20 years I have answered to the title of Lord Ted of Ed.

Eldest of five children with Dad on the Means Test throughout the thirties, I had passed my eleven plus exam and finished at my elementary school as Top Boy; and started the romance with the Co-operative Movement in 1939, with the passion undimmed after 64 years.

War Service saw me join the Royal Marines, but whilst preparing for D Day in May 1944, I was badly wounded (in Wales) and saw no action.

The Workers Educational Association formed the Tyneside Youth Parliament in 1948, and I cut my debating teeth there while serving as the Prime Minister, before going on to a year at the Co-operative College to become qualified in Secretarial and Management skills. Always feeling 'that I had a degree in me' I eventually got through the Open University and in 1976 became the first – and today still the only – Member of Parliament to do so. I was later awarded the Honorary Degree of Master of the University.

Becoming a Councillor in Enfield in 1960 I went on to become Leader, and then to serve for a time as Leader of the new London Borough of Enfield when it was created in 1964. During this time I fought my first Parliamentary Election – against Iain Macleod in Enfield West, and in 1974 entered the Commons as Member for Edmonton. At that time I was the National Secretary of The Co-operative Party.

I served as the Private Parliamentary Secretary to Alan Williams, the Minister for Consumer Affairs in the department headed up by Shirley Williams, and when Jim Callaghan became Prime Minister he put me in the Government Whips Office where I served as a Lords Commissioner to The Treasury (Senior Whip).

Losing my seat in 1983 Michael Foot sent me to the Lords and straight into the Whips Office there. All told when I came out of that office in 1997 I had served in Labour Whips Offices for more than 20 years, seven of them as Opposition Chief Whip in the Lords from 1990 to 1997. It is during that period that much of what follows is based.

'The Usual Channels' is the euphemism given to describe the way in which business is done by the Party Whips Offices. Without going into detail, it will be said on the Floor of both Houses that a particularly knotty problem 'will be dealt with via the usual channels' meaning that the Chief Whip of the Government will initiate discussions with his counterparts and present their solution to the Leaders – and the House – for action. It is rare that this device fails to come up with an answer to a potential problem. Whilst the Chief Whips carry into the discussions their view on an ultimate solution, the Private Secretary to the Government Chief Whip (also known as the Business Manager) will play a crucial role, especially when progress of legislation is the subject under dispute. Appropriate Ministers and their Opposition numbers will also become involved. The idea is that instead of issues becoming a scrappy knock down and drag-out manner of resolving matters, compromise is reached 'via the usual channels' where frank speaking can take place, positions are changed, but at the end of the day agreement is reached and honour satisfied in a civilized manner.

Absolute trust in any agreement reached is always taken as read. Even when the advice from the 'usual channels' brings dismay to one side or the other, it is almost always accepted by the House. Not that it is automatic. There have been cases where the advice is rejected and overturned – but only rarely.

It has to be appreciated that business cannot proceed without those agreements, for if there is insistence – mainly from the Government Chief Whip – for a certain course – unless it is accepted it will be brought onto the Floor of the House, and thus publicly revealed that the 'usual channels' are not working. That very rarely happens.

The most serious charge that can be made is that of cheating, or reneging on an agreement. All know that it is the duty of the Opposition Chief Whip to inflict defeats on the Government as often as can be delivered but always 'within the rules'. The Government Chief Whip must – in the absence of any prior agreement – keep his guard up and be prepared for 'an ambush' or 'a secret vote'. A late night roster to ensure that a snap vote to 'count the House out' is not successful is part of the standard equipment for Government Chief Whips, but it is the art of the Opposition to wrong-foot the Government, and call votes at unexpected times and not always on the most obvious of issues.

There may be some who take the view that such behaviour is childish or petty. To some this may be so, but when there are men and women who have dedicated their lives to a cause, it is legitimate to fight and frustrate. A judicious mix of faith and guile allied to a pinch of opportunism brought the 'old soldiers' pictured in this book more than one unexpected victory. They may not have changed the world – but it was fun!

Acknowledgements

Inspirations

'WHY WRITE A BOOK' I hear the cry. 'Why not?' I reply. Why not indeed, and so here goes. In part it is to set out the record – not that it is not straight, but for my own satisfaction. At some point in one's life there begins to grow a feeling that you have reached the stage you have due to the way in which others have been kind, or considerate, and this needs to be recorded. For my part, the initial inspiration to put pen to paper came about in a conversation I had with my boyhood friend Ted Grey and his wife Irene. 'What are you doing to fill your busy life?' I enquired of Ted in 2001. 'I'm writing a sort of life story – not for me, or my children, but largely for my grandchildren. I was born in the 1920s in a Newcastle-on-Tyne long since gone. It isn't easy for my children to relate to it all, but it is almost impossible for my grandchildren to understand what "born in the twenties and living on Tyneside" means, and so I am setting it down and, in a very limited edition, I will present them with "My Life".'

That set me thinking. Thinking of the episodes which make up my life, and those who have played a part in it. I rue the fact that I have never kept diaries and have relied on memory or the printed word (Hansards do come in useful!). It will be far from a complete account, either of incidents or of personalities, but it tries to reflect the journey from my Newcastle of the twenties to the House of Lords, a journey I could not have undertaken without much, much help – and inspiration.

My co-operative friends

That I have retained into the present day my unofficial title of 'Mr Co-op' wherever I go is due to the support and comradeship of many, beginning with my Youth Club days. Laurie Pavitt (later to become a Member of Parliament); Harold Campbell whom I succeeded as the National Secretary of the Co-operative Party; Johnny Jacques, a former miner who achieved high status as a Retailer and came to the Lords and served with distinction; Robert Leckie Marshall who served as the Principal of the Co-operative College at Stanford Hall, Loughborough and who trained and inspired generations who served the Co-operative ethos here and abroad; Dennis Landau and his successor as Chief Officer of the Co-operative Wholesale

Society, Sir Graham Melmoth, who were always supportive; Dame Pauline Green who is the Chief Officer of Co-operatives UK, formerly Leader of the Socialist Group in the European Parliament; David Dickman, a senior Official at the Co-operative Bank and who led the United Kingdom Co-operative Council with verve and drive when I was Chair; Max Wood, Bernard Rhodes, John Gallacher and John Tilley who were the voice of the Co-op in Whitehall whilst mine was heard elsewhere, and back to Joan Straker, who, as a 15-year-old took me on at the age of 14 – when my Co-operative life began in 1939. She has been my friend to this day.

My political friends

I was inspired in part to write this book arising from my time as the Opposition Chief Whip in the Lords. There I worked with men and women who at some time had been heroes or heroines of mine, had given great service to the nation and the Party and yet, some into their nineties, were not prepared to lie down – yet. Many are mentioned later, such as James Callaghan, Ernest Shackleton, Barbara Castle, Harold Wilson, Douglas Houghton, Arthur Bottomley, Frank Longford, Pat Llewelyn-Davies, John Mackie, Nora David, Bea Serota, Myer Galpern, Charlie Leatherland, Eirene White. These illustrate one of the themes of this book – with the option of 'retiring' onto the red leather benches of the Lords, they all chose to try to fulfil their life's work – to work for the return of a Labour Government.

I owe a debt to Ivor Richard who was Leader of the Labour Peers Group whilst I was the Chief Whip. His wide experience in international affairs, his legal training and his shrewd and deft political touch was comforting to us all – but especially to me.

I served in the Government and Opposition Whips Offices in the Commons, and the Opposition Whips Office in the Lords. If I had served in the Government Whips Office in the Lords I would have had that rare achievement of serving in all four Offices. I owe a debt to many fellow Whips, too numerous to mention, but I humbly do so now. In all places and at all levels I enjoyed the camaraderie of being at the centre of events and helping to shape them. It was both a privilege and a pleasure – and hard work!

Supporters – I've had a few

There are those who have rendered great service to me while they got on with their work and I with mine. Damien Welfare has played a part in shaping this book, using his long experience in Local Government first at the GLC and latterly as a special adviser to Ivor Richard. Mathew Evans used his knowledge of the book trade to give me valuable advice. My principal secretaries in the Lords and friends over the past twenty years have been Shirley Sheppard, Marieanne Morris and Ryma Howard. All played a major part in putting this book into some shape and I am grateful to them – and others. For the help given me by my Research team in Opposition; Robert, Elizabeth, Clare, Victoria and Christine I say 'thank you' – and also to the brilliant team of researchers in the House of Lords Library. Thank you all. To all at The Memoir Club – especially my editor Sheila Seacroft, a big 'thank you'.

Finally – my family

If life on Tyneside in the twenties and thirties was tough, it was made less so by the love given to all of their five children by my Mam and Dad. They had precious few worldly goods, but we all got a share. Lastly, to my wife Margaret and my sons Martin and Ian I would say that I could not have lived the life I have without neglecting them more than I should have. I ask forgiveness. 'Regrets? I've had a few', but for me the words of Hilaire Belloc say it all:

> From quiet homes and small beginnings,
> Out to the undiscovered ends,
> There's nothing worth the wear of winning,
> But laughter and the love of friends.

I'll drink to that.

Introduction

THE WRITER and Labour peer, Ted Willis, was fond of recalling how someone had described the House of Lords as 'God's Waiting Room' and those who visited can be excused if they came away with the impression that many of those sitting on the Red Benches were indeed waiting for something to happen. In fact, now we know that appearances can be deceptive, for this is the story of a band of brothers – and sisters – who had no right to expect to be able to shake the Thatcher and Major Governments to its foundations – but did just that.

When the Liberal Government at the beginning of the last century challenged the Tory Government of the day with the election slogan – Who Governs Britain? – it achieved a ground breaking shift in the distribution of power between the Commons and the Lords. The Lords, then even more dominated by a Tory majority than it was in the eighties and nineties, backed away from that challenge in the sure knowledge that if the issue was to be decided by the people it would have effectively finished the powers of the Lords. Their motto was 'He who runs away lives to fight another day'. But although it was stripped of most initiatives and of powers what it then had left to compete effectively with the Commons was the power to delay. Thanks to the huge inbuilt hereditary system it remained a stumbling block to progress and a satrap for the Conservatives, especially when Labour was in power. The record shows that the number of defeats for a Labour Government in the Lords was infinitely greater than when it was a Conservative Government. (See P.Q. 14/7 2002)

Although defeats for a Government in the Lords can almost always be reversed when the amendments come to the Commons, the cost of doing so is to use up that most precious of parliamentary commodities – time. At the best of times a government struggles to complete its legislative programme in October/November when numerous Bills have to complete their passage between both Houses.

The evidence shows that the Labour Governments of Attlee, Wilson and Callaghan all suffered from this. Once Labour lost power in 1979 there was a clear determination to address this constitutional issue when next power was achieved.

This came in 1997 when the current changes were begun. In the meanwhile the Labour Peers Group which was meeting at the beginning of the Eighties had to take stock of the situation. Although the political realities were well understood, (a Labour total of little more than 100 in a House of more than 1000) it soon became clear that the situation was there for the exploiting. Many of the Labour Peers had come from the Commons and were experienced in parliamentary warfare. The impact of the Life Peerages Act of 1958 was creating opportunities for Labour Leaders to put into the Lords those without ostensible political experience but who brought to it their organizing, plotting and manoeuvring. They were game for it.

The size of the task was not underestimated. Nor was the skill of the Government Chief Whip, the redoubtable Lord Bertie Denham. When he retired in 1992 he had served in the Conservative Whips Office for more than 30 years in Government and in Opposition. Yet subsequent to the repeated defeats for his Government it is said that after each defeat, and on Mrs Thatcher hearing the news on the *Today* programme, he was resigned to receiving the expected call from No 10 for an explanation.

The period of the Conservative Government from 1979 to 1997, whilst bleak for Labour in the House of Commons, saw many a shaft of light for it from the House of Lords.

For with little or no prospect of victories in the Commons it became commonplace for Labour Peers (with a little assistance from their friends) to inflict defeats in the Lords, which were great morale boosters not only there but also for Labour supporters in the country. Once the technique for staging a successful 'ambush' had been perfected – and there were many – elderly Labour Peers into their nineties would cheerfully stay long past their bedtime in the almost certain knowledge that they were making the best contributions to the cause – inflicting injury on the enemy.

It was the same band of brothers and sisters who were there to welcome long needed reinforcements in the shape of new Labour Peers who joined them after 1997. Newcomers however could not experience the thrill and satisfaction of 'the ambush', for with their combined strength Tory and Liberal Democrat Peers could defeat the Labour Government by staging their votes at a sensible time, up to 7.00 p.m., in the certain knowledge that they would win. The place of the Crossbench Peers during this period is examined too, for whilst on the whole there was a tendency for their majority to support the Government of the day, the support of a handful who could – and were – persuaded to wait until late and vote with the Labour Peers helped at times to make the difference.

This is also the story of one of those Labour Peers who was born and bred in the heart of working class Newcastle on Tyne in the twenties and who rose to play a crucial part in the organizing of the victories which so delighted the Labour Movement.

As I once put it 'The pleasure on the faces of Labour giants who had rendered great service to the State as I carried the wand of victory to the Woolsack was enough for me. It meant that a lifetime of working for that Labour victory which came in 1997 was coming about before my very eyes'.

But above all else this is a story dedicated to ordinary men and women who found themselves in a place and in a position most of them had dreamed they would one day fill, and which they did with pride, humility and joy.

PART I

Early Days and Life Before Westminster

CHAPTER 1

Early days

YEARS LATER, when I was made a freeman of the Worshipful Company of Butchers, I could tell my fellow Freemen that I had known of the meat trade all my life. On my birth certificate the profession of my father is stated as 'Meat Porter'. It may be easy to summon up a picture. In the 1930s of my childhood much meat was imported from Australia, New Zealand – and Argentina. It came into the Tyne and was transported up and onto the meat warehouses and salerooms in Marlborough Crescent, which is 100 yards from Central Station, at the beginning of Scotswood Road and at the foot of Westmorland Road – and opposite the cattle market. When it reached its destination, 'humpers' – like my Dad – would carry it off the lorry and place it on the huge scales. By knowing exactly where it should rest on his shoulder he would walk to the scales and, with a shrug, would deposit the side of beef onto the weighing hook. When the meat was bought by the retailers he would then carry it from the shop and heave it into the retailer's lorry. That job done, he would be told by the owner that he would see him in the nearby pub, and there he would receive his 'tip' – not in money, but in free pints. Thus my Dad, and others, were never short of a pint – but were always short of cash. That's the way it was.

The firms I could recite to my audience of 60 years later were Swift, Sansinena, Tweddle, Wilson and Armour. They were the giants of that industry, but the work was hard and relatively unrewarding. Dad worked from 5.00 a.m. to noon five days a week for just under £2.00 a week. When he later stopped working and went on the dole, his wage was just a little more than the dole. I can recall that with five children and with himself, and my mother, he received thirty-seven shillings a week to feed, clothe and care for the seven of us. However, there was a camaraderie amongst those who had worked in Marlborough Crescent. One of my regular visits to butchers such as R.A. Dodds in the Grainger Market was to do as my Dad had told me – 'Ask for Cyril and tell him you are Tommy's boy and could he give you a parcel'. Dad's pals always did. The parcel would invariably consist of a sheep's head, a rabbit, some sausages and some chops or a small joint. A feast fit for a king! Mam would use them all with great economy. The sheep's head would make broth, rich in vegetables and rather light (for us children) on meat. Dad always had the brains, Mam the tongue and then we would have the jawbones and the like. I have happy

3

memories of sitting around the table – all seven of us. With a loaf of bread to soak it up we went to bed that night (usually Mondays) with a full belly and a contented smile on our faces. Happy days!

One of my pleasures was to visit the cattle market (again, on a Monday) and see the drovers drive their cattle in, stand them in the pens and watch the auctioneer sell them, and then follow them into the slaughterhouse – in those days open and inviting. Seeing pigs slaughtered and hauled into a vat of boiling water never put me off liking pork!

Whenever people ask me where I come from I say Newcastle, and when they press – and even when they don't – I go on to say that I come from Scotswood Road. It is an area of Newcastle that is well-known, not least because it figures prominently in the Tyneside Anthem, 'The Blaydon Races'. Blaydon is at the end of the Scotswood Road, and the Scotswood itself is that main road out of Newcastle. My memories of it are from the 1930s and it was a bustling place and always 'busy'. With the river Tyne down on its left as you travel from the Central Station, and the streets leading up to Benwell, thence up to Westgate Road and finally up to the West Road and out to places like Denton Burn, Throckley, Walbottle and on to Corbridge and Hexham, you would soon be on the Military Road originally built by the Romans, and along which Hadrian built his Wall to keep out the marauding Scots.

Because there were no cars on the roads, the trams were in full flow before we entered the age of the trolley bus in the 1930s. From wherever you flowed you gravitated down to 'the town', the centre of Newcastle. Here the main streets became known to you, that is, if you wanted to roam around, as I did. Northumberland Street was the mecca for me and those I hung around with. It was in Northumberland Street that Marks & Spencer and Woolworth dominated the shopping scene, but the department store, Fenwicks, gave them both a run for their money, with Littlewoods close too. One of the ways in which you came to know your town was to remember the landmarks. In some places the map was marked by knowing where the churches were, and I knew that too. Then, in other places, it was known by the pubs. I have been told that there was a pub on every corner along Scotswood Road, just as I was later to be told that there was a Co-op shop on every corner. I learned that that was not strictly true, and the same applied to the pubs, but it was mostly true. Along in what became known as Cruddas Park there was a pub called 'The Gun', for it was opposite the entrance to the great armaments factory simply called 'Armstrongs'. It was one of, if not the greatest, suppliers of jobs in Newcastle although of course those other great industries of shipbuilding and engineering ran it close. It was in 'The Gun' that I came across a souvenir of my childhood years later.

The Newcastle Chronicle *cartoon.*
By kind permission of the Newcastle Evening Chronicle

I attended a school called 'Cambridge Street' at the bottom of Rye Hill, notable for the fact that the playground was on top of the school – land was in short supply in those days! It was at Cambridge Street that I played in goal for the school team, and we must have been passable because in my year we won our league. At that time the *Newcastle Chronicle* had a cartoonist called 'Bos' and each week it published a cartoon of a successful football team. In time he drew our cartoons, but to see them you had to buy the paper. Years later I popped into 'The Gun' and there on the wall was the cartoon framed and in pride of place. Years later, too, I obtained a copy of the cartoon and it hangs in my home as a reminder of my athletic success!

'The Gun' was managed by Seaman Tommy Watson, a native of Newcastle who had fought for the world lightweight boxing title, and had lost on points. Another boxing connection came from my school football days, for our centre-forward who scored most of our goals was 'Ikey' Moses, who was the younger brother of Mickey Maguire who fought Kid Chocolate for his world crown, only to be beaten on points. Even though I was still a schoolboy, I loved to force my way into St James's Hall, the Newcastle Boxing Hall, which stood opposite St James's Park, the hallowed ground of 'The Magpies' – but more of that later. My time of being a devotee of boxing stretched over the war period. Then I saw Nel Tarleton, Tom Smith, Stan Hawthorn, and Billy Thompson amongst others. I was later, by extraordinary coincidences, to see other world famous boxers in action. When I was hospitalized during the war (more later) I saw the legendary Freddie Mills fight Jack London for the British Heavyweight title at Belle Vue, Manchester in September 1944. Although not given much of a chance, Jack London won. He defended his title against the then impressive Bruce Woodcock on the Spurs ground at White Hart Lane, Tottenham in July 1946 and, by chance, I managed to miss my train down to Devon, where I was stationed, and thus attended that fight – which Bruce won by knocking Jack out.

Bethnal Green and York Hall, London, provided me with the opportunity to see Tommy Farr and Eric Boon – both nearing the end of their careers and making something of a comeback, and both heroes of mine from days of yore. Again, by a fluke, when I was in hospital near Warrington I managed to notice that both Joe Louis, the World Heavyweight Champion, and Billy Conn, who had given him what was up to then one of the hardest fights in his career, were giving a boxing exhibition in the Parr Hall in Warrington. They were doing this for the American troops who were stationed at the nearby huge camp at Burtonwood. It was during this period – 1944–45 – that I managed to get to see two other boxing legends in The Stadium, Liverpool – Peter Kane and Ronnie Clayton – all this before I was 21!

My final boxing story comes a lot later. While I was a member of the House of Lords I helped BECTU, the union led by Alan Sapper, and one day I attended their Annual Meeting in Congress House, and thence on to lunch at a nearby hotel. During the meal the chap sitting next to me said to a person across the table 'I will let you have a copy of my book on my father's life story when it is published'. Curious as to who I was sitting next to, and who was to write the life story of his father, I glanced at his name card to find that it was said 'Monty Lewis'. 'I am pleased to meet you,' I said, and he glanced at my card and said, 'One of my best friends is a member of the Lords and his name is Ted Willis'. I told him he was a great friend of mine (coming from nearby Tottenham) and then he told me that his father was Kid Lewis! He had at one time held three world titles simultaneously, and was a boxing legend. He later sent me a copy of his book. Fabulous!

Life along the Scotswood Road

My grandparents lived in George Street, which runs down from Westmorland Road to Scotswood Road. In and around here is my first memory of 'community', a feeling of belonging and feeling that this is my patch. Dad and Mam had come to No 49 and had a room to themselves when they were married, a usual way in which to begin married life. Wide cobbled streets were the order of the day and, with relatively few cars, the streets became the playground. I often think, as I discover an area and note the names of adjacent streets, what it was that influenced their naming. Around and from George Street I remember there was Duke Street, Blenheim Street, Churchill Street, Blandford Street – and I have a good guess that the streets were built in the early nineteenth century. It was at the top of Churchill Street that the Salvation Army reigned supreme, and from there that their evangelists sallied forth and sang their songs on every street corner – with me and my mates following them and joining in.

It was in the basement of the Salvation Army Hall that soup was served on a Thursday lunchtime. It was a soup kitchen in every sense. My recollection was that no money was asked for and so, out of school and home to collect a manageable jug, we would charge and push and shove until we eventually collected our share from a great vat of very nourishing broth!

Later a broken jug comes to my mind. When we lived in the Suttons Dwellings my job was to race home and collect a jug and get to the Pease Pudding shop on Stanhope Street and get it full – for threepence. But if the crowd there was huge, I had a sixpence in my pocket so that I could go to the fish shop on the corner for sixpennyworth of chips. Unfortunately one day I was climbing over the railings around Sutton Dwellings and smashed the jug. Going home with chips but without the jug earned me more than a ticking off!

Moving away from Scotswood Road 'up the Hill' to pastures greener was fine, but the shopping habits of Mam meant that every Friday evening I was sent back down to Scotswood Road for shopping. Coming up Rye Hill, I was accosted by two boys who demanded my bag of shopping. I had with me my sister, Alma, and brother Ken. Of course, I refused, whereupon a boy called Bincliffe pulled out a knife and stabbed me within a fraction of my left eye. I certainly could have been blinded – or worse. Fortunately, there was a doctor's surgery within yards whose doctor clipped together my injury. Mam was paying him at the rate of threepence a week for a long time after.

Another couple sharing the haven of 49 George Street was my Auntie Ginnie and my Uncle Syd. He was Jewish, and they were devotees of health and beauty. They had two daughters, Miriam and Hazel, whom I rarely met, but I knew about. Miriam married Tom Stoppard, and Hazel married Preston King, a philosopher from Georgia, USA. Their daughter was called Oona, and went on to become Oona King – the Member of Parliament for Tower Hamlets! More on this theme later.

Here are some indications of the general level of life in the Graham household in the years before I left school at the age of 14. Dad was on the 'Means Test' which I understood to mean that after unemployment entitlement had run out, you were then in receipt of benefit, but only after 'your means' had been subject to stringent tests and searching inquiries. If life was hard, I did not feel it, for Dad was a great provider and Mam was a genius at making the best out of what Dad brought home. In the thirties I can remember going to a local bakery with the bread Mam had made in tins on a tray. All the boys were doing the same thing. We would hand the tray to the baker and come back two hours later, give him 2d and we had bread freshly baked. Bread figured largely in the diet of families in the Sutton Dwellings.

Monday morning saw me get to the front of the queue at Poritts the Pawnshop to pawn my Dad's one and only suit. Friday would have seen me 'retrieve' it – the 'pledge' going in was usually worth seven and sixpence, and getting it was 8 shillings. Sometimes the pawnbroker would give me less than Mam had asked me for – and that shortfall of a shilling would be felt in the Graham household that week! Sunday morning would see scores of boys and girls trooping into the Congregational Church in Bath Lane. We sang our hearts out – for we knew that when the service was finished we would be given a potted meat sandwich and a cup of cocoa. When I served in the Royal Marines years later, and was asked what denomination I was, I told them that I was a Congregationalist. They were impressed!

Geordie Bowman ran a Mission in Prudhoe Street to which we would go on a Thursday evening. For attendance you were given a numbered small card and, if you had the requisite number, you were entitled to a trip to the coast in the summer, and a place at the table for the Christmas Party. You may think that our devotions were being bought and, if they were, and it made your belly full in the process, it was a good thing!

One day, when I was about 10, a policeman came in, to the classroom at Todds Nook School. He whispered to the teacher, who then called out 'Alfie, Billy, Teddy, Charlie and George – go out with the policeman'. We were all scared stiff – what on earth had we done – or been found out doing? When we went out, the policeman stood by a large wicker basket, and brought out pairs of boots and tossed them to us. 'Try these on for size,' he said. All of us had on what were called 'sandshoes', but others would call plimsoles. I raced home with my prize and told my Dad and Mam that I had been given them by a policeman. I was questioned closely, given more than one smack, and told to take them back. After convincing them of the truth, my Mam cried. Years later I asked her why she had cried, and she told me that the teacher must have singled out the poorest boys in the class, and she felt ashamed that her son was one of them.

It was then that I felt the stirring of a political anger which has never left me.

Educational yearnings

I have always supported education, not only as the way out of conditions such as I experienced on Tyneside, but also for its own true value to the individual. All this made sense for me, rather late in the day, but when it did it brought to me a great sense of achievement which will never leave me.

In 1976 I was awarded the degree of Batchelor of Arts by the Open University. BA! Letters after my name! By then I had already got some 'letters after my name'. Fellow of the Royal Society of Arts (FRSA); Fellow of the British Institute of Management (FBIM); Co-operative Secretaries Diploma (later with Management Endorsement – CSD and CMD). Of course, MP and, subsequently, letters before my name when I was made a Member of Her Majesty's Privy Council (Rt Hon).

I had spent nine months at Stanford Hall, the Co-operative College, in 1949–50. Then there were hundreds of thousands of returning ex-servicemen and women who had been deprived of their further education. Although I could have been counted in that category, I had started on 'catching up' by myself. In 1935 I took my 11 plus examination, and passed. I rushed home with the piece of paper that the teacher had given me, and shouted to Mam and Dad that I had passed my exam, which was to get a place at Secondary School – I was then at an Elementary School. Twas not to be. Dad smiled and Mam cried. We were 'on the dole', and to find the money, not only for books but for uniform and other expenses, were beyond them. But I must have yearned for a place, because two years later, there came the chance to sit an exam to go to a technical school – at Atkinson Road Tech. I passed that too, but again could not go.

I finished my formal education at Westgate Road School within a month of my fourteenth birthday. This is what J.L. McAndrew, my teacher, wrote on my leaving testimonial:

> Edward Graham is a thoroughly reliable lad and I can, with confidence, recommend him to any employer. He is well above the average: he is honest and truthful and is willing and obliging. For the past year he has been in the position as Head Monitor of the School, and he has always been trustworthy. He is too good a boy to go into a casual or blind-alley job.

Clutching a green card from the Employment Exchange I was given a slip to go to Templetons, the carpet manufacturers, in Eldon Square for a job as a warehouse boy at ten shillings a week. After six weeks my Mam told me that I was to go for an exam to be an errand boy with the Co-op – or 'Stores' as it was called in Newcastle. I always did what my Mam told me. In June 1939 there were more than 100 boys taking that exam. I was one of about a dozen who were chosen. The fact that to this day I am still working for the Co-op clearly indicates that I eventually started in what was not a blind-alley occupation! I took my first exam in further education studies and did not finish until more than 35 years later! – in all, more than 30 certificates and diplomas of one kind or another. Great! Whatever bug bit me, it has never left me to this day.

The Open University has been called 'The University of the Second Chance', and it has certainly been for me. In 1976 I completed my studies, and when I was interviewed after the press conference, at which they had invited a docker, a taxi driver, a nurse, a professional footballer and an eighty year old lady – and me – I was asked how I studied. 'Victoria Line' I replied, and this was true. When I had enrolled in the second year in the life of the University in 1972, I had to travel from my home in Enfield to Buckingham Palace Road, near Victoria Station. Thus I had almost an hour travelling each way. Whilst others read newspapers or books, gossiped or slept, I got out my study outlines and did rough reading, marking passages, highlighting bits and pieces, ready for the serious work at the weekend. When I had to make journeys to Glasgow or Edinburgh, I would opt for the train journey rather than the plane, because it afforded me hours to read OU work. When I went on holiday I took 'recommended reading' rather than novels. Once the OU gets under your skin, it never lets go! It was absorbing as well as rewarding. It opened up vistas not previously seen. When, in 1976, I completed the course, I was then the only Member of Parliament to do so whilst being a sitting Member and now, 30 years later, I am still the only Member of Parliament to have completed the course whilst being a Member of Parliament. Others have come in with a degree, and many have left Westminster and gone on to earn a degree, but not whilst sitting as a Member! Being a backbencher in Government means that you are prevailed upon to keep your mouth shut, but be there for the vote. As the votes often did not come until the small hours, there was time to study. I have always felt that I had a degree in me – and so it proved!!

Michael Foot gave me a place on the University Council as a Government representative and, after three years, this was renewed by Willie Whitelaw. I became an unofficial cheer-leader for the OU in the House of Lords and absorbed all that I could about it. Harold Wilson once told me that if he had to be remembered for one act whilst being Prime Minister, he would have no hesitation in saying that it was the creation of the Open University. One of my great joys later, when I went to the Lords and served in the Whips Office, was to find that I had amongst my flock Jennie Lee, who was the Minister for Arts and credited with 'starting it', and with Ted Short, who had been the Minister for Education when it was created in the late sixties. And I was to make great friends with Walter Perry, the University Vice-Chancellor. All glory to OU! 'Open as to People', 'Open as to Places', 'Open as to Ideas', 'Open as to Methods'. Now the largest university in the United Kingdom, since 1971 more than 2 million people have studied there and, currently, its student population accounts for 25 per cent of all part-time higher education students in the UK. Last year 8000 people with disability were students with the university. In 1990 I was awarded the Honorary Degree of Master of the University (MA) and did it alongside Melvyn Bragg, who received a doctorate. Magic! We met again later in the Lords!

Melvyn Bragg receiving Honorary Doctorate from the Open University when Ted received his Honorary Masters Degree.

CHAPTER 2

All roads lead to Newgate Street

STARTING WORKING LIFE in 1939 for the Newcastle-on-Tyne Co-operative Society – and still working for the Co-op some 65 years later – must say something of what that start meant to me. It meant everything. Not only was I a 14-year-old boy in need of comfort and guidance, but I needed a star to guide by. That star turned out to be 'Co-operation', and when I look back I can see that I have made my way in the world due in no small measure to the solid start I received when I had the good fortune to become an errand-boy in the Greengrocery department of 'The Stores'. Darnell Street, Benwell High Cross and finally, North Elswick (all now gone) were the branches in which I served before landing my job in the General Office. I had already survived as one of a dozen for that job of errand boy in April, 1939 – out of a roomful of other hopefuls numbering more than 100!

It being the way things were, two years later, at the age of 16 you then were made redundant, unless you were successful in being 'taken on' as a Junior. There were but four vacancies in the General Office, and, after competitive examination, I got one of them. Wartime conditions may not have been the best in which to start, but it was a happy atmosphere, save that from time to time colleagues were called up for Service, and my turn came in 1943 on my eighteenth birthday. That was not before I had served The Co-op by doing fire-fighting duties in both North Elswick (it was on Westgate Rd and Hartington Steet – and as I lived at 41 I had had experience, for incendiary bombs dropped on 41 and I had to carry one of them out with a shovel and a bucket of sand!) I regularly did firefighting duty at the Co-op Warehouse opposite Manors Station in New Bridge Street. Getting up onto the roof to watch the night action was a thrill – but also potentially dangerous, for I witnessed the demolition of the Apollo cinema in Byker but a few hundred yards away!

This was the time of The Home Guard and I joined what was officially called the Local Defence Volunteers LDV – for Look – Duck – and Vanish! We were fortunate in having the Manager of the Central Menswear Department, Bill Richardson, to hand. He had been a Captain in the Great War, and was the Commanding Officer of the Newcastle Co-op Home Guard. I was proud to be a member one of many 17-year-olds serving with veterans of the Great War.

The family, pictured at my sister Alma's wedding to Ken, flanked on the left by Ken's parents, on the right by Mum and Dad. Back row: my brothers Rob and Dick, Joan (Ken's sister), myself, brother Ken

All my contemporaries in the General Office went to serve. Jimmy Charlton, Syd Ainsley, Joe Grey, George Henderson, Stan Woodmass, Jack Moffat, Billy Waton. In that time we were 'mothered' by a great band of girls who looked after us, saw us off, kept in touch and welcomed us back. It was then that I began to appreciate just what 'comradeship' was – and what being a Co-op Employee meant. Whenever we came home on leave we would seek out Roland Yates and he gave us a few pounds from the benevolent fund. Knowing you were part of a family meant at lot in those days!

I comment on my war service elsewhere – and on the start of my political activities – yet when I returned from service in the Royal Marines in 1946 I was glad to have my old job back. I knew that one day I would 'fly the nest' but when where or how was unknown. I got stuck into my studies, and as I worked as a clerical worker, it was into evening classes at Cambridge Street School and in correspondence courses that led me to a period of bliss – a nine months course in Secretarial studies at the Co-operative Movement's very own College – Stanford Hall, near Loughborough. I talk about that elsewhere, but it was thanks to a scholarship from the Newcastle Society

Student days at the Co-operative College. Myself 2nd from right, back row

which paid my wages that enabled me to go – and go on to higher things. You do not forget such generosity in a hurry!

I attended my first ever Co-operative Congress as a delegate representing the Society Employees in 1949 when it was held in Scarborough. I made my first 'Address to Congress' there, and some forty years later I was proud to have been elected to the highest honour bestowed by the Co-operative Movement – as the President of the 1987 Congress held in Harrogate – with the Halle Orchestra and Nigel Kennedy as the Sunday night Concert! Along the way I had worked for the Cooperative Movement in one post or another, mainly in the south. Having married Margaret in 1950 she came north to live but it was not too long before I realized that life in the south had its attractions! When I left Tyneside in 1952 it was a wrench, for my family were there and my many friends, especially in Newgate Street, the main premises of the Society. On Tyneside in those days, if you said to almost anyone that you worked at Newgate Street they knew that you meant the Central Premises. Established in 1861 as most Co-ops were, through the sheer poverty and unfairness of the world around them, working people saw their salvation in starting and running their own shop. By the turn of the century 'The Stores' was not only established, it was powerful and successful. 'The Board' of Management – the Directors – were elected by the members and although they may not have had the education nor the business skills of their competitors, they had something the business men did not have – dedication, idealism and determination to make their Society the vehicle for bringing about that change in Society that they would not be able to do by themselves. 'One for All and All for Each' stood them in good stead.

The unique tool that was fashioned by the Rochdale Pioneers – the fore-runner of most successful Co-ops – was the distribution of profits made in proportion not to the Shares held, but to the purchases made – the Dividend. Merging with 30 other Societies in 1969 to form the North-Eastern Co-op Society it has served the population of Tyneside and beyond for almost 150 years.

I owe a debt to it that I can never repay. In my Congress Address I paid tribute to those serving now and then for all it meant to me. I hope they are as proud of me as I am of them.

Dividend day at the Newcastle Co-Op

Long before I began to work at the Newcastle Co-operative Society in 1939 I was no stranger to a Tyneside ritual – Divi Day. At the time I was but dimly aware of the significance of it nor, indeed, of other aspects of the Co-op. In Newcastle a Co-operative Society had been formed in 1861 and over the years, by amalgamation, had grown into a substantial economic force. The headquarters was in Newgate Street and the departmental store, built in the 1930s, was an outstanding building, and protected. In those days, it seems there was a Co-op shop on every corner and 'The Stores' were into everything. Not only groceries, but all provisions – coal, clothing; household goods – and it paid a divi! Contrary to popular belief, that dividend could be calculated in advance, for the Newcastle Co-op was known as a 'two bob Co-op'. Prices were set so that after expenses had been met etc the dividend, when announced at the end of each quarter, was 'two shillings in the pound'. For my Mam and thousands of others, this anticipated return was the main way in which they saved, both for a rainy day and for other things.

I would participate in the quarterly payout. Mam would fight her way, with me by her side, up and along the second floor corridor and into the General Office where she would first of all exchange her purchasing record and collect her dividend book into which there had been recorded the exact amount of dividend due. Then she would stand before a 'Teller' and draw from her book what she wanted. The Co-op Passbook was the main savings for the working class families of Tyneside for, besides drawing out what she wanted, she left in what she could afford, and this accretion of undrawn dividend was for the 'rainy day'. It was also the way in which most Societies could have access to cheap capital for, whilst it earned a modest rate of interest, its use by the Society gave it access to capital for expansion at a lower rate than had to be paid if borrowing from banks.

Each day for a six or seven day period 10,000 members were told to be 'in line' and would shuffle patiently to the front of the queue. Once in possession of their cash, Mam and I and hundreds of others would dive into the Aladdin's Cave that the Departmental store was. New shoes, new towels, curtains, pots and pans, cups and saucers, they were all bought with the Divi.

'The Board' of the Co-op were held in the highest esteem – and awe. Elections for 'The Board' were fiercely contested, and forces at work could be the Guilds, men, women's or mixed and employees, both internal and of the CWS, for Newcastle was a depot with salerooms, printing works, the bank etc. To be a member of 'The Board' was far more prestigious than being on the City Council. Fees were infinitesimal – the aphrodisiac was power! And prestige! Quarterly meetings in the City Hall were always full, and if the dividend was cut or the General Manager was sacked or under a cloud, you could expect a full house. The City Hall held 2000!

Years later I was the 'Teller' who stood behind the counter and paid out the divi. That period – Dividend Week – was always a hectic period and we had to work very quickly. There was a sort of rivalry amongst us Tellers as to who could pay out the most in any one day, but we also had to be careful. The amounts we paid out had to be entered on a running total sheet, and at the end of the day what we paid out had to balance with the amount we received from the Chief Cashier. If it did not, then we began to sweat, for any shorts had to be reported, approved and, if there were too many, then a black mark was entered on your record.

In the middle of a very busy period a man thrust a Passbook across the counter and said 'Can I get anything from this book?' I looked up, and froze. There in front of me was not only *my* idol, but the idol of Tyneside and beyond. It was Jackie Milburn, the brilliant Newcastle United footballer, who was at the height of his powers. It was either 1948 or 49. All the other Tellers were staring at me. I looked at the Passbook and noted that it was in the name of his wife. I told him that I could not pay him out, but if he cared to have the form I gave him signed by his wife, I could pay. 'How much can I get?' he asked, and I told him that he had to leave three shillings in the book to maintain the membership. There was £8.17 shillings in the book, and I could therefore pay him £8.14 shillings. He told me that that was as good as a week's wages! He came back the next day and I paid him. His final words to me were that if ever he could, he would do me a good turn in return. I told him that one day Newcastle United would be in the Cup Final and I would like to think that I could write to him for a ticket. He made no promises. In 1951 Newcastle got to the Final (the first of three in 1951/52 and 55) and I wrote to him at St James's Park with a plea that if he could send me a ticket I would be very, very grateful, and enclosed a three shilling postal order (the price of a standing ticket) and a stamped, addressed envelope. Within a week I had my response: my three shilling ticket, and my postal order returned, as was my stamped, addressed envelope – with a Newcastle United compliments slip! What a gentleman! He had burst onto the football scene just after the war, and alongside such as Charlie Wayman, Ernie Taylor, Bobby Mitchell, Frankie Brennan, the Robledo brothers and a host of other 'heroes', he illuminated the gloom of that immediate post-war period. When he died of cancer in his early sixties the route from St James's to St Nicholas Cathedral was lined six deep as a tribute to 'Wor Jackie'.

I have many memories of Newcastle footballers, my first 'hero' had been Albert Stubbins, a dashing centre forward with carrot coloured hair. Of course, also Len Shackleton and, later, Kevin Keegan who has done so much to make St James's Park the mecca for all United fans. Later as the host for dinners in the Lords, I was to meet Kevin, Alex Ferguson and Arsene Wenger. Happy, happy days!

My Co-Operative journey

From the cradle to the grave may be apt, but as the journey is still going on, I will resist that tag! Whilst the main thrust of this story is, as the dedication says, 'to honour the work of Labour Peers in Opposition' it must owe something to the events that shaped me the better to assist in the telling of that story.

Following on from my early days with the Newcastle-on-Tyne Co-op Society, the next part of that story relates to the opportunity it gave me to enter into the world of Co-operative Democracy. Even before my war service I began to understand how ordinary people – the members – could participate and influence events if they attended Members Meetings and voted in Elections. It may also have helped me to learn how to argue in public, and prepare myself for that period I served in the Tyneside Youth Parliament.

Certainly, the time I had as a student at the Co-operative College (1949/50) must assume great significance, for it not only opened my eyes to what educational endeavour can bring, but it started many friendships which have lasted until this day. I pay tribute to Bob and Beryl Marshall elsewhere, but I can never say enough about their major contribution to my development.

My first real job from the shelter of the General Office was when I became the National Secretary of the British Federation of Young

Home Guard, 1942. Myself 2nd from right in 3rd row

Co-operators in 1952. It brought me in touch with the great names within the Co-operative firmament, attending Education Convention and Co-operative Congress. Amongst those who influenced me were Harold Campbell, Laurie Pavitt and Peter Shea. We continued to meet – with our children – and still do! We called ourselves 'The Walk and Talk' Club, because that is what we did, meeting, walking to the nearest pub, arguing and putting the world to rights. Of late, due to deaths we finally decided to change our name from the 'Walk and Talk Club' to 'The Shuffle and Grunt' club! But the comradeship of the BFYC helped to form character.

It was during my service with the Enfield Highway Co-operative Society in the 1950s that The Independent Commission was established in order to better guide the future for Co-ops, following the first century after the Rochdale Pioneers in 1844. Both Hugh Gaitskell and Tony Crosland helped to fashion the future for us, but as is the way within Co-operatives it would be many years before positive changes were seen. Not perhaps until the Commission was reconvened in 2000 under the chairmanship of the TUC Secretary John Monks. I was to play my part in the sixties when I became a Co-operative Union Official. With that doyen of Co-operatives, Johnny Jacques helping to reshape the Co-operative Map by urging amalgamations of societies right left and centre! I saw the inside of more than 30 Co-operative boardrooms, some of whom heeded my advice while others did what they always did – nothing!

The great changes which abolished the full-time Board of Directors of the CWS came in the 1960s, as did the tragic death of Phillip Thomas; appointed to wield virtually supreme power over – everything! A survey of the Durham Societies which indicated disaster staring them in the face forced the creation of the North Eastern Co-operative Society in 1969, the greatest amalgamation by 31 separate societies, never to be repeated, but it set a pattern and a goal which still shines to this day.

It was in 1967 that I succeeded Harold Campbell as the National Secretary of the political wing of the Co-ops – the Co-operative Party. By then I had served on the Council of the London Borough of Enfield, been its Leader and fought my first parliamentary contest against Iain MacLeod in Enfield West, so I was equipped to do the job. It took me far and wide throughout the British Isles proselytising on behalf of the Co-op, but also preaching the doctrine of the trinity of the working class – Labour Party, Co-operatives and Trade Unions. I served on the National Council of Labour, which brought the leaders of all three wings together. It taught me the art of conciliation and of the sober fact – that the credibility of the Co-op case was in direct proportion to its standing in the Market Place or on the High Street. At that time it was an uphill struggle.

With the aid of the North Eastern Co-op and my Co-op Party friends I tossed my hat into the ring at Morpeth, only 15 miles out of Newcastle – and lost the selection by two votes. However, frustrating as that was, it left me free to be selected on my own patch for Edmonton, which I won in 1974.

My life as the MP for Edmonton is stated elsewhere, but I always remembered that I was in the Commons only as a result of the support of the Co-operative Movement. Under strict financial terms in an Agreement known as 'The Hastings Agreement' my constituency party benefited and in return I was able to assist the wider Movement in many ways from my perch, not least in the Government Whip's Office from 1974 to 1979. I hope the names of the present members of the Co-operative Parliamentary Group are as well known today as were those whilst I was in the Commons. Bob Edwards, Laurie Pavitt, Dick Douglas, John Rankin, John Tilley, Ioan Evans, Barry Sheerman, Arthur Palmer, Bert Oram, George Darling, Frank Beswick, Sydney Irving, Alf Morris. Both Johnny Jacques and Bob Palmer (Lord Rusholme) helped to forge an identity for the Co-ops of which I am proud – as were Co-operators throughout the land. Dividends can come in many ways! But in 1983 at the age of 59 I was out of the Commons with my pensions not due to kick in for another 6 years. Thanks to negotiations by David Wise, who succeeded me as Party Secretary, I was made a Consultant to Co-operatives and with goodwill all round I happily did this until I became the Opposition Chief Whip following the death of Tom Ponsonby in 1990. It saved my life and I will always be grateful to those who had faith in me. And being elected President of Co-operative Congress in 1987 certainly helped!

It was during the time in the Lords and before I was elected as Chief Whip that I discovered the world of Consultancy. Whilst as a member of the Commons you receive a salary and other reasonable expenses to carry out your duties, in the Lords that is not the case. No salary, just expenses and only if you are recorded as having attended that day. Each day is taken separately. For those with generously paid outside interests the modest regime of allowances in the Lords may suffice, but for those like me with no such source it was crucial that other means of 'earning a living' were discovered. And so I happily assisted the interest of such as USDAW, Ancient Order of Foresters, the Prison Officers Association, The National Federation of Market Traders and the British Retail Consortium. All these helped to keep the wolf from the door, and they gave me a wide range of interests and made many new friends. It was an exhilarating time!

In my years in the Lords I have been closely involved with a number of All-Party Groups. Having served on the 1983 Mobile Homes Act I continued my support for those who live on Park Homes. I act as a co-ordinator for those MPs who have a constituent feeling aggrieved at the manner in which they have been treated by Metropolitan Police.

When Dennis Carter succeeded me as Chief Whip, he resigned as the Chair of The United Kingdom Co-operative Council, and I succeeded him. Born out of the time when the Co-operative Union was fighting for its life, and unable to carry out some of its functions, the UKCC has been a haven for the 'other Co-operative Movement' outside the Consumer Movement, such as Housing, Employee Ownership, Credit Unions and Care Co-operatives. It was during this time that I learned to value the encouragement of Terry Thomas (now Lord), who, as the Chief Officer of the Co-operative Bank encouraged other central organizations to back it. Other Co-operative Bank Officers such as Peter Walker and latterly David Dickman have proved to be real towers of strength, and I owe a lot to both of them.

On the advice of Tony Blair the Prime Minister I was made a member of Her Majesty's Privy Council, a great honour, given normally to all Cabinet Ministers and other senior backbenchers to mark seniority.

From 1939 to 2004 I have never forgotten my roots. They were planted in the conditions of Scotswood Road in the twenties, the Newcastle Co-op of the thirties, and the reborn Co-operative Movement of today. There is always a part to be played by willing hands, and mine will continue to work for these causes for a very long time!

They call it friendly fire!

'A Life on the Ocean Waves' is the regimental march of the Royal Marines, and it was in April 1943 that I enrolled, but I never saw the sea. Initial training at Lympstone, near Exmouth, was a bonding experience, for my Training Squad (672) and my first instructor (Corporal Ransome) still evoke a memory almost 60 years later. In 1943 we were very much in war mode. None of us knew what the future would bring, but we knew that it could lead to action – and that is what most red-blooded young men expected, and wanted. I was no exception.

In late '43, together with others in my training battalion, I was asked to attend for interview and found that the first and, in my case, the only question we were asked was if we could speak French. I could not, and was out. Others were in, and they quickly disappeared for 'special training' and I have no doubt that they had been chosen for operations in France. Towards the end of the year, I was drafted to the Royal Marines Depot at Deal, which was the main place for the training of NCOs and, in December, I passed out as a corporal. That's as high as I got!

The Royal Marine Commandos was the place we all longed to gravitate to, and the training camp at Spean Bridge, Achnacarry, near Fort William the goal, where you passed out and were then attached to one of the Commandos – either 40, 41 or 45. We all knew that D-Day could not be far away, and we all yearned to be in action. However, before that could happen for me I was sent to the War Office Advanced Handling and Field Craft School at Llanberis, North Wales where I worked with others from a variety of Units and was initiated into the skills required for I know not what. It was there that my war service was effectively terminated.

I was just over my nineteenth birthday on 4 May 1944. Ten of us travelled in a three ton lorry, and we alighted on the edge of the lake at Llanberis at the foot of Snowdon. We erected a canvas boat and, as we stepped into it, our instructor told us to keep our heads down. It was good advice, for he then told us that a fixed line Bren Gun would open up and fire about a foot over our heads – with live ammunition. We needed no further incentive for, as we rowed across the lake, we could hear the bullets flying above our heads. When we arrived at the shore on the other side, and got out of the boat, our instructor told us that we would be taking a position about 50 yards up a hill. Before that he would fire a Very Pistol, whereupon the firing would stop, we would 'take the position' and the firing would continue as we ran down the hill on the other side. As we stood there he fired his Very Pistol. Bearing in mind that it was 8.00 a.m. in the morning, we were at a lakeside and it was misty. Whether he fired the wrong colour cartridge, or whether the Bren Gunners could not see, the fact was that as we charged up the hill the firing opened up and I fell, shot as the 'Certificate for Wounds and Hurts' recorded in the following terms:

'Corporal T.E. Graham was then actually on His Majesty's Service in that he was attending under instruction a field firing exercise and sustained the following injury on May 4th 1944:

1. Gun shot wounds lower abdomen wall with prolapse of small intestine.
2. Gun shot wounds left thigh, entrance and exit wounds with some destruction of the muscle. A severe injury.'

It is now called 'friendly fire' and when it happens today it makes news, but in the Second World War it must have been more commonplace. I certainly held no great anger, feeling that I was lucky to be alive. My life was saved by the prompt action of my instructor. It turned out that he had seen action in the Middle East, and when he was called to help me he immediately tore away my trousers and stuffed my field-dressing into the gaping hole out of which my intestines had protruded. Not many people can say that they have had their guts in their hands – but I can! I was taken away to the Waterloo Hotel in Bettws y Coed about thirty miles away where a field hospital from the Middle East was resting prior to being sent to the Second Front. Not having had pain relief for more than two hours it was a relief to be dealt with by a Mr Anderson from Sheffield. When I thanked him later for saving my life he said that he had been dealing with similar wounds for the past six months and it was no big deal for him. It was for me!

When I recovered I was sent to a Military Hospital in Winwick outside Warrington. Half of it remained what it had been for many years – a lunatic asylum – and the other was the Military Hospital. I saw out my service at the Pay Corps of the Marines and left the service in October 1946.

There was one other memory with dramatic overtones during my service. In September 1943 I was on training out of the Royal Naval College in Dartmouth. We would be taken in landing craft and land on terrain which I now know was similar to that in Normandy. As we spluttered out of the craft we would be up to our armpits in water and we had to fight our way ashore, sometimes for hundreds of yards. We were training alongside American Rangers who suffered one of the tragedies of the war. German intelligence had found out about this training and, in May 1944, they devised a plan which placed their boats between the incoming American Rangers and the shore. As the landing craft were approaching the shore – but miles out, the E-boats pounced and shot the helpless craft to smithereens, sending more than 700 young American soldiers to their deaths. When the bodies were washed ashore, the local populace was sworn to secrecy and the relatives were later advised that their loved ones had been lost during the landings on D Day. Investigative journalism uncovered this episode years later. The place was called 'Slapton Sands', where now stands a huge memorial to the episode, and the men who lost their lives.

Prime Minister at 23

Memories of periods in my life are scattered throughout this story, but perhaps the first 'memory' I have stems from joining the Co-operative Youth Club. In 1941 the Government initiated a call for young people to be involved in meaningful activity and in wartime Britain that was not difficult. The Cooperative Movement responded by establishing The Co-operative Youth Movement, and as I was then working in the Central Premises of the Newcastle Co-op I quickly learned of this, and joined. It was to lead to a most rewarding part of my life.

'The Guildroom' in those central premises at Newgate Street became the hub of my universe for the next ten years, save for that period when I served in the Royal Marines from 1943 to 1946. I became the Club secretary and found that I had a flair for organizing others – something which developed a lot in later years! I found that I enjoyed debates and

Myself, extreme left, back row, manager of Co-op football team, Cowgate

chancing my arm in arguments and was soon fluent – at least at a Youth Club level. It led to my becoming a Public Speaker and I was let loose on the many Guilds and Groups associated with the Education Committee of the Co-op. I found that I enjoyed cycling and rambling with others, and that there was excitement in attending Week-End Schools and Rallies with others of my own age. In those days, the Week-end School was all the vogue.

The atmosphere for a 16/17-year-old at that time was electric. I can recall listening spellbound to a lady straight from the Russian battlefield who had become an expert marksman and was feted throughout Britain. I can recall listening to Ernest Bevin in the City Hall telling us all about the National Effort. I can recall travelling through to Sunderland to hear and be inspired by Harry Pollitt the Secretary of the British Communist Party. I remember with affection the nights we would go straight from the Co-op Youth Club to the boisterous meetings of the Young Communist League in Trafalgar St. I never joined, but at the age of 16 I joined the Labour Party and have never left it – or thought of leaving it now for more than 60 years. Those were the days! It was in the Youth Club that I first met my friend Ted Grey and his future wife, Irene Appleby. Club members were all of the same age and so it was that almost every week we would find that one or more of our members had departed into the Armed Forces. My best friend Ted went into the

Royal Air Force, and I went into the Royal Marines. I did not have a link with 'The Royals'. My dad had served in the 1914-18 war, and had been called up in the last general call-up in October 1941 at the age of 41.

After wartime service I returned to work in the General Office of the Newcastle Co-op, and joined the successor to the Co-op Youth Club – the British Federation of Young Co-operators or 'the Bific'. It was during my life there that I heard of an initiative that was to lead on to greater things. The Workers Education Association (WEA) was responsible for setting many a young or not-so-young person on to educational progress, and in 1948 due to the inspiration of the District Organizer, Mr Abrahart, it established the Tyneside Youth Parliament. As Labour was in Office at Westminster, so would the TYP have a Labour Government – which would change as and when it did at Westminster.

Procedures and Standing Orders were modelled on Westminster with Questions and debates. The backbone of the Government side was made up of Young Socialists and Co-operators – and besides my friend Ted Grey becoming a Cabinet Minister – I became the Prime Minister! All this was a step up in the League but it was fun, for whilst all of us were politically aware we were far from experienced. But neither were the other participants, and so we were launched into a venture which for me led from the British Restaurant in the Haymarket where our Parliament was held down to Westminster into the Commons and eventually into the Lords!

Along the way, I attended the National Youth Parliament in Beaver Hall, Mansion House, the venue for the first meeting of the Parliamentary Party after the victory of 1945. There I was to meet some whose paths crossed mine in later years. As a student of Co-operation I had read avidly *A Century of Cooperation,* a standard text-book by G.D.H. Cole. His son Humphrey was the leader of the National Association of Labour Students Organizations (NALSO) in the Youth Parliament. The Leader of the Young Communists was Les Cannon who went on to become the President of the Electrical Trade Union, and who died tragically young. The Young Conservatives were led by John Hay who went on to become the Tory MP for Henley. When those of us on the Labour side met we chose a young delegate from Wallasey to lead us, Fred Jarvis, who went on to become the General Secretary of the National Union of Teachers (NUT). Years later I met Arnold Kettle when I did my Open University courses. His wife was the Speaker of the Parliament, and Martin Kettle is their son and a fine journalist. Prominent in the Tyneside Parliament was Peter Cadogan who emerged later as the Secretary of the Committee of 100 led by Bertram Russell.

All told, those Youth Club days were great. They gave me lifelong friends such as Ted and Irene, and Norman Sherry who went on to become Professor of Literature at the University of Texas and the authorized biographer of Graham Greene, but they also 'blooded' me for the life I was to lead later. You never know where a present-day experience will lead to – and perhaps it is just as well!

1951 was Festival of Britain Year. I had been married in 1950 and so one of my journeys from Newcastle that year was to visit the Festival site and to be pleased to see that at last the hard work of Herbert Morrison and his Cabinet colleagues had come to fruition. Festival Hall and the Festival Gardens were a must, and I still retain happy memories of that visit.

Within my store of 'Co-operative' memories of that year was a first visit to the City of Sheffield. Outside the City stood Wortley Hall, the ancient home of the Earl of Wharncliffe. It had been left to go to rack and ruin, but at that time the Labour Movement in Sheffield had devised a scheme whereby it was bought for the purposes of providing a 'home' for Schools and Activities. The grounds even in their sorry state were a sight for sore eyes, but the main building had been a problem. All the trades deployed to renovate a building had been pressed into working on it, and after many activists had spent many, many hours, it was ready for occupation. The very first booking at Whitsuntide 1951 was for the British Federation of Young Co-operators – and I was the National President – a big moment for me!

One just does not appreciate what will happen in life. I have always been amazed at how from small beginnings significant happenings occur. This time, it was to lead from Wortley Hall right up to Westminster. It was traditional for our conference to invite the Labour League of Youth (then Labour's Youth Wing) to send a fraternal delegate and this happened on the Sunday morning. We had a delightful greetings from a sparky lass who made a deep impression on us all, not least for her jolly demeanor and her optimistic message, remember that we were in the dog-days of Clem Attlee's second term. It was Betty Boothroyd, then just 21, and she cheered us up no end! The rest, as they say, is history. Although I watched the ups and downs of her political career from afar, we finally met when I went to the Commons in 1974, she having arrived a short while before in a by-election.

Within the BFYC in Sheffield it was the Munn family who shone. In 1998 Reg Munn a long time friend invited me to come back to Wortley Hall on International Co-operators Day on the first Saturday in July. What a transformation! It was a great credit to the Labour Movement in Sheffield, and I honour them now. I shared a platform on the back of a Co-op lorry with John Prescott and John Monks. The event was organized by Dick Caborn, now a successful Minister in the Government. The story is complete when I tell you that Reg's daughter, Meg, is now the Labour and Co-operative Member of Parliament for one of the Sheffield constituencies! Talk about a small world!

CHAPTER 3

Rewarding times in Enfield Highway

EARLIER I SPOKE of the 1960s as being rewarding for me, but the 1950s were full of incident. As the Education Secretary of the Enfield Highway Co-operative Society I was given the opportunity to serve the educational and cultural needs of more than 60,000 members. Of course, most of them were content to be shoppers and paid little attention to the other benefits of being a member, but for those who wished Co-operative Education was often the gateway to higher and better things.

The territory I covered started in Edmonton to the south and went up into Buntingford in the north. The Society had been started by those working as 'Lockies' at the Enfield Lock Small Arms factory in Ordnance Road in 1872, running through such places as Waltham Cross, Hoddesdon, Hertford, Chingford, Bush Hill Park and Enfield Highway. It had a reputation for providing opportunities, and one of the main vehicles was the Cooperative Women's Guilds. There were then 15 of them and they provided a haven for working class women to discuss the events of the day and to learn how to conduct meetings. They were a principle source for sending into the wider world, women who had been given confidence, public-speaking skills and a thirst for knowledge. Many a councillor and Member of Parliament owes it to the Guilds for their earlier training. When I organized a course of lectures one year it was on the emerging freedom for British Colonies. One of my lecturers was Jim Betts, the brother of Barbara Castle, recently returned from colonial service.

It was there, too, that I was responsible for the Enfield Highway Orchestra, the Enfield Film Society and the Wheatsheaf Light Operatic Society – Gilbert and Sullivan to you. One day I was introduced to the producer, Harold Abrahams. His wife was Sybil Evers, a former G & S star who died tragically after being stung by a wasp in her garden in Hertfordshire. The Cambridge athletic link led to the McWhirter twins coming along to the shows and I enjoyed the relaxed atmosphere – that is before Ross went on to contest the Edmonton seat, but who was tragically killed by the IRA on the doorstep of his home in Bush Hill Park. He it was who officiated when the Orchestra of the Latymer School in Edmonton played itself into – the Guinness Book of Records!

I first met Jeffrey Archer in the sixties. I served on the governing body of the Enfield Grammar School, where another governor was Iain

MacLeod, then MP for Enfield West. We had invited Chris Chataway as the principal guest for our prize-giving, but then we got a note to say that as the newly appointed Chair of the Inner London Education Authority he could not come, but sent along his then 'bag carrier' Jeffrey Archer. Howsoever Chris would have performed, Jeffrey had them eating out of his hand! We were to meet later in both Commons and Lords – but that is another story!

My debt to Margaret

My life in the 1950s was largely domestic. I married Margaret in 1950 when I was 25 and she was 23. She had been a West Ham girl, bombed out and settled in Becontree, Dagenham. We met through our membership of the Co-operative Youth Clubs and she has been an anchor to me in many, many ways. At the times of crisis or despair the need for an anchor may be taken for granted and it is only later that you realize how you have been sustained through difficulties. Margaret has never let me down, although I know that I have far too often put my politics before my family. I hang my head, not in shame, but in gratitude. She had worked at the May and Baker Pharmaceutical factory in Dagenham and it was there that she was a member of the Works Netball team, playing for Eastbury and being very involved. One of my early memories of married life was to accompany her to netball matches, and enjoying it! She was a sportswoman and remembered with affections that in 1948 she had attended Wembley for the Olympic Games and seen the splendid Dutchwoman, Fanny Blankers Kohn who won four gold medals. We went on to have two sons, first Martin born in 1957 and then Ian born in 1959. A joy has been to be able to celebrate both our Ruby and then our Golden Wedding anniversaries on the Terrace of the House of Lords with friends we have made over the years.

Mention has been made of the Co-operative College at Stanford Hall, Loughborough where I was a student in 1949 and Margaret in 1951. It has been a huge influence on our lives and we still meet some of those from that time. Bought by the Co-operative Movement to commemorate the birth of the modern movement in Rochdale in 1844, it served the national and the international Co-operative cause for more than 57 years, but was deemed to have served its purpose in the year 2001. The major influence on the nature of the College and on the thousands of men and women who were trained for Cooperative service was without a doubt the Principal and Chief Education Officer, Robert Leckie Marshall, known as RLM to all who valued the institution.

He and his wife, Beryl took Stanford Hall from being just another stately home turned to other uses into a thriving community which sent converts

Margaret and I – first election photograph, 1974

and disciples throughout the land and into many an emerging nation, where ex-Co-operative students filled important posts in Government and Government organizations. Within the Co-operative Movement, the highest accolade that can be bestowed on a Co-operator is to be elected to be President of the Co-operative Congress, and this honour was fittingly bestowed on Bob Marshall in 1976. No one before or since has more richly deserved it. That honour – President of Congress – was awarded to me in 1987. The 1960s were good to me. In 1960 I was elected to the Enfield Council and when the London Boroughs were created in 1964, I became Leader of the London Borough of Enfield – a great honour. In 1966 I was selected as the Labour and Co-operative Parliamentary candidate for Enfield

West where the sitting MP was Iain MacLeod. At the Labour selection conference I had only one opponent – Anthony Lester – who went on to become a prominent QC and who is now in the Lords with me, but sitting on the Liberal Democrat benches! And in 1967 I became the National Secretary of the Cooperative Party. Great! I was now the spokesperson for the Co-op within the Labour Movement.

High – or low – lights as a councillor

I became a member of the Council in Enfield in 1960 and spent eight very happy years there. After two years I became Leader of the Council. This was what turned out to be the run-up to the 1964 General Election which Harold Wilson won by a whisker. I learned, with experience, that being the Leader of a Council with a population of almost 300,000 was a good grounding in the arts required to lead a group, face the lively opposition and to deal positively with the officers. Enfield was Council No 32. It was made up of the solidly Labour Edmonton, the solidly Conservative Southgate and the left-leaning Enfield. Proof of this is that with the first of the London Borough elections it resulted in a division of councillors by 31 to 29 in favour of Labour. When people ask 'Where were you when you heard the news of the assassination of JFK?' I would reply that I was at a committee meeting in the Council Chamber at the Enfield Civic Centre, and to the next most 'where were you?' – I was at the count itself when Michael Portillo bit the dust!

One of my abiding feelings of satisfaction is to have been a founder-member of the Lee Valley Regional Park formed in 1966 with Bill Fiske of the GLC as its first Chairman, and the athlete Ron Pickering as its first Sports Director. The inspiration for the LVRP had been Lou Sherman, a Hackney man, who served on the Borough Council and on the GLC and who earned his living as a taxi driver. As I visit the Park to enjoy the facilities we dreamed of now 40 years ago, I taste the feeling of satisfaction at what one can achieve with good ideas and community support – and I am content.

It was Mary Tudor who said that when she died the word 'Calais' would be found on her heart. For me it would have been 'Lavender Hill'. There is a 'Lavender Hill' in many parts of the country. Mine was an allotment site which was owned by the Enfield Parochial Charities and which they decided to get rid of, as the income from letting it to the Council for civic allotments brought in peanuts. The Charity Commissioners deemed that it had to be disposed of by 'Dutch Auction', sealed bids. As the only likely user of this land, which was zoned as statutory allotment land, the Council felt confident that it would acquire it, but when the two envelopes were opened, the Council was bested by another bid. Trying to obtain approval from the District Valuer to make a further and final bid, we were again bested, and the land passed into the ownership of a company only registered weeks before. Under the planning procedures, although paying 'allotment value' they proceeded to ask the Minister – Sir Keith Joseph – for a Certificate of Alternative Use for Housing, which he then granted. Thus, land which was worth but £7000 became worth more than £300,000. The land was then developed for council housing and Harold Wilson used the issue during the 1964 election most effectively. Now you know why 'Lavender Hill' is engraved on my heart!

In 1969/70 Will Owen was to figure large in my life. Will was the Co-operative sponsored Member of Parliament for Morpeth in Northumberland, and he announced that he would not be standing at the next general election, which was likely to be in 1970. Coming from that part of the world, I decided to put my hat into the ring as the Co-operative candidate. The miners held the seat when Will, a miner and an activist of many years standing, contested it, and won. They took his standing down badly, and made it clear that they were determined to win it back. I won the Co-operative selection, and the miners' candidate was George Grant, a union official in the area and a local man.

I knew that it would be a hard fought contest, and so it proved to be. After the first ballot George had 38 votes, I had 34 and Gordon Adam (who went on to become an MEP) had 12 with Jim Murray, the nominee of the AEU, with 2. That meant that to win I had to get not less that 43, but I got 42 and George 44. We parted in friendship, but the atmosphere I tasted in Ashington that day made me relieved that I would not have to justify my victory to my own Party, if that had turned out to be the case. George came to Westminster but, sad to say, he succumbed to illness within ten years and died.

Meanwhile Will had been arrested and was now in Brixton Jail. He faced charges of espionage, for using his membership of the Commons Defence Select Committee to give secret information to the Czechs. At the time I was the National Secretary of the Cooperative Party, the political wing of the Co-operative Movement. One of our members was Tom Williams QC, who rang me and asked me to visit Will in Brixton. He was arrested on a Thursday and I visited him on the Saturday morning. (I was in fact later to visit Brixton Jail in the 1980s as the Parliamentary Consultant to the Prison Officers Association, one of several jail visits to better understand the conditions under which Staff were operating). He was depressed and drained, a shadow of the man I had known for almost 20 years. We did not discuss any aspect of the charges facing him, but he asked me to go at once to see a prominent person who was known to many – including me – for his links with Eastern European Governments. I was to ask that this man should stand as a Guarantor when Will applied for Bail, but when I saw him in his flat in Belgravia he said bluntly that in no circumstance would he do so. Although he had plenty of money, he said that too close an association with Will would not be in his interest. Not Will's, but his own.

Rebuffed in this way I went back to see Will. Arising out of that conversation I went to see a mutual friend John Jacques who was from the heart of the Morpeth constituency, Ashington, had had an illustrious career within the Co-operative Movement and was now a member of The House of Lords. Together we decided that jointly, we would stand surety for Will, and my contribution was to put my home in Enfield at the disposal of his legal team. I never hesitated, for Will had been a good friend, and I was convinced that he would honour any commitment.

Bail was refused, and so Will stood trial at the Old Bailey in April/May, just before the General Election of .June, 1970. I attended the Trial almost every day and by the time of the verdict there was not much cheer about. Will had a brilliant legal team. Leading for him was James Comyns QC who pushed the evidence provided by the Prosecution all round the Number 1 Court. The two prosecuting personalities I recall were the Treasury Solicitor, a Mr Cousins, and the Head of the Scotland Yard Flying Squad, Commander Wilson. Such as it was, the evidence consisted of Will making available extracts and reports from Parliament, which was proved had been freely available as Parliamentary Papers, and not secrets at all. Will acknowledged that he had contacts with members of the Czech Diplomatic fraternity and had accepted gifts of spirits and other things, but denied that they had led to him disclosing secrets of any kind. He didn't have any to give! It later transpired that Will had been named by a Czech defector who was subsequently totally discredited.

On the morning on which the verdict was to be given I was phoned at home by the Junior Counsel to James Comyns, Mr Jeffrey Thomas, QC who was a rising star of the parliamentary Labour Party. He was the Member of Parliament for Abertillery. He said that the night before, James Comyns and he had reviewed the case, and had come to the conclusion that Will was facing a sentence in the region of ten years imprisonment. Could I alert and warn Ann, Will's wife? Whilst I could do that I decided not to do so – and subsequent events proved that that was a good decision.

I sat in the Gallery as the Jury returned. Will faced six charges. 'Members of the Jury, have you reached your verdict?' 'We have'. 'How say you to the first charge – Guilty or Not Guilty?' 'Not Guilty'. 'Members of the Jury, have you reached your verdict on the second charge?'. 'We have'. 'What say you to the second charge?' 'Not Guilty'. And so on, right through and to the sixth charge – Not Guilty to them all! Pandemonium!

Of course I was delighted. Will asked me to accompany him to his home in Carshalton in order to assist when, as we both knew, the Press would be there in force. They were! Later that same evening I went with Will to the BBC Newsnight studio when David Dimbleby interviewed Will. He acquitted himself well, but by then he was a broken man.

In 1972 Austin Albu, who was the Member of Parliament for Edmonton, suffered a major operation for cancer and announced that he would not stand at the next election. On the short list I faced Will Howie, John Dunwoody and Donald Anderson (all ex-MPs). I won the nomination and entered the Commons in February 1974. There began one of the-most hectic periods of my life, but I would not have had it any other way.

Out into the wider labour movement

As Co-operative Party National Secretary, I worked closely with the National officials of the Labour Party. Reg Underhill was the National Agent and with Reg I would agree the formula to be applied before each General Election to the number of Co-operatively sponsored candidates who would be allowed to bid for 'winnable' seats and the proportion of 'unwinnable' seats that we had to fight. Labour and the Co-op had a National Agreement fashioned in 1927, so that the possibility of fielding both Labour and Co-operative candidates was avoided. In earlier days Co-op sponsored candidates (and subsequently Members of Parliament) included such as A.V. Alexander, Alf Barnes, George Darling, Frank Beswick, Joyce Butler and John Stonehouse – who was later to disappear sensationally, only to surface and earn a prison sentence for fraud. The job took me into the House of Commons on almost a daily basis and thus I became very familiar with the operation of Parliament. Reg would in time enter the House of Lords, as did Joyce Gould, another Transport House official as did, too, Betty Lockwood, with whom I had established a friendship at that time which was to last.

I became the main propagandist for the Co-op which meant that in time I learned the quickest way from all the main railway stations to the city Town Hall, Co-op Hall or Trade Union Centre. I also learned to avoid catching trains back from such as Manchester, Leicester, Newcastle or Birmingham at the same time as the supporters of Arsenal, Spurs, Chelsea or West Ham were travelling – especially if they had lost! That meant that in sneaking onto a train before they travelled, I would be travelling to London with the just married couples on their way to London to start their honeymoon!

At this time I started two ventures which helped to cement both Co-operative politics and the relationship with the Labour and Trade

Unions. Co-op Societies sustained Cooperative politics by a subvention based on their membership, but we had only a handful of MPs. The better understanding of what we were trying to do at Westminster was important and we would invite the Chief Officials and Presidents of the Co-op Societies to a one-day seminar to discuss with members of the Co-operative Parliamentary Group current worries and ambitions. This was much appreciated.

A series of conferences was also organized throughout the country with a speaker from the Labour, Trade Union and Co-operative organizations with the audience drawn from the local members. I shared platforms with such as Harold Wilson and Peter Shore and with trade union leaders such as Jack Jones, David Basnett, Vic Feather, Jimmy Knapp and Hughie Scanlon. On one fraught occasion we had organized an event at the Central Hall, Westminster with Harold Wilson as the star turn, and he had just opened up when there was a bomb scare. Everybody out!

PART II

Setting the Scene and Entering
Parliament

CHAPTER 4

The 1974/1979 parliaments – an overview from the Whips Office – the gathering storm

Being elected to the Commons in February 1974 was intended to be for a five year parliament. Instead by 10 October I had fought for Edmonton for the second time within 9 months, increasing my majority on both occasions. So had Harold Wilson. Ted Heath had surprised the country by winning in 1970 but he had had to endure a period of militant industrial turmoil, so that when he finally decided on 7 February to call the General Election for 28 February the prime issues were clear – who governs Britain? Sadly for him, he finished up with a result from the electorate which clearly did not endorse him as the Governor.

When I fought that February election I can recall some of the major issues, and as always they were not what the Labour Opposition would do if returned to power, but related to the series of crises which were the order of the day under Heath. The crisis in the Coal Industry; the continuing reign of terror emanating from Northern Ireland; matters relating to the EEC and the spin placed on that by Enoch Powell; Industrial Relations and the Wilson pledge to produce a new Social Contract with the Unions. In that February election there was, by today's standards, a high turnout of 78.8 per cent, and gave Labour 301 seats, Conservative 296, Liberals 14, and others 23, although, with the quirks of the British electoral system Conservatives had 37.9 per cent of the votes to Labour's 37.2 per cent. I was to learn that the 'first-past-the-post' system was to figure large over the next few years.

It is intriguing to reflect that one of the possibilities at that 'stalemate time' was that Jeremy Thorpe was offered a seat in a Conservative Cabinet in a desperate attempt by Ted Heath to get the Liberals on side. 'Twas not to be, and so when I first sat on the green benches it was to sit on the Government side of The House, and behind such Labour luminaries as Harold Wilson, Denis Healey, James Callaghan, Barbara Castle, Michael Foot, Roy Jenkins, Tony Benn, Ted Short, Roy Mason, Shirley Williams and Tony Crosland. These were men and women who had waited but four years to get back into office, many of them serving in Harold Wilson's 1964 to 1970 Cabinets, unlike those who marched into Downing Street in 1997,

Wooing the voters – and taking the Tories to the cleaners, October 1974

having waited almost 18 years for their chance. The intake on the Labour side who entered with me in 1974 turned out to be every bit as fitted for high office later, but at the time they were unknown quantities: Robin Cook; Margaret Jackson (soon to be Beckett), Ann Taylor. All three served in the 1997 Cabinet. Such as Bruce Grocott (Chief Whip – Lords), and his now deputy, Bryan Davies; Bryan Gould who left after 1992; John Macintosh who tragically died early; Jeff Rooker now Housing Minister, Lords. Others of the 1974 intake to note would be Robert Kilroy Silk and David Penhaligon (tragically died early).

Of course, with such a fragile grip on the key to No 10, no-one expected that parliament to last very long, and so it proved, for during the Long Recess, Harold Wilson announced that the General Election would take place on 10 October. This, however, was not before his Ministers had began to lay the foundation for solid achievements to be built upon in the next parliament.

- A Prices Bill introduced by Shirley Williams giving the Government increased powers to regulate retail prices through a Prices Commission.

(Alan Williams – Shirley's Minister of State – asked me to be his PPS, which brought me into the Department.)

- Roy Jenkins announced an amnesty for illegal immigrants in Britain.
- Michael Foot introduced the Trade Union and Labour Relations Bill repealing the Industrial Relations Act in favour of pro-union law protecting the closed shop.
- Flesh was put on The Social Contract which was devised to bring about restraint in wage demands in return for control of elements in the cost of living. The General Council of the TUC approved wage restraint coupled with social and economic reform.
- It was proposed to bring into public ownership the Offshore Oil and Gas Industries.
- Michael Foot announced the establishment of a Royal Commission on the Distribution of Income and Wealth.
- Denis Healey reduced VAT to 8 per cent, eased dividend controls and increased food subsidies.
- Tony Benn made a commitment to nationalize the shipbuilding and associated industries.
- Tony Benn issued a White Paper 'The Regeneration of British Industry' proposing a National Enterprise Board (NEB) to take over selected private companies and to draw up planning agreements with the larger companies.
- A White Paper on devolution proposed directly elected assemblies for Scotland and Wales.

The flurry of activity from the Government did the trick. From a minority, Labour emerged from the General Election with an overall majority – but only just. 319 Labour, 276 Conservative, 13 Liberal, 26 others.

Labour's share had gone up from 37.2 per cent to 39.2 per cent while Conservative declined from 37.9 per cent to 35.8 per cent. Overall, there was a decline from 78.8 per cent to 72.8 per cent. But Labour's troubles were just beginning.

I was in the Department of Prices and Consumer Protection when the news came through that Harold Wilson had announced his resignation. Our departmental head, Shirley Williams, was at the Cabinet Meeting, but I was with the Minister of State, Alan Williams. I knew immediately that in the forthcoming fight for the Leadership I would be supporting James Callaghan, and quickly contacted Jack Cunningham his PPS and volunteered my support, which he accepted with alacrity. I could contribute from my background as a London MP, a 'Geordie', but especially being sponsored by the Co-op. We met every day in Jim's office behind the Speakers Chair, sometimes under the guidance of Merlyn Rees when he could escape from his responsibilities in Northern Ireland. Jim was meticulous in thanking every single one of his colleagues who was reported to him as pledging their support, always writing a 'thank you letter' immediately.

As expected it was a run-off between Jim and Michael Foot in the end, and with Jim as the victor I was soon invited by him to serve as a Senior Whip under Michael Cocks, which I gladly accepted. And so began the most intense and exhausting time of my life.

Not everyone appreciates that being a Whip entails more than simply sitting on the Frontbench and assisting the Minister to get the business through. The Committee work was heavy in that period. The first Committee I served on was with Shirley Williams and it was in that period where the Conservative Opposition were still smarting after being ejected from Office. It was there that I came across Jeffrey Archer again, having first met him in 1967 when he was a member of the GLC. I also served on a Health Committee with Barbara Castle and her very able Minister of State Brian O'Malley, who tragically died early in life.

One of my memories of that period – 1974 to 1979 – was the number of deaths recorded – especially of Labour members. 22 Members in all died, of whom 16 were Labour and 6 Conservative. Of our 16, of course as a Whip I had dealings with them all. Most had reached a good age, such as Hugh Delargy, Willie Small, Marcus Lipton, Arthur Irvine, Tom Swain. The pressure and strain placed on all Labour members was intense. I can recall standing in the Division Lobby one night (at 3 a.m. in the morning) looking at Tony Crosland coming through. He looked ghastly. He had been in Brussels for three days, had been forced to come and vote – and the next morning would have to attend the Cabinet Meeting. He died within a few days. Millie Miller was worn out. Bill Hamling died of exhaustion. Alf Broughton died of a broken heart – more of that later. Within six months of becoming Prime Minister Jim Callaghan had to face the fact that at this rate, having already lost the overall majority – he would lose a Vote of Confidence. The way in which he and Michael Foot clung to office via the Lib/Lab Pact makes interesting reading.

During that first year of the Callaghan Government votes were more often won by single figures, but one of the debilitating aspects of life at that time was the ability of a small number of Tory backbenchers to keep hundreds of Government supporters out of their beds till the small hours. Unless the issue was one deserving of applying a Guillotine the debate would be sustained by a group of Tories who enjoyed the game. Such as Ian Gow, Norman Tebbit, Roger Moate, Hugh Dykes, Maxwell-Hislop were masters at feeding off each other by the simple device of interventions. Thus we would stagger towards the time of the vote – only

With Jim Callaghan in 1979

to find that a division would not be called. As our troops were released you can imagine the epitaphs flung the way of those who had made us miss our sleep!

I have referred to the pinpricking of Labour members voting against the Government, often to no avail because they did not attract support from any other quarters, but in February 1977 22 Labour MPs helped to defeat the Government when their votes supported those of the Opposition Parties on Devolution legislation, and the Government lost a Guillotine motion by 312 votes to 283. This led directly to the creation of the Lib/Lab Pact, for that defeat emboldened Margaret Thatcher to put down a vote of no confidence, which she lost by 322 votes to 298. With defeat for his government likely, Callaghan 'did a deal' with the Liberals, which gave him their support at crucial times, in return for undertakings for regular consultations over policy and the holding of free votes on proportional representation for the elections to the European Parliament.

A sub-plot to all of this was the reality that it was the undermining of his ability to govern caused by a handful of Labour MPs that forced Callaghan to trim. In the Whips Office we were constantly faced with the need to work on winning the vote – often by one or two – instead of being able to get about delivering the good policy which had been promised in the Election Manifesto. The record shows that in the course of less than two months (from 19 June to 30 July 1976) the Government was defeated in the Commons no less than 17 times.

If the Parliamentary Labour Party was shown as divided on policies such as the Common Market, Devolution and Northern Ireland there was an inevitable cost to pay in terms of public confidence. In a mining constituency (Ashfield) Labour lost a by-election, losing a majority of 22,915 to a Conservative one of 264. A similar disaster followed when Fred Peart went to the Lords, and his seat at Workington went to the Tories. While the ability of the Government to govern was underwritten by the Pact, that came to an end with the end of the 1977/78 Session. In the Whips Office it was felt to have served its purpose. It had avoided the inevitability of a Thatcher Government – for the time being. In the Whips Office we could never understand why Jim failed to 'go' in October 1978.

Once I had entered the Government Whips Office I entered another world. For whereas before I was largely left to my own devices save that I had to respond to calls on my time to serve on Committees or vote, as a Whip I was subject to what looking back I would call a harsh regime. Moving from my home in my constituency of Edmonton, I had to be available no later than 9.30 a.m. for Committee work and would be on duty until the House went down – more often than not, at two or three in the morning. This on top of the burgeoning volume of work in the constituency made for a heavy workload, but one which was shouldered cheerfully.

There was a meeting of The Whips every day at 2 p.m. before the start of Business in The House. Early on when a controversial issue was raised, Michael Cocks the Chief Whip would hold up his hand when a colleague argued that it was a matter of principle:

'Principle! Principle! Whips are not concerned with matters of principle! We are about numbers and votes. All we are concerned with is to ensure that we win the vote! Now get out there and make sure that everyone of your group goes through the right lobby – the Labour Lobby!'

As will be shown elsewhere, from those early days in the Callaghan Government we were about ensuring that we won, and it was often down to winning by a vote – or two. It was the job of the Deputy Chief Whip, Walter Harrison, to report on the likely outcome of the vote. He would give us a round-up from the minority parties with whom he had established a reciprocal rapport and with whom he could obtain favours – providing he could deliver favours in return. In time, the supporters of the minority parties would become hostile to deals done for the purpose of keeping in power a Labour Government which was losing its appeal, but in the early days he would report that the Northern Ireland Unionists would be short by two or three due to problems with delayed aircraft or missed trains – and that was well before the MPs were due to begin their journey! Or perhaps a demand for support from the Government for some public service was to be announced in a day or two to the satisfaction of a Nationalist MP who would find that it was convenient to put a pressing constituency matter before being in Westminster.

I was given two specific tasks. One was to check, as the ten o'clock vote was due, to see if there were any Labour colleagues 'detained' in the toilets. Once I had ascertained that the body in the cubicle was Labour I would hammer on the door until I got a response, but if I had ascertained that the body was other than Labour I would tiptoe out of sight. I was designated as 'The Upper-Floor Flusher' – Jock Stallard was the 'Lower Floor Flusher'. I was also given the job of ensuring that Tories who had been paired did not emerge from the Division Lobby, by memorizing the handful of pairs and watching out for them. I saved more than one vote that way! Invariably the error was due to a mistake – but mistakes count!

My memory of the atmosphere in the Commons during the period after Callaghan came to power and the striking of the Lib/Lab Pact about a year later is one of toil and trouble. Although it was exhilarating to find that we were in Government, for many of our backbenchers it was a time of frustration – even disillusionment. Without a proper job, used mainly as lobby-fodder and having to defend a slowly discredited government, there was a resentment building up. The Tribune Group was being formed into a constant thorn in the flesh of the government, although the fact that Labour leftwingers were voting against their own government was not normally the signal for the Conservative Opposition to try and defeat the government. I am indebted to Professor Phillip Norton (now Lord Norton of Louth) for this table showing the extent of Government defeats during the period 1970–1983.

Government defeats in Parliament 1970–1983

| | Number of defeats | |
Parliament	House of Commons	House of Lords
1970–74	4	25
1974	17	15
1974–79	42	347
1979–83	1	45

Source: P. Norton, 'Behavioural Changes' in P. Norton (ed.) *Parliament in the 1980s* (Oxford: Basil Blackwell, 1985, p. 27.

The decision to hold a Referendum in July 1975 and to give Labour MPs a free vote undoubtedly saved a huge split within the PLP, the issue of the Common Market unquestionably dividing the Party both in the country and at Westminster. It was thought that by the device of the Referendum it would settle once and for all where Labour stood on the issue, and although Harold Wilson and George Brown won it by more than two to one, the issue rumbles on to this day. When I fought (and lost) the 1983 General Election it was on the policy of bringing Britain out of the Common Market!

The table above however shows that the Tory Party used its majority in the Lords to an inordinate degree, and even though most of Lords amendments are overturned in the Commons, they do take up time when time is the most valuable commodity.

That Labour would lose the May 1979 Election was not a forgone conclusion, despite the serious collapse in the Public Services caused by the breakdown in trust between the Trade Unions and the Labour Government, and although backing for the Labour Party remained strong in Scotland and the industrial North of England, it was the electors in the Midlands and the South of England who swung decisively to the Conservatives and sealed Labour's fate. Labour's total of seats in 1974 had been 319, yet at the dissolution this had been eroded to 306, and in the General Election, even further down to 268.

After the 1974 election the Conservatives had 276 seats, at the dissolution this had crept up to 282, but was increased to 339 at the General Election. The Scottish Nationalists paid for their stand on Devolution, going down from 11 seats in 1974 to only 2 at the General Election. As the Whip for Outer London and the 'Odds and Sods' such as Plymouth, Bristol, Norwich and the Medway Towns, I sent off 31 in my flock in May 1979. When we returned there were only 15. When I saw them off into the General

Election of 1983, only 3 returned. From 31 down to 3 – that was the size of the task facing Labour in opposition – even just to get back to parity with a Labour PLP with a bare majority. That it did so in 1997 was some sort of a miracle, to be repeated in 2001.

Thus began one of the most unhappy episodes in Labour parliamentary life, for it saw the coalescing of the disparate groupings which were 'fringe' or leftwing organizations, the most prominent being those calling themselves 'The Militant Tendency'. This all led first to the election of Michael Foot as Leader when Jim Callaghan stepped down in 1981, and to the election of Ken Livingstone as Leader of the GLC, together with the target of opposition to the Tory Government being seen as work for the extra-parliamentary forces of the Left outside Parliament. All over the place with our policies, we went into the 1983 General Election with a Manifesto described by Gerald Kaufman as 'The longest suicide note in history'. In that parliament I had remained in the Opposition Whips Office for 2 years, then at the invitation of Roy Hattersley became his deputy at the Department of the Environment. When he went to the Home Office he invited me to go with him and take on the responsibility for Prisons, but I was content with the brief for Local Government, etc, so was happy to serve under Gerald Kaufman until the election. In that election we plummeted down to 209 seats, partly due to the loss of Labour seats turned over to the newly formed SDP whilst the Conservatives went up to 397 seats from 334. The other great influence on the result was the successful war in the Falklands which brought Prime Minister Margaret Thatcher great kudos. Labour's subsequent new Leader – Neil Kinnock, who had my full support, had nowhere to go but up – which he did in 1987. My seat went in 1983 but I was saved when Michael Foot sent me to the Lords. Michael gave me a new life, for which I will always be grateful.

Women MPs post 1945 with special reference to 1974

Since 1945 there have only been two parliaments when Labour was not the Party with the largest number of women MPs, 1970 and 1983. Until the breakthrough year of 1997 when there were 120 women and 101 of them were Labour, the number bobbed around in the 20/30 region. Much can be said about the style or culture of women until 1997 and I can well recall the sheer joy on attending that historic meeting of the Parliamentary Labour Party in Church House in May 1997 and being bowled over by the multi-coloured throng as they crowded around Tony Blair for what was, by any standard, a historic picture. Even more so, looking down from the Strangers Gallery in those first heady days I could not help but be proud of the fact that it was Labour who had pioneered the shock breakthrough. It brought back memories of that 1974 parliament when I had made my own Maiden Speech sandwiched between Rhodes Boyson and Lynda Chalker. Of course, that 23 years had made a substantial difference in appearance, and for many a Labour woman MP it must have been a daunting time. Many of them had either not started their family or had had their first child, yet in the case of Yvette Cooper and Ruth Kelly within 7 years they were looking after more than their first – or even their second!

It was Helene Hayman who created the situation of babysitting in the Whips Office, for having got married just before entering the Commons in October 1974 she became a mother some years later and she then must have been some kind of ground-breaker in the maternal stakes! Of course there have been many women parliamentarians who attained motherhood whilst being a sitting member, but it is more usual today than it was in 1974.

I entered the Government Whips Office as a Lords Commissioner to the Treasury in April 1976 on James Callaghan becoming Prime Minister and, as is the way of organizing Whips to look after certain groups (usually – based on geography), there were a number of women in my flock, but there never was any distinction made or shown between men and women. A quick run-through of the Labour women MPs who served in the 1974 parliaments will be of interest:

Betty Boothroyd; Joyce Butler; Barbara Castle; Maureen Colquhoun; Gwyneth Dunwoody; Judith Hart; Helene Hayman; Lena Jeger; Joan Lestor; Joan Maynard; Millie Miller; Jo Richardson; Renee Short; Shirley Summerskill; Ann Taylor; Shirley Williams; Audrey Wise. Some of these deserve special mention, but I am moved to say that, looking back, I am struck by the maturity of most of my women colleagues, the depth of their experience and service before entering Westminster – and the long and distinguished service they rendered in the years after 1974.

CHAPTER 5

Into parliament and into government

THE TWENTY-FIVE YEARS before 1974 were my formative years as far as getting ready for my life in Government later. In 1952 I left my employment with the Newcastle on Tyne Cooperative Society and came to London and took up the post of National Organizer for the British Federation of Young Co-operators and this led, eventually, to obtaining the post of Education Secretary for the Enfield Highway Co-operative Society, where I spent nine happy years before switching my Co-operative emphasis from Social to Commercial aspects on becoming the Southern Section Secretary for the Co-operative Union, the national federal body for Co-operative Societies.

My interest in politics and 'changing things' must have been born out of the conditions on Tyneside as I grew up. I can remember someone telling me that if you are a socialist you are either an idealistic socialist – one who was persuaded to embrace the creed and the need to organize for power out of reading, discussing, arguing and finally coming to the conclusion that the way to do it was through socialism, or you were an environmental socialist. That is, someone who took in the conditions in which they were born, brought up, educated and worked in and concluded that the only way to change things for the better was through socialism. I was and remain an environmental socialist. The 1945 General Election came at the right time for me. The forces were in every sense a melting pot, a cauldron of ideas. In that period 1945 and 1946, there was time for lectures, discussions and the overwhelming feeling was that we would not go back to the old ways. It was truly a time for change, and there was excitement in the air.

When I first entered the Commons in 1974 Shirley Williams was the Secretary of State for Prices and Consumer Protection, her Minister of State was Alan Williams and the Parliamentary Private Secretary in the Department was Bob McClennan. Bob Mitchell was Shirley's PPS and, within two weeks of entering the Commons, I was invited by Alan Williams to be his PPS – the first rung of the ladder, unpaid and unseen, but it got the PPS into the inner sanctum of the Department. Shirley was an inclusive minister and I learned a great deal. I was there when Harold Wilson announced his unexpected resignation in March 1976, and I immediately became a member of Jim Callaghan's campaign team under the leadership of Merlyn Rees and Jack Cunningham. When Jim was finally

47

elected he sent for me to go to No 10. I hadn't a clue what job I might be offered, and it turned out that it was to go into the Whips' Office, under Michael Cocks, as a Lord Commissioner to the Treasury – a senior Whip. One of the perks of so being was that I went onto a very restricted list of about 52 who – twice a year – received a haunch of venison from the Royal Parks. Needless to say, other Whips shared in this bonanza!

The partnership of Michael Cocks and his Deputy, Walter Harrison, was a combination of Mr Nice Guy and Mr Nasty – they could reverse the roles at the drop of a hat. Within four months of Jim Callaghan's Government starting, it lost any majority that it had by deaths, and we entered the period when very sick colleagues were brought by ambulance into Westminster to be 'nodded through' at 10.00 p.m. for the vote. Add the name of Jack Dormand, the Pairing Whip and that of the Leader of the Commons, Michael Foot, and we came to that fateful vote of no confidence in March 1979 which brought it down.

Following the Referendum on Devolution in Scotland in March 1979 the Scot Nats blamed the Government for its failure and immediately tabled a Vote of No Confidence. Having done this herself – and alone – before, Margaret Thatcher immediately signed up to that vote, and thus the size of her party vote was strengthened by that of the Scots Nats and the Liberals, who had ended the Lib-Lab pact some time before. In the Whips' Office we knew that we could not win – and yet, and yet . . .

Walter Harrison, as Deputy Chief Whip, was the master of putting together coalitions for an issue, calling in rain checks for services rendered and making promises for the future. He, with Michael Cocks and Michael Foot, knew how we were getting on but, in general, the mood was that we would not survive – unless, unless . . . We suddenly learned that there would be some dramatic switching of support amongst the Irish and that happened, but we were made aware that the hitherto solid support from Gerry Fitt and Frank MacGuire SDLP could no longer be relied upon due to a breakdown in trust between Gerry and Roy Mason, the Northern Ireland Secretary of State.

'Doc' Broughton was the Member of Parliament for Batley and Morley. In five years I had only seen him three times, slipping into the Whips' Office at 10 p.m. when there was a very heavy three line whip – and he was gone in ten minutes. I was told that he suffered from emphysema and breathed with the utmost difficulty. When he was brought down to the House it was always without the approval of his doctor. When Walter Harrison spoke to his doctor about bringing him down for this crucial vote, he was told bluntly and forcefully that if he was brought down it would kill him. Those with the responsibility took the decision not to bring him down, and we lost the vote of No Confidence by one vote – 312 to 311.

Jim Callaghan, in the debate, said that the Scots Nats were 'like turkeys voting for an early Christmas'. When Doc Broughton was told that we had lost by one vote he was broken hearted, and died within days. The right decision had been made. If he had come down and we had survived, but he had died, the job of carrying on would have been impossible. Jim went to the country on 3 May and Labour lost by 268 to the Tory 339. We were out.

Singing 'The Red Flag' in the House of Commons

I am often asked what was the most dramatic moment – or event – in my years in the Commons, and this inevitably leads to my time in The Government Whips Office. Without a doubt it has to be the night of 30 March 1979 when Labour lost its majority on a Motion of Confidence and which precipitated the May General Election which saw Margaret Thatcher enter Downing Street. I deal with those dramatic events elsewhere, but running that night a very close second has to be the night Tarzan came into his own. It was the night that Michael Heseltine, golden locks flowing, picked up the Mace, the symbol of parliamentary authority, and was in the act of no-one knows what, when he was stopped in his tracks by his colleague, Jim Prior. Jim restored it to its rightful place, only to place it the wrong way round! Michael did not 'swing it' – rather he advanced towards the Labour benches 'below the gangway' from where most noise was emanating – but I get ahead of myself!

First, the background. In those long ago days (only thirty years!) it was the habit of the broadsheets to give very full accounts of proceedings in parliament, and so I can do no better that to use the excellent reports from *The Times* of the day, and let David Wood, that great parliamentary reporter and Political Editor, set the scene.

> Wild disorder broke out in the Commons last night when the Government won by one vote the division on a government motion to suspend standing orders so that a Speaker's ruling declaring the Aircraft and Shipbuilding Industries Bill as a hybrid, could be sidestepped. Fifteen minutes earlier there had been a tie of 303 votes and The Speaker, following precedent had voted with the Government. When the tellers came back into the House after the second division to announce the Government victory by one vote, for the first time since the Labour land-slide of 1945, Labour backbenchers began to sing The Red Flag (and I was there!).
>
> Mr Michael Heseltine, Opposition frontbench spokesman on Industry, seized the mace (memories of the Clydesiders in the 1930s,) and behind the Bar of the House blows were exchanged, elder statesmen like Geoffrey Rippon abused Government backbenchers in the roughest words. The

Speaker had to suspend the sitting of the House for 20 minutes after the Sergeant at Arms had separated MPs who seemed to be threatening to come to blows, (That was only the half of it!)

The anger of the Conservative Opposition, frontbench and backbench passed all bounds. They had managed to bring all the Opposition parties into agreement that the Government could not ride roughshod over parliamentary procedure to carry its Bill against the Speaker's ruling yesterday that it ought to be treated, prima facie, as a hybrid Bill. They knew that Mr Peter Fry, Conservative MP for Wellingborough, in spite, it is said, of three warnings, was reported to have left for a holiday in Corfu.

But for that, the combined Opposition would have defeated the Government on the first vote. The Ulster Unionists and the Scottish Nationalist Party, with Mr Grimond and the Liberals had kept to their bargain to oppose what they considered to be a trespass on the principle of parliamentary procedure, by which a minority opinion is given protection under the hybrid standing order that the Government was seeking to suspend. Then, in the second division, according to Mr Humphrey Atkins the Opposition Chief Whip, the Government won by one vote (304 to 303) because Tom Pendry, a government Whip, broke a pair.

Asked to comment on how the Government raised its vote between the two divisions from 303 to 304, Mr Atkins answered that it was a deliberate Government decision so that the Speaker would not have to give his casting vote at the second time of asking. In fact it was no secret that, following precedent, if there had been a tie in the second division on the Government's motion, the Speaker would have voted against, and thereby ensured that his ruling on the hybridity of the Bill, prima facie, would have been sustained.

So much for the bare facts, and even they are still to this day the subject of dispute and interpretation. What David Wood could not do in his excellent summary of the matters to be resolved was to convey the atmosphere in and around The Chamber that night. Picture the scene. More than 600 Members of Parliament crowded into a space used normally for 400, and many of them as they say, having dined well. At stake was the future of the Callaghan Government – and that less than two months old. Don't forget either that for many if not most of the MPs, there was the question of whether they would hold their seats at the consequent General Election if the Government fell.

George Thomas had been in the Speakers Chair for just a short while and undoubtedly this was the first major test of how (and whether) he could assert his authority. As he explained in his autobiography *George Thomas, Mr Speaker – the Memoirs of the Viscount Tonypandy*, he had been visited by all the major players in this drama before, during and after the event, but he had decided that he would stick faithfully to the precedents laid down by a previous Speaker, Speaker Denison in the 1860s.

Different solutions applied to the various stages of a bill's passage through the Commons. Denison had ruled that if it was a Second Reading (this is a general debate on the merits of the Bill) – he would vote in favour to give the House time to look at it again. If it was in committee (where the Bill is subject to detailed scrutiny), and there was a tie, the chairman should vote to keep the Bill as it was before it came to the committee. At the Report Stage in the House, the Speaker would vote to keep it as it left the Committee, but if it was the Third Reading, the last chance the House had to consider the bill, and the House failed to give it a majority, the Speaker would go against it and the bill would fail to pass. This last principle applied to motions too. Denison had taken the very sensible view that it was not up to the Speaker to 'make up the House's mind for it'.

In the Labour Whips Office there was relative calm. At that time I had been a Whip for some six weeks and was still bedding down, getting to know my flock, learning the trade, finding out what makes things – and people – tick. My fellow Whips were Michael Cocks (Chief) Walter Harrison (Deputy) Joe Harper, Jimmy Hamilton, David Stoddart, Donald Coleman, Jack Dorman (Pairing), Tom Pendry, Tom Cox, John Ellis, Peter Snape, Frank White, Jock Stallard, Alf Bates and Jim Tinn. Michael Cocks operated on a 'need to know' basis. At the regular Whip's meetings, held every day at 2 p.m. there would be a general review of the Business of the Day, but such things as stratagems and highly confidential information was kept very close to his chest. Thus, our task as Whips was simply to ensure that every possible 'voter' knew exactly what was expected of them, and to be in or near the Chamber at the appointed time. Crucially, Jack Dormand as the Pairing Whip held the vital information of who would be missing, including the sick and the Ministerial absences which were unavoidable. His task was to register with the Tory Pairing Whip (John Stradling Thomas) those it was agreed would be 'paired'. Although many names emerged after the event as playing some part in the excitement of the night, none fingered Jack – but he held – and still holds – key information surrounding the uproar.

To the event, told none better than by Ian Aitken and Peter Cole in *The Guardian* of Thursday 27 May under the banner headline 'Red Flag is waved at the Tory Bull':

Against an unprecedented background of fisticuffs, the singing of The Red Flag and a Conservative attempt to run away with the mace, the Government sneaked home to an unprecedented victory of one vote in its battle to overrule an attempt to destroy its nationalization plans for the shipbuilding industry. Nothing like it has been seen in the Commons chamber for more than 40 years. As soon as the Whips announced that a Government majority had been achieved by 304 votes to 303, Labour MPs stood and began to sing The Red Flag.

As they reached the words 'We'll keep the red flag flying here' Mr Michael Heseltine, Tory Spokesman at the conclusion of the debate, jumped up and seized the mace from its rack beneath the Speaker's Chair, As he waved it aggressively towards the Labour benches his Shadow Cabinet colleague Jim Prior wrested it from his hands and replaced it in its rack the wrong way round. While Mr Prior was changing ends, so to speak, a fracas developed in front of the Tory Front Bench. Mr Geoffrey Rippon, a former Tory Minister, seemed to be in full physical conflict with Mr Dennis Canavan, Labour MP for Stirlingshire West. Mr Canavan was pulled away by Mr Peter Snape, a Labour Whip. But as the altercation turned into something very like a brawl in the middle of the floor of the Commons, the Deputy Speaker, Sir Myer Galpern rose and declared 'The House is suspended for 20 minutes'.

Normally such a move would have ended the disturbance. But within a matter of moments, as MPs were moving out of the Chamber, yet another outbreak of scuffling took place. Mr Tom Swain, a miners' MP from Derbyshire, was seen fighting with a Tory member Mr Michael Spicer, Worcestershire South (and currently the Chair of the 1922 committee).

The origin of the majority of one soon turned out to be highly suspect. It was alleged that the Government secured its extra vote only when Mr Tom Pendry, a Labour Whip, deliberately broke a pairing arrangement with a Conservative member in order to go into the Government lobby to save it from defeat. As soon as it became known to the Conservative Whips, the Tory Chief Whip, Humphrey Atkins issued what amounted to a declaration of total war for the remainder of the present session.

The Government last night flatly denied the Tory allegations that a broken pairing arrangement had provided Labour with its majority of one in the second and most vital division. It insisted that it had discovered that Mr Fred Peart, the Minister of Agriculture, had not been included in a general ministerial pairing deal with the Opposition, although he was abroad on departmental business in Denmark.

The floor of the Commons on that night had to be seen to be believed – and even then you would not have believed it. It was a solid mass of Members pushing and shoving. When the singing started, together with every other Labour Member I gave vent to my pent up emotion and joined in the singing of The Red Flag. It was tribal. It was emotional. It was the only – and right – thing to do at the time. I witnessed all of the incidents as reported in *The Times* and *The Guardian*. I could not have done otherwise. Michael Heseltine wanted to apologise that night, but had to wait until the next day when he – unreservedly – apologised for his part in the shambles. The break-down in relations was total and placed great strains on everyone in the Commons. All I can say is that if the House had been televised it would have been a sad day for Parliament and democracy.

Memories of Edmonton

I was elected as the Member of Parliament for Edmonton on February 28 1974 and lost in the election of June 9 1983. Those almost ten years were some of the happiest and most fulfilling of my life. I had one of the best agents in the Labour Party. His name was Ted Pain. He was the National Secretary of the Labour Agents Organisation and was a well-known and respected figure within the Labour Party. Edmonton had been solid Labour for many years, but had now become part of the London Borough of Enfield, along with Southgate and Enfield. It was without a doubt the poorest part of the London borough and along the eastern part of the borough provided much of the industrial strength of the area. The Great Cambridge Road (the A10) was a ribbon along which great firms were perched – Fergusons Television, Belling and Lee, Samgamo Weston, Ripaults.

I had succeeded to a majority from Austin Albu of just over 2000, but Edmonton was always seen as a Labour heartland. When I inherited it I knew every school, every pub, every street and every factory from the days when I was the Leader of the Council. I made it my business to be seen as widely as I could. One of the highlights was the Silver Jubilee of the Queen's Coronation in 1977. I had had a card printed wishing Her Majesty all happiness and this featured largely in a wide circulation. I quickly found out that Edmonton was one of those places which loves a street party and before I knew it I had been invited to 83! My wife, Margaret and my agent did 40 and, together with Evelyn my agent's wife, I did 43 – both over two days. I have a lovely album of photographs and even today, more than 25 years later, I still get stopped as I go round Edmonton Green Market by young women with their children who tell me they remember my attending their street party in 1977! The wedding of Charles and Diana in 1981 brought similar pleasure and activity, although not on the same scale. Happily, into the year 2002 I still got five invitations from my old patch to attend their Golden Jubilee celebrations!

I held a 'surgery' at my offices in Broad House every other Friday and there were times when I had to squeeze in an extra one. The record for two Fridays and an extra one was in excess of 100 cases. I know from other places that this was not exceptional, but the workload flowing from surgeries was heavy. In those days the assistance one received by comparison to that available now for MPs was poor. I do not begrudge modern day MPs a penny of what they get. They need the support they are granted. Neither do I grudge the present generation of councillors, who are paid generous allowances, while in my day we did not get a penny. In Edmonton the greatest problem was housing, either the lack of it or the

Local workers present a petition at Westminster

Boxing Clever!

Doing what comes naturally to a politician – kissing babies!

In at the deep end – swimming for the British Heart Foundation

state of it. Edmonton was one of those Labour Councils which had its own direct labour building force and was a pioneer in municipal housing and enterprise. But times they were a-changing and, when you've got to go, you've got to go!

Two memorials of horror

I declined trips abroad, more often than not, on the grounds that as far as I was concerned Westminster is where the action was. Although I appreciated the value of visiting foreign countries, I would rather be at home. I have been a member of the Inter-Parliamentary Union (IPU) and the Commonwealth Parliamentary Association (CPA) for almost 30 years now, and those are the main sources of securing membership of a delegation, but I was never on either a CPA or IPU delegation. However, there were two trips which turned out to be of great and lasting impact.

The first was a visit to Japan. Sir Julian Ridsdale was the Conservative Member for Harwich and a gentleman. He was able, thanks to his diplomatic connections, to arrange through the Whips Offices for a joint delegation paid for by the Japanese Government, and I went on such a trip in 1981. It gave me an insight into that country and the ways it was, by virtue of its culture, in the ascendancy industrially. It also gave me the opportunity to visit Hiroshima and to stand on the spot where the epicentre of the H-bomb had been. The way in which that country had reconstructed its life had been breath-taking, but it was an awful reminder of war.

I have always been a sincere supporter of the State of Israel, and have been a Member of the Labour Friends of Israel for thirty years. Paying our own travel costs, but being guests of the Government, I visited Israel in 1978 along with John Macintosh, Brian Sedgemore, Dennis Canavan, Bruce Grocott and Robin Corbett. One of the most dramatic events was a visit to the place where millions of victims of the Holocaust are commemorated – Yad Vashem. Two happenings haunt me. We approached the memorial by walking through an avenue of trees. This is called the Avenue of the Gentiles. Here every tree is dedicated to a non-Jew who saved Jewish lives during the war. There is only one dedicated to an Englishman, and this is because it was on the European mainland that the most terrible crimes were committed. Charlie Coward had been a full-time soldier who was captured and found himself in a Labour Camp attached to Auschwitz where he saw the skeletons of people who had been incarcerated there. He devised a scheme whereby hundreds of Jewish people were smuggled out to freedom. Charlie Coward lived in Edmonton! I went to see him on my return. By then he was destined to die shortly, but it was humbling to meet such a hero.

Later, when I visited Yad Vashem with my wife, we were viewing the graphic pictures, one of which showed prisoners with their prison numbers tattooed on their arms. A young boy asked his father why they had to do that, when a man standing nearby thrust his arm forward and rolled up his sleeve to show his prison number. He was now happily settled in New York, but that number would remain with him all his life – and in my memory too.

Up the Lilywhites

I have never pretended that I was other than a 'Magpie'. As I spend time in my garden I can be sure that some time a magpie will appear, and I will see immediately that its black and white plumage and cocky strut is the image of the Magpie who paraded around St James's Park now almost 70 years ago. Every team has a mascot, invariably dressed in the colours of the team. The black and white stripes of Newcastle United are famous and bring me warm memories of great games that I have watched – and cried over! But when I moved to Enfield and represented Edmonton in Parliament, I began to see more and more of Tottenham Hotspur than I had done previously. I had first stood on the terraces of White Hart Lane in 1946 when I had watched Bruce Woodcock knock out Jack London for the British Heavyweight title, but when I moved there in the 50s it was to see such as Len Ducquimen, Ronnie Burgess, Billy Nicholson, Danny Blanchflower, Dave Mackay, Pat Jennings and Alf Ramsay. Incidentally, Alf had been employed by the Grays Co-op Society and played for the Society team. I can remember seeing the first game that Jimmy Greaves played for them, and it was a real thriller. Was it 60,000 or 65,000 attendance, with almost all of them standing?

When I spoke to the pupils in an Edmonton school, I would chat for a bit and then ask 'Who supports the Spurs?' when about half the hands in the class would shoot up. The other half looked despondent. I would then ask 'Who supports the Arsenal?' and half the hands would shoot up again, and the rest looked despondent. I would then say 'My team is Newcastle United' and the whole class would boo! When I looked around the class I could see myself some 60 years before, except that most of those in my class had no shoes let alone football boots! I would then get them talking so that they would not stop. I would ask them where they had been for their holiday that year, and would then be given a tour around the world. Edmonton and Enfield were heavily influenced by Greece, Turkey and Cyprus, so there was always a good proportion who had been to Larnica, Paphos, Limassol and Nicosia. I had visited Cyprus in 1976, only two years after the division of the Island following the invasion. I met Archbishop

Makarios and the leaders of the Greek community, but it was always more difficult to meet Turkish Cypriots, although I had met Ralph Denktash frequently when he visited Westminster.

The Indian sub-continent provided many pupils for Edmonton schools, and they had all assimilated the culture of supporting a local football team, either the Gunners or the Lilywhites.

I had always been made very welcome at White Hart Lane and was a frequent visitor to the Directors' box where I enjoyed their hospitality. It was there that I met Gordon MacKeag who was a power in the Newcastle boardroom at the time. His father was Alderman MacKeag and with Stan Seymour had led the Newcastle United of the post war period, when they did very well.

The Spurs were as famous for their exploits in the boardroom as they were for their play on the football field. They enjoyed the patronage of vast areas of north London and attracted many well-known personalities. It was there that I met, and enjoyed the friendship of Warren Mitchell and of Ted Willis and his wife, Audrey. He was Tottenham born and bred while she was from Enfield Highway, part of my patch when I worked for the Enfield Highway Co-op. They were as passionate for their club, the Spurs, as I was for my club, the Magpies and we always had friendly banter about the relative merits of teams over the years. Ted was to get to the Lords before me and, after being there for a while, he christened it 'God's waiting room'!

It was in 1981 that I had one of the most enjoyable experiences of my life. The dream for a top club is to bring off 'the Double' and in 1981 Spurs got to, and won the Cup Final. As is fitting, arrangements had been made to celebrate this happy event with a reception in Tottenham Town Hall, and it was to start from Edmonton Town Hall. As the local MP I was invited to greet the players, and it was great – Ossie Ardiles, Ricky Villa, Glen Hoddle and all the stars of the day. In addition, their manager at the time was Keith Burkinshaw who had previously been the manager of Newcastle United. We got on very well. The Mayor of Enfield was Clive Goldwater and he invited me to ride to Tottenham Town Hall in the Mayoral car. What a treat! Short-lived though, for he had to tell me that the Town Clerk had turned up and there was no seat for me. I was not upset, but Keith Burkinshaw overheard the conversation and invited me to travel on the top of the open-deck coach with the team. Fabulous! Somehow or other they managed to get a piano on top, and Chas and Dave were banging out the team song for that time – 'We are on our way to Wembley, Spurs are gonna do it again'. And there I was, beaming down on a sea of delirious fans who were all my constituents. How lucky can an MP get?

It was bedlam, but happy and abandoned. We passed the Charrington Brewery and two boys, clinging on to something, held up a huge poster which read 'Thatcher not the only one with Crooks at No 11'. Garth Crooks was then one of the stars of the team and he told me later that that was not the first time that Labour supporters had done exactly the same on other happy days!

As we got to Tottenham Town Hall, there waiting was the Civic Party. As I got off the coach I went slap bang into the open arms of my parliamentary colleagues Norman Atkinson and Reg Race, whose faces were a picture! We all went into the Town Hall and had a marvellous time enjoying the hospitality of the Tottenham Council. Spurs went on to win the FA Cup the next year but, for me, it just was not the same.

My cousins – Hazel and Miriam

One day, I was speaking to my Mam when I was already an MP. She said that she had seen my cousin on the television. I was surprised and asked her who she meant and she said, 'Miriam – Miriam Stoppard'. I said that I knew that I had two cousins – Hazel and Miriam – and they were the daughters of my Aunty Ginny and Uncle Sid. 'Well' she said, 'Miriam married this chap Tom Stoppard and she is always on the telly with programmes regarding health and fitness matters'. I was very proud of the fact that THE Miriam Stoppard was my cousin!

Then one day I received a letter addressed to me at the House of Lords from a girl in the Sixth Form at Haverstock Comprehensive School asking if I would take some of her classmates around Parliament as part of their studies. She concluded her letter by stating, 'My mother tells me that we are related because she is your cousin' and signed herself Oona King. Of course, I was on the telephone like a shot, making the arrangements for the class to visit Parliament, and also asking that her mother – my cousin, Hazel – and her daughter, Oona, come and visit us. They were both lovely, and a joy to meet – and relatives too! Of course, I wanted to know all about the family, especially my Aunt Ginny, not least because when I was lying in hospital after being shot, she had accompanied my mother to see me, and I would always be grateful for that. We then went to see them both when they lived in Belsize Park and, to my delight, my Aunty Ginny and Uncle Sid were there too. And brother Slater. Sadly, Hazel's marriage had been ended. Her husband was Preston King, who was a Philosophy lecturer at the University of Lancaster.

Margaret and I, with my two sons, Martin and Ian, visited Miriam in their lovely home where they and Tom Stoppard got on famously. We also met Oona's best friend, Quincey Whittaker, whose father was known to me as Ben Whittaker, the former MP for Hampstead and Highgate, and whose lovely wife, Janet, was made a Peeress in 1999. What a stimulating turn of events, to find that my two cousins had done so well. Hazel was a teacher of Special Needs in a local school and she subsequently has gone to live in France. And Oona?

When I met her, she was still a schoolgirl but I knew from what she told Margaret and me that she had already done (picking coffee beans in Costa Rica, for instance!) that she would one day be a star. And so it has proved. She next popped up on the Terrace of the House of Commons at a lunch hosted by Robin Cook – because she was assisting his Health team in Brussels. That's where she met her husband – and we all met again at her wedding and where I also met many of my relatives, long lost but delightfully found! Neil and Glenys Kinnock were there too, and before long, I was to greet Oona at Westminster, when she entered the Commons in 1997. I do believe in fairy tales!

When you've got to go

The period from 1979 to 1983, when I lost my seat, was not a happy one. Some of my fellow Whips took the opportunity to leave the Whips Office but I stayed on, the main reason being that I wanted something to do and the second reason is that Michael Cocks asked me to. He had had experience of being in an Opposition Whips Office and wanted reliable colleagues he could trust to 'lift the moral of the troops'. That is what he told me.

Just before Jim was to resign as Leader, he asked me to join Roy Hattersley at the Department of the Environment, which I did gladly. I was, and still am, an admirer of Roy's. When he bid for the Deputy Leadership in 1983, I was on his team. When Denis Healey bid for the Leadership against Michael Foot, I was on his team. Opinions differ, and I love Michael, but in that period after 1979 and before 1983, Denis was without doubt the Parliamentary giant who, I believe, would have held the Party together. Those who broke away to form the SDP used as their final excuse to justify doing so, the election of Michael as Labour Leader. It is said that some of them had made sure that Michael would be elected Leader by voting for him in the Leadership contest, whilst sadly, with the militancy within constituency Labour Parties, some of my colleagues succumbed to pressure and voted for him against their better judgment. The outcome was that Michael became Leader of a very divided party and had little chance to bring unity.

In that period, besides beginning the processes of rolling back any advance made by Labour since 1945, Margaret Thatcher faced the greatest challenge to a Prime Minister's authority it was possible to imagine – the Falklands crisis. By June of 1982, with victory to hand, she had the ideal launching pad for a further term of office, which duly came in 1983. Labour had had a disastrous campaign – categorized by the remark of Gerald Kaufman that Labour's Manifesto was the 'longest suicide note in history'. In Edmonton, I began that campaign in sober mood. My majority inherited from Austin Albu had been 2,030, which increased in the elections of 1974 to 5,000 and then to 6,500 but had dropped to 1,970 in 1979. Crucially, boundary changes took good bits out and put bad bits in, and I knew I had a fight on my hands. In the event, I lost by 1,200. Outer London had a reputation for dealing harshly with the potentially defeated Party. As I listened to results coming in, and hearing that Joan Lestor had lost Slough, and Stan Newens Harlow, I knew we would lose Edmonton. And so we did.

After the General Election in June 1983 I was fifty-eight and had no job to go back to. Gentle enquiries to various Co-operative sources, whilst sympathetic, told me that they were in a process of 'slimming down'. I was wondering what would happen, when I took a call from Tom McCaffery, the Office Organizer for Michael Foot. Would I be interested in going to the Lords? I had to think. I felt that having lost Edmonton and waiting four or five years meant that I would be sixty-two or sixty-three at the next General Election and there was no guarantee that I would either be selected – or elected. It turned out that the comrade who did fight the seat in 1987 (Bryan Grayston) lost it by more than 7,000, so my chances would have proved slim indeed! Sounding out a number of friends in various parts of my interests assured me that it was a chance too good to miss. I rang Tom back and he was happy, but pointed out that Michael was putting forward a number of others and that there was not certainty that I would get there. I was content.

Usually, the arrangements on numbers and parties takes about a month but after six weeks, there was still no news. Items appeared in the gossip columns that Margaret Thatcher objected to some of those on Michael's list, especially those who had only climbed the ladder as high as becoming a Whip! She held to the view that at the very least candidates for the Lords had to have been of Cabinet rank or material. We were told that Michael had put forward more than twenty Labour nominees, many promised before the Election, and other, like me, casualties of the battle. In the event, Labour was given seven Peers, with the Tories taking nine. Of Labour's seven, four of us were from the Whips Office: David Stoddart, Jock Stallard, Joe Dean and myself. Others in the list included Joel Barnett, David Ennals and Neil Carmichael. Some ex-Cabinet Ministers had been excluded but came in on later lists.

Altogether I was very satisfied. I could continue my Parliamentary life and at least had the base for earning a living until my pensions kicked in when I was sixty-five. I took my place on a Tuesday, made my Maiden Speech on the Wednesday and spoke from the Front Bench on planning matters on a Thursday! I had willingly accepted Tom Ponsonby's invitation to join the Labour Whips Office and served there for the next fourteen years. Added to my Whips Office experience in the Commons, this means that I had served in Labour Whips Offices for almost twenty years, and on both sides in the Commons and in Opposition in the Lords. I am proud of that!

What impressed me most on entering the Lords? Meeting so many I had known in the Commons, I suppose, and the generally more relaxed ambience. Tom operated a rota, which meant that I had to stay often till the end of the business with no car to take me home, as in the Commons, but that was taken in my stride. My local government experience put me alongside Alma Birk, with whom I struck up a lasting friendship. She was a real professional and I learned a lot.

CHAPTER 6

A Chief Whip's lot

Timing is of the essence

O NE THING THAT YOU LEARN in the Whips Office is the supreme importance of dates and their relationship to recesses and especially as they impinge on the end of a session. Whilst currently there is discussion on Bills being enabled to be 'carried over' from one session to the next, as a general rule, a Bill which starts in one session must complete all of its stages in both Houses before Parliament is prorogued. The art of the business manager – in both Houses – is to time when Bills start and to take account of the minimum days required between each stage in both Houses so that time is programmed in for the number of Committee stage days, Report stage days – and, in the Lords, days for Third Reading as well, not part of the procedure in the Commons. It is true to say that the main weapon in the hands of the Opposition is to delay, and if it is possible to so delay the passage of a Bill as the session end nears. It is what an Opposition dreams of!

In the spring of 1997, John Major was boxed in. The Parliament was due to end in May and with Easter looming, the date whereby Bills had to complete their passage in both Houses was realistically seen as the end of March. In the Lords, we had inflicted defeats which required the Commons to deal with amendments and then send them back to the Lords – with the possibility of 'ping-pong' emerging, and the business managers of the Government had landed themselves in a right old mess. As the Opposition forces in the Lords had played no small part in arriving at this situation, we left for the General Election, the date for which we had helped to influence, in good heart. I spent the campaign period visiting about fifteen constituencies around the M25 and spend a lot of time in Edmonton and Enfield. Southgate was not even a twinkle in Tony Blair's eye! Stephen Twigg soon put that right and I was there at that count to see Michael Portillo make a dignified exit from front line politics.

Two days before the election, Ivor Richard rang me to come in immediately. Tony Blair had asked for his list of Ministerial appointments. We both took the view that having ended the previous Parliament with a Front Bench that had performed out of its socks, we would recommend that they be appointed Ministers – to begin with. He would recommend me as his Chief Whip, on the assumption that he would be invited to be the Leader of the Lords. We asked Tony to note the special qualities of Liz Symon, Helene Hayman and Larry Whitty. And so to bed. To dream!

A Chief Whip's lot can be a happy one

When the dust had settled after the appointments had been made to Labour's Front Bench in the Lords, I was no longer Labour's Chief Whip. I could not, nor did I, complain. I had been elected as their Chief Whip by Labour Peers in 1990 and had enjoyed my seven years 'at the top'. Tony Blair rang me the Monday after the General Election to tell me that I would not be serving. I asked him who it would be and he told me that it would be Denis Carter. I said, 'He is a good man, and he will not let you down.' He thanked me for that, as did Denis when I told him. Denis had stood as Chief Whip when Tom Ponsonby had died in 1990 and I had been chosen by Labour Peers, and beat him. He became my Deputy and we had then, and later, worked in harmony.

As the lists were scrutinized, it was seen that a criteria for appointment in that first list had been age. It is difficult to appoint younger Peers in a Group where the average age in 1995 had been seventy-one. I was seventy-two at the Election and no-one was appointed in the Lords who was as old as that. I was sorry for my Deputy, Brian Morris. He came into the Lords from being the Principal of Lampeter College in Wales. He was a lovely man and did great work for the Prince of Wales. He was one of the acknowledged experts on Shakespeare and would bring the House to laughter when he rattled off extracts from many a classic. He just could not get his head round the political world where doing a good job – a very good job – in Opposition did not mean that you got the job in Government.

Other casualties were Maurice Peston and Charles Williams. Both had been part of the backbone of Labour's successful attacks on the Government, and outstanding in their demolition of Government policies in detail and ad infinitum. They, however, were both over sixty.

Andrew McIntosh was a special case. In Opposition, he had performed persistently with the Home Office brief and had the measure of all Tory Ministers. He, together with Patricia Hollis, were the outstanding performers from Labour's Front Bench in Opposition. He deserved an appointment, but it went to Gareth Williams, who too was an outstanding, even brilliant, performer 'at the box' – the yardstick whereby all Parliamentary performers are judged. When the post of Deputy Chief Whip remained unfulfilled in stepped Andrew and he never looked back. He carried a number of Departmental Briefs, and was the star performer in that first administration.

Flying back from holiday in New Zealand in 1998 when I got off the plane I was developing a Deep Vein Thrombosis, which was dealt with splendidly at the appropriately named Whipps Cross Hospital. Later I was able to raise issues related to DVT, and to encourage the establishment of a Selection Committee in the Lords to which I gave evidence as did Dr John Scurr, a leading consultant in the field, and relatives of those who had died as a result of a DVT were called. Finally, a report was issued which was accepted by the Department of Health as a working basis for improving the situation. By this time, there were many additional cases publicized which would have gone unknown without the Inquiry. I played a modest part in the whole affair – except that without my being directly affected when I got off that plane, I doubt if the Inquiry would have got off the ground. And so, when I reflect on the value of my time in the Lords, I do not think of the drama, the Bills, the speeches; I close my eyes and think of clots, only to wake up and find myself amongst – oh, never mind!

Another 'campaign' from which I get much satisfaction concerns blind Magistrates. I had become interested in magisterial affairs when Margaret, my wife, became a Magistrate and served on the Highgate Bench. This work absorbed her interest for many years and she enjoyed the work. Laurie Buxton was the Chair of the Highgate Bench and had been a friend for many years. Until he retired, he had been the Maths Advisor to the Inner London Education Authority and a highly respected figure in the academic world of the University of London. Sadly, he died in 2001.

In developing his research into inhibitions facing disadvantaged aspirants for the Bench, he drew my attention to the fact that if a person was blind, that barred them from consideration to become a Magistrate. Nothing ventured, nothing gained, so I took him in to see the then Lord Chancellor, in whose gift these matters were. He was James Mackay, Lord Mackay of Clashfern, and a lovely man who made courageous decisions which did not always please the Judiciary. He expressed sympathy and explained that the issue had been examined many years ago, and he would cause it to be examined again.

Came the General Election of 1997 and a change of Lord Chancellor. He was now Derry Irvine, Lord Irvine of Lairg, and I requested that he meet Laurie and me to see what the position now was. He readily acceded to my request but this time, Laurie was accompanied by another who he introduced as the Chairman of the National Institute for the Blind. The Lord Chancellor said that he had examined the papers and was minded to consider having an experiment by appointing a limited number for a trial period. In the course of the conversations, the case we made had been immeasurably strengthened by our companion, who turned out to be – a Judge! Although blind, he nevertheless was able to satisfy the authorities that he was competent. The main argument against putting blind people on the Bench was that they were unable to see the person in the dock, and so were unable to detect whether they were telling the truth! As was pointed out, a blind person develops many other senses so that by concentrating on not only what the Defendant looked like, but how he sounded – and avoiding being impressed unduly by how he looked – could make a good decision.

Some years later, the Lord Chancellor announced that he was authorizing eight persons to be appointment Magistrates for a trial period, and he did this at a Press Conference in his Department and was kind enough to invite me to attend. It was one of the most satisfactory times in my life, to see the men and women who had been chosen, standing there full of apprehension but at the same time, proud that they would determine if this progressive move was to succeed. It did, and a year later, more blind persons were made Magistrates. My inquiries proved to me that with their fellow Magistrates that they had been made welcome – and felt very satisfied.

The Whips Office – powerhouse or powerless?

It can be confidentially stated that all Parties at Westminster look upon the operation of their Whips Office as a crucial part of the operation – that is either to sustain the Government, or to bring it down. Because by tradition – at least in the Commons – Whips take a vow of silence as they go about their masters' business – little comes into the public domain, save when the spotlight is shone into the dark and murky places they call the 'usual channels'. But in the Lords it is somewhat different. Because of the paucity of Peers who actually want to be visible and/or articulate there is a convention that Whips double up as not only a member of the team of Whips, but also as Spokespersons. In Government, this means that they are surrogate Ministers, both answering parliamentary questions and also taking part in debates. There are a host of other duties shared between both Houses, and, at all times, ensuring that the Minister has by his or her side a Whip who ensures that the Minister can concentrate on the business in hand while the Whip is in charge of 'House matters'.

But without a doubt, the character and ability of the Chief Whip can make or mar the performance of the Whips Office. Only those on the inside can have a sound idea of precisely how they operate – or how successful they have been. The glamour and the rhetoric parades outside the Whips Office – on the Floor of the Chamber or in the headlines and press releases, yet it is in the delivery of the vote to support and sustain their Party that the Chief Whip is seen to be on form. So many things can happen. The ideal would be to record a vote which matches the known strength of the Party, yet there are so many ways in which that committed vote does not appear in The Lobby.

One thing is for sure. With the use of pagers and emails used both by the Whip and by the Member it is far more likely that the outcome of a vote is known before it is announced now than it was even thirty years ago. In this, the role of the Pairing Whip is absolutely crucial, especially in the Commons, for in the Lords there is no system of 'pairing'. The Pairing Whip in the Labour Whips Office in the seventies was Jack Dormand (now Lord Dormand of Easington) who had that job when Labour had not only no majority, but was actually 'in deficit'! And although it is between the two main parties – Labour and Conservative – that the balance has to be known, in those days there were the Liberals, the Scot Nats and the Irish, all of whom were capable of upsetting the apple cart, and as a consequence had to be kept 'on board . Here, in my days in the Commons Whips Office, the work and skill of the Deputy Chief Whip, Walter Harrison was critical. He had the task not only of knowing which of those groups would be present, but also which members could be persuaded not to be present! The reality was that although each of the minority parties had to maintain a public position, there was always room to 'do a deal'. And deals were done!

The first of my 'Chief Whips' was Bob Mellish. I had first met him when I was the Leader of the London Borough of Enfield Council in 1965. He was the Minister for Housing, and he was accompanied by Evelyn Dennington who was the Chair of Housing in the Greater London Council. They came to Enfield as part of a drive to build more houses in the public sector. They did not need to knock on our door too hard, for Enfield was a great Housing Authority. Partly as a result of their enthusiasm we set ourselves a target of building 1000 units a year by 1970. Alas, by then we had lost office in 1968, but that target was achieved. Later all three of us would meet up again in the Lords when I arrived there in 1983 – but that as they say is another story! Bob was a brilliant Chief Whip. He was down-to-earth, could bark out his orders and was Labour to his fingertips. Unfortunately for him, when Harold Wilson announced his retirement in March 1976, Bob backed Michael Foot for Prime Minister – and lost. The price for that was that Jim Callaghan replaced him with Michael Cocks.

One of the successes of the new Tory Government was to create the Urban Development Corporations and one of the first to get off the ground was the London Dockland Development Corporation. Michael Heseltine was the Secretary of State and in 1981 he invited Bob to be Deputy Chairman to Sir Nigel Broakes. Bob had to consider leaving his seat at Bermondsey in the heart of Docklands to take the post. I can recall a vicious meeting of the Parliamentary Labour Party when this became public knowledge. Bob was pilloried for helping the Tories to make a success of – anything! Labour under Peter Shore had spent more than 5 years trying to get the Riparian authorities with frontage onto the Thames, together with the Labour GLC, to agree on a way to create the structure to bring that derelict and blighted part of London into life, but to no avail. Local petty jealousies prevailed, and when Michael Heseltine got his hands on this and other areas such as Liverpool docks, he was armed with planning powers over local government, and drove his schemes through. Although I was deputy to Gerald Kaufman at the time, and deployed all the arguments against the schemes, I now know and say that without the ruthlessness of Heseltine (and Thatcher) it would not have happened. As I look at Canary Wharf and the splendour of the revitalized London Docklands today I know they were right, and we were wrong.

By one of those twists of fate, in 1986 I was approached by Sir George Young who was the Junior Minister at the Department of the Environment with the invitation to consider being appointed as Bob's successor. The offer had the approval of his superiors, Kenneth Baker and Patrick Jenkins, and the job carried a salary of £22,000 for a three day week, at that time and with no other income a tempting offer, but I would have been restricted in my political activities, and I declined. Later, and now in the Lords, my next Chief Whip was given the job – Michael Cocks. A small world!

In the seven years I was the Opposition Chief Whip there were four Government Chief Whips. First was Bertram Stanley Mitford Bowyer, The Lord Denham – Bertie to his friends – with hereditary links going back to 1660. He has what must surely be a unique record of having served in a Whips Office – in either House – for more than 30 years, having entered it in 1961 until he retired from it in 1991. The Office carries the title of Captain of the Honourable Corps of Gentlemen at Arms, and, whilst Deputy, the title of Captain Yeoman of the Guard. He was also a writer of thrillers, with such titles as 'The Man who Lost his Shadow', 'Foxhunt' and 'Black Rod'. He was – and is – a gentleman, a martinet who knew procedures and protocol backwards. We never had a falling out over trust. He remains a friend to this day.

He was succeeded by Alexander Hesketh, an altogether different kind of fish. Whilst Bertie was one of nature's Whips, Alexander wasn't. If I say that he suffered fools badly it would not be an understatement. It was during our 'sparring' time in the early nineties that we both had to endure many long and excruciatingly boring hours well into the small hours of the morning. We both helped to give the Lords a bad name. He it was who had the impossible task as a Minister of State of bringing in 'The Football Spectators Bill'.

Nicholas James Christopher Lowther, the Second Viscount Ullswater came next. He had succeeded his great-grandfather and was educated at Eton and then Trinity College, Cambridge. He had been a Captain in the Royal Wessex Yeomanry and was at one time the Chairman of the Wincanton Races Co. – an interest much shared with others on his side of the House! By the time he became the Chief Whip, Conservative Peers had been in government for 14 years and their spirit was somewhat dimmed. He had a difficult task, but he stuck to it manfully. We respected each other and never had a cross word. He failed to win the election to decide those Conservative Peers who gained a place after 'the cull', but made his name into the history books when he became the first of them to be elected back when a vacancy occurred on a death.

The last of my opposing Chief Whips was Tom Strathclyde. He is blessed with the names of Thomas Galloway du Roy de Bilcqay Galbraith and must hold the record of being both the youngest Chief Whip and subsequently the Leader of the Opposition in the Lords. He came second in the poll to retain Conservative Peers and is extremely popular – and able. His combative style at 'the Box' when in Government marked him out as a personality to watch. That he recently was voted 'Peer of the Year' by his colleagues underlines his qualities.

Michael Cocks had the almost impossible task of sustaining the Callaghan Government with a declining majority which disappeared completely within a year of his assuming office and which led to the Lib/Lab Pact. He could not afford to be other than dedicated. In my mind that Government was sustained by the efforts of Jim Callaghan, Michael Foot, Michael Cocks, Walter Harrison and Jack Dormand. This was the High Command. At other levels, such as the Cabinet and within the Parliamentary Labour Party there were others who helped. Cledwyn Hughes for instance who, as the Chairman of the PLP was a bulwark against those on the wider extremes of the militant left who tried almost every week, yet never succeeded in breaking through the barrier. Labour was driven from Office in May 1979 due not to the failure of that High Command, but by the smell and signs of decay wrought by what became known as the winter of discontent, and to what extent that was a self-inflicted wound only history will tell. No-one was more dedicated to saving that Labour Government than Michael. Even then, though, he had to contend with bitter strife within his own constituency of Bristol South. After losing the 1979 election, Tony Benn who represented another Bristol seat was the sweetheart of the Labour left in Bristol – and of many who were to the left even of the Labour Party. Michael had the task of defending his Government, often alone, and soon became a target, especially when Tony Benn lost out in a boundary redistribution and left Bristol at the 1983 General Election. From then on

Michael was undermined within his own constituency, and lost a bitter reselection contest in 1987. For my part, he was a victim of that destructive virus which consumed the Labour Party during the Callaghan Government, and which was only halted when Neil Kinnock made his unforgettable denouncing speech to the Annual Conference in Bournemouth in 1986. Michael was a good man.

When I came to the Lords in 1983 the Labour Chief Whip was Tom Ponsonby. He had succeeded the charismatic Pat Llewelyn-Davies. Tom was a hereditary Peer, although he had tried to find a seat to fight more than once in the past. Amongst other qualifications he brought to the Lords was a spell as Secretary to the Fabian Society, a post held by, amongst others, Shirley Williams and Bill Rogers of 'gang of four' fame. Tom knew how to handle a Hereditary House, and did so with consummate skill. Amongst his skills was that of tact and diplomacy, which had led him to become the Chairman of the Football Panel, via his links within the House, with Football Trust colleagues. This was the Panel which met every Saturday throughout the season and pronounced the result of matches which had not taken place! Together with Cledwyn Hughes he formed a partnership of the highest order in which the reputation and successes of the Labour Peers Group became a legend. When he died in 1990 I was his Deputy, and in the election to succeed him I beat Dennis Carter – who went on to be appointed by Tony Blair in 1997. As others have said, it's a funny old world!

Whips I have known

I served in the Labour Whips Office in Government in the Commons for three years and for two years in the Commons in Opposition. I served in the Labour Whips Office in the Lords for 14 years, seven of them as Opposition Chief Whip – 19 years in all. To say that I had enjoyed every moment of it would not be true, but to look back on that period in my life gives me immense satisfaction. Often described as; 'the power house' it has to be able to deliver that which the Leader and/or the Prime Minister demands. Congeniality amongst colleagues is absolutely essential and getting the chemistry right is the job of the Chief Whip. Beggars can't always be choosers, and in both Houses men and women arrive there at the behest of the overall plan of the Leader or Prime Minister, When Jim Callaghan sent for me on his becoming Prime Minister in April 1976 he invited me to go to the Whips Office as a Senior Whip with the title of 'Lords Commissioner to the Treasury' which was very acceptable, especially when he told me that he had discussed the composition of the Whips Office with Michael Cocks the new Chief Whip, and he told me that Michael was happy for me to join the team. Geography plays a big part in the Commons, for it is crucial that 'the flock' have their own regional shepherd – they can talk the same language and share common knowledge about the region. As a Geordie Michael allocated me to a vacancy for the Northern Group, but they resented the fact that although I was more from the region than many who represented Northern seats, I was not 'one of them'. I represented Edmonton, a London seat, and so had that allocation – plus what we called the 'odds and sods', such as the Medway Towns, the South West and Outer London – the Home Counties, making up the share of about 30. Having been active in London politics and a Leader of a London Council helped.

The make-up of my group would be little different from that of others. It included current and ex-Cabinet Ministers, long serving and newly arrived colleagues, men and women, left and right. The trick for the Whip is to get to know what motivates each and every, one of his group, to earn their confidence – and be trusted. Colleagues who hear rumours or jump to conclusions need some-one they can rely on. That person is their Whip. There must be complete trust between them. I'd like to think I had that.

In my time we would meet every day the House sat at 2 p.m. for 30 minutes before the start of business. Here the Chief and Deputy Chief Whip would go over that day's business, take us through the problems which then always were about how to get a majority when no such thing existed! Michael Cocks spent little time on persuasion. 'Policy? Arguments? Principles? Get the buggers into the Labour Lobby – quickly!'

Tom Cox, Jock Stallard and I were 'London Whips'. It was then essential to do Friday duties. Jack Weatherill was the Tory 'Friday Whip'. With Jack we 'managed' Friday business amicably. We learned to trust each other implicitly, and that trust has lasted into the Lords to this day.

If, as I was, a Whip was whipping a Committee in the morning, then my day would start by leaving home at 8 a.m. and last until 2 or 3 in the morning – night after night after night. The fact that there was general agreement with the Parties led during the nineties to a complete revolution. Don't get me wrong. The hours worked then were ridiculous, but today and not only for the Whips, life in the Commons is no longer the depressing slog that it was. But although there has been common agreement on the changes in the Commons, they would never have been contemplated without the huge changes in culture. The intakes of 1997 and 2001, especially from the Labour benches, indicated quite clearly and forcibly that they would not tolerate the ludicrous working conditions that had been tolerated – and protected – for many, many years.

Until 1997 the position in the Lords meant that much was expected from Labour Peers. From 1979 until 1997 there was little if no chance for the Labour benches to triumph in the Commons, yet Labour was desperate to fight back against first the Thatcher and then the Major governments.

Astoundingly, despite having only 120 members in the Labour Peers Group against a total House of more than 1200, time after time, the Government was defeated. A table elsewhere shows the details. This is a story of how the Labour Whips Office worked during that period, to ultimately drive the Major Government up against the buffers in March 1997 when there were four major bills unable to be completed in time for the dissolution of parliament in March/April 1997.

First of all, we had a precious commodity to hand, in that most of the Labour Group were very keen to inflict injury on the legislation, whilst at the same time, the Tory Peers staggered towards March 1997 not only weary, but fed-up with the quality of the legislation they were being asked to support. Until the great influx coming after, 1997, the majority of the Labour Group had been there some time, many of them coming from the Commons with service then going back years and years. The Earl of Listowel (Billy) had been a member of Churchill's coalition Government, Frank Pakenham served in Attlee's administration, Arthur Bottomley likewise. After a successful 'ambush' which brought a Labour victory I received a note from Eddie Shackleton congratulating me on its organiz-ation and saying 'it was so exciting – just like the old days in the Commons!' The point I wish to make is that Labour Peers needed little stimulation to turn out for an ambush – they, enjoyed tweaking the nose of the Tories!

Note should be taken that Whips in the Commons were all nominally full-time politicians. They were on the payroll. Invariably they had ambitions. Sworn to a kind of silence they rarely if ever spoke in the Chamber. They played a key role in managing the progress of business, needing to be on top of the job – and if they fell asleep or were distracted and failed to give the correct response when business is called by the Clerks, there can be real trouble. It is different in the Lords.

The only person on the payroll in the Lords is the Chief Whip, and whilst there is a carefully crafted number of Whips in each Whips Office in the Commons, this does not apply in Opposition in the Lords. However, in Government in the Lords each Whip is on the payroll, and is substantially part of the Ministerial team, with departmental responsibilities. The average age of Labour Peers was 71 years of age and care had to be taken to recognize this when manning the Whips Office. Many of my Whips were into their seventies. The Chief has a free hand.

In 1983 when I entered the Whips Office in the Lords, the Chief was Tom Ponsonby, a hereditary Peer of the best kind. He was a consummate political figure. He had forged a first-class working arrangement with the Leader, Cledwyn Hughes. His deputy was the redoubtable Nora David who even then – in 1983 – was seventy years old; She is still going strong. She was succeeded as deputy by Wendy Nicol, one of the Cambridge mafia, coming into the Lords with Andrew McIntosh fresh from his defeat by Ken Livingstone for the Leadership of the GLC in 1981. When Wendy retired I succeeded her as deputy which lasted until 1990 when Tom died and I was elected by the Labour Peers over Dennis Carter who had been in the Whips Office and who then served as my deputy for a number of years.

Knowing that a stint in the Whips Office was no sinecure, nor, in Opposition could it lead to greater things, I was always grateful to those colleagues who without question accepted my invitation to 'help out'. I refer to the likes of Joe Dean, Patricia Hollis, Margaret Jay, Jenny Hilton (formally a Deputy Commissioner of the Metropolitan Police), Brenda Dean, Joyce Gould, Derek Gladwin, Alf Dubs, Tony Berkley, Brian Morris (my deputy), Josie Farrington, Simon Haskel . . .

Their job was to be a shepherd to a portion of the Labour Peers Group, to encourage them and to understand that for some while the heart may be strong, physical problems – for them or their partners – had to be known and taken fully into account. I count it one of the outstanding achievements on the night they managed to get more than 75 per cent of Labour Peers to vote. Magic! The Government Chief Whip has the responsibility for ensuring that the business of his Government proceeds at a pace which will ensure than all Bills received from the Commons are cleared and receive the Royal Assent before Prorogation, Ultimately, if agreement cannot be obtained 'through the usual channels' there is no other alternative but to bring the disputed piece of business onto the Floor of the House and try to force it through by weight of numbers. Even if this was achieved it would almost certainly be counterproductive, for the loss of trust and harmony would devastate the normal smooth passage of business. Very rarely is this breakdown in relationships exposed.

From the State Opening of Parliament when the broad outline of the legislation to be brought before the House is revealed, there is a continuing series of discussions between 'the business managers' from all Parties in which accommodation for the points of view expressed is sought. This normally revolves around dates for stages of Bills and timing, leaving the politicians to fight their corner on the Floor. But it is not just legislation that is dealt with through the usual channels. The Administration of House Matters and such important matters as accommodation, car parking, dining facilities and many more land on the desks of Chief Whips. In my time I had the happy experience of working with four Conservative Chief Whips. They were Bertie Denham, Alexander Hesketh, Nick Ullswater and finally Tom Strathclyde. They were all most considerate of the views of Her Majesty's Official Opposition, and I can't say fairer than that! You need to be scrupulously fair and steer clear of anything resembling sharp practice, but as is reported elsewhere, if one of the tasks of the Opposition Chief Whip is to defeat the Government whenever he can, then stratagems have to be devised to do just that. The number of defeats for the Tory Governments of 1983 to 1997 was hailed as significant when we upped it to double figures. Now this Opposition does not hesitate to use its inbuilt majority to inflict defeats at a much higher level. But we have plans for dealing with that situation!

Unlike one of my colleagues, I was sent to the Lords by Michael Foot to work for and vote Labour. I could not do anything else. After each General Election there are always a number of colleagues who resign at that election on the high expectation that they would come to the Lords. One of them, a Cabinet Minister, failed to do so, but was sent there on a subsequent New Years Honours List on the recommendation of the Prime Minister, Margaret Thatcher. Once, when I spotted him leaving before a crucial vote and asked him to stay he pointed out that he was not sent here by Labour, but by Margaret Thatcher and he had no obligation to stay and give support to me! I thought how sad it was that a comrade who had given long and valuable service to The Party should turn sour, after being the recipient of so much patronage. It takes all sorts!

Being in two places at the same time

Every Standing Committee in either House is manned by members in proportion to an agreed formula, Ministers and a Whip. If you are a member of the Whips Office you can expect to serve on more than one Committee during a session, and often it will be two or three. If you have special knowledge or required skills you will be the Whip on important Committees where the Minister in charge may make a special request that he – or in this case, she – requests that the Whip on their Committee be you. Therein lies this problem.

Walter Harrison was a great Whip, and in demand. John Silkin (Chief) told Walter that both Barbara Castle and Roy Jenkins had specifically asked for him to Whip their committee which were scheduled to follow each other in Standing Committee. However, as can happen there was a change of plan, and Walter found that the committees were to meet concurrently – in adjoining rooms on the Committee corridor, Rooms 9 and 10. Walter contrived to ensure that he would vote in one and then race into the next room to be ready for votes there, but of course he was rumbled. The Tories contrived to call votes at precisely the same time – the same moment – in each committee. Knowing Walter, he managed to escape calamity more than once but nemesis loomed. One day he voted in one committee and raced into the Finance Standing Committee – only to find that the policeman behind the door proved an obstacle. 'Lock the Doors' cried the chairman, and the policeman, doing his job, sought to do just that. Walter was almost in but his leg was caught outside the room.

Pandemonium! Amid the hiatus Iain MacLeod who was leading for the Tories sought to have an explanation for the uproar, and appealed to the Chairman – John Jennings – asking what was the status of Walter who by then was inside the room. The chairman asked Walter to explain what had happened, and Walter told him that in seeking to enter the room in time, he had been almost through – except for his leg – when the doors were closed. The Finance Bill Committee is always large, and when the vote was called it resulted in 22 for the amendment – and 23 against – including Walter, Whereupon the Chair declared the vote to be 22 – to 22! Not carried! Walter saves the day, even though he was out on a limb!

Hansard records the episode thus:

Question put. 'That the amendment be made' The Committee divided Ayes 22 Noes 23'. 10.15 p.m.

Mr Iain Macleod. 'On a point of order. Since there is a difference of only one vote in that Division, would you, Mr Jennings, be good enough to enquire from the policemen at the lower door whether the hon. Member for Wakefield (Mr Walter Harrison) whom we greatly respect and who has an enormously difficult job being a Whip in two Committees, did or did not enter this room after a clear order was given to lock the doors and after the doors had been shut?

The Chairman. It is a valid request. I observed some form of scuffle at the door. Perhaps the hon Member for Wakefield (Mr Walter Harrison) would clarify the situation.

Mr Harrison. Certainly I can clarify the situation Mr Jennings. I am of the opinion that the greater proportion of my body was through the door. Unfortunately, below the left knee it was not quite through. Not getting through made me fall onto the floor. I must apologize for the disturbance, but I consider that my vote was valid. That is entirely up to you, Mr Jennings, but I consider that the greater proportion of my body was through the door at the time.

Mr Macleod: Further to that point of order Mr Jennings. We are much obliged to the hon. Member for Wakefield. I would not have raised this point of order if it had not been the question of one vote, but the Committee will understand that one vote matters on this occasion. I made, with respect what I think and what you Mr Jennings said was a perfectly valid point, and I ask whether you would consider all the circumstances. I am absolutely content to leave it in your hands. If you wish to make an investigation and announce the result later we will naturally accept that.

The chairman. I could announce the result now: it is 22¾ to 22. The hon Gentleman was in the process of coming through the door. Therefore I rule that his vote is valid. If it is any comfort to anybody, may I say that if it had been a tie the result would still have been the same, because as Chairman I should have cast my vote for the Government.' (Standing Committee A Finance Bill, 29th May 1968).

Later in my Whipping days in the Commons I landed an almost similar situation when I was deputed to be the Whip on both the Education Bill, and a huge Planning Bill. I started one Bill in November and when that was finished started on the other which took us into June – more than 6 months continuously in Committee! Being tied to the Committee can be a nuisance, but one adapts and makes good use of the time. I was fortunate in that Peter Brooke was the Whip for the Tories on both Bills and we struck up a respect for each other which lasts today into our time in the Lords.

PART III

Life – and Death – in the Lords

Chapter 7

The tide turns

T HE QUESTION OF WHAT to do with the House of Lords had been on the agenda of the Labour Party constitutionalists now for almost one hundred years. Ever since the early days of the Liberal administrations of the early Twentieth Century, with the clash of the Commons versus the Lords in which the threat of going to the county on the slogan 'Who governs Britain' saw off the bolshie attitude of the built-in Tory majority – there had been about the place the smell of unfinished business. The Tory Party paid scant attention to the need to either reform or modernize during the intervening years. Given that it was only really under threat when Labour had a majority in the Commons – and as statistics will show, not even then – it relied on the Labour Party getting on with its own domestic agenda while the diminished Centre Party – now the Liberal Democrats – could play little part in serious reform. Until now.

History will show that the mood change of the British electorate during the 1990s after the sloth by the Tories during the previous thirty years propelled the question of 'Who governs Britain' from somewhere near the bottom to being somewhere near the top once Labour regained power under Tony Blair in 1997. Whilst the Tories could ignore the need to redress the democratic deficiency which allowed them so much power, it was the excesses of the Thatcher Governments which propelled the issue before both the public and the Labour Party policy makers. It was not only the fact that it was unfinished business to be returned to. Especially during the 1990s, the ability of the Opposition Parties to inflict damage on the Tory Government's legislative programme brought to the public the fact that the House of Lords was not just the second chamber, not just a resting place for retiring politicians, but was also the place where the excesses of the Commons majority could be thwarted or delayed. For this to happen, there had to be a combination of any number of situations.

First of all, the legislation brought to the Lords from the Commons had to be capable of being attacked as being bad. There not only had to be the normal resistance to any Government legislation but that opposition had to strike a chord with the public – or part of the public.

Next, there had to be a body of help to the Opposition Parties not previously experienced, for as the services and facilities made available to members of the Commons grew – and grew, and grew – those on hand to aid the Opposition Parties in the Lords remained woefully inadequate. Two things brought easement. The first was the arrival in the Lords of a version of what became known as 'Short Money'. Established under the Leader of the Commons, Ted Short, it was a way of giving financial support to the Opposition Parties based on their support at a previous General Election. Meagre as it was – and still is – it provided the then Opposition Parties, Labour and Liberal Democrats, with funds to engage staff to undertake research and general support. Overnight, the proficiency of Opposition Front Benches improved. The circle was completed in July 2002 when it was announced that the main Opposition Party in the Lords would henceforth receive £390,000 a year. When the Leader of the Lords, Lord Williams of Mostyn made the announcement, I said:

> **Lord Graham of Edmonton:** My Lords, the Government and the Leader of the House should be congratulated on the proposal before us. When the governing party was in opposition, there was no such thing as Cranborne money. Cranborne is the son of Short. When Labour were in government in the other place, Ted Short – now the noble Lord, Lord Glenamara – initiated the Short money principle. That principle arose in response to the fact that the governing party had a wide range of support from Whitehall but the opposition parties had none. In opposition, Labour had to rely in the House of Lords on obtaining, and pleading for, a small amount of Short money from the other place.
>
> It is to the everlasting credit of the noble Viscount, Lord Cranborne, that, within a year of what I assume he knew would be a change on the Benches, he proposed Cranborne money. The first amount to be allotted was £60,000 a year, and £30,000 was made available for one half-year. After five years, the case for a five-fold increase has been made by the Leader of the House and accepted by the Treasury. I do not consider that to be over-generous because the money needs to be spent and it needs to be validated. I do not want to feel that any shortcomings of the Opposition in this House are due to a shortage of cash; they are due to other reasons.
>
> *http://pubsl.tso.parliament.uk/pa/ld200102/ldhansrd/vo020730/text/20730-04.htm 21/07/2004*

During the eighteen years of Conservative Government until the end, always with a substantial majority, those from outside Parliament who sought to influence the course of events found that the Opposition in the Commons were often powerless to alter legislation, let alone stop it. But in the Lords, the situation was somewhat different.

The turning point came in the midst of the battle to abolish the Greater London Council – and with it the Inner London Education Authority. In 1981, Labour regained control of the GLC. This brought into national prominence the figure of one Kenneth Livingstone. Ken came to the GLC having broken his teeth on London politics with stints on the Councils of Lambeth and Camden. In preparation for what turned out to be the Labour victory of 1981, he and his friends had carefully – and successfully – ensured that the Labour candidates in many a likely Labour winning seat were sympathetic to his style of leadership. Prior to that election, Sir Reg Goodwin had been the Leader of the Labour Group, with Andrew McIntosh as his anointed heir, but at the first meeting of the Labour Group after the election, the coup to elect Ken as Leader came about. Margaret Thatcher and her Government were then subjected to a constant and highly publicized running battle with the GLC. The Metropolitan Councils – and there were five others – had been the creatures of previous administrations and were designed to give their regions a voice and a place in the devolution of power from Whitehall. But with the return of a Conservative Government with Margaret Thatcher as Leader in 1979, the scene was set for confrontation – nowhere more than in London itself.

Ken Livingstone and his colleagues relished the fact that in the absence of a Labour Government, they provided the frontline of Opposition to the Tory Government and there was many a row between Whitehall and County Hall. Instead, however, of relying on the hitherto democratic practice of seeking to vote out an administration which had been voted in – in 1981 – it was decided by Margaret Thatcher that not only the GLC but all other Metropolitan Councils would be abolished, and this plank appeared in the Tory Manifesto for the 1983 election. A main policy of the Labour GLC had been a policy called 'Fares Fair', an attempt to hold down the cost of transport, particularly on the London Underground. When the legislation to abolish the GLC was produced, it sailed through the Commons but it was a different story when it came up to the Lords. A daily battle was fought through London, largely between Patrick Jenkins, the then Secretary of State for the Environment, and Ken Livingstone and, from all accounts, Londoners were by no means as convinced as was the Government that the GLC had to go. But Ken knew that winning the battle of the billboards and the opinion polls did not count. What did was damaging or even halting the legislation itself. Thus, the most ferocious search was on to find members of the House of Lords who had the most precious of commodities in a democracy – the vote. The potential lying dormant on the benches of their Lordships' House came alive.

The appeal made by the Labour GLC to Lords who had become strangers to the Chamber was both direct and crude. As a Patron or President of a charity or association which relied on grants from the GLC to survive, it was your duty – to the charity – to attend the debates but, more importantly, to vote – on the issue of abolishing the GLC and ILEA. For that, GLC had for good policy reasons spread its largesse around liberally to such an extent that it not only propped up many an existing group or cause but it had initiated many new ones, covering almost every aspect of life. It was to these worthy men and women that the appeal was made, and not surprising, many of them were on the Crossbenches and on the Conservative Benches too.

Remember the arithmetic in the Chamber at that time. Ostensibly, the Government had an overwhelming majority with almost the whole of the hereditary element on its side, and a majority of the life Peers too. The purpose of the exercise now being carried out by the GLC was to persuade Conservative backbenchers to at least abstain on important issues and for Crossbenchers to vote positively in support or retention of the GLC and ILEA. There had indeed been other times when a direct appeal to what could be called 'the backwoodsmen' had been made, especially on the issue of religious education. A famous stand against Government policy had been made when the Education Act 1981 was before the Lords and the Duke of Norfolk led a rebellion largely because the effect of the legislation was detrimental to Church-aided schools – and he won the day.

Starting in the mid-eighties, we can see that lobbyists of all kinds were turning to the House of Lords in an attempt to secure changes in legislation denied their masters – mostly pay-masters – by the large Government majority in the Commons. After the battles over the GLC and ILEA, there came battles later in the eighties to scupper the Poll Tax legislation, in which a former Commons Minister, Sir Tufton Beamish, played a prominent role. This was before Michael Heseltine made such a strong case for its abolition in his battles to secure the Prime Ministership as the eighties turned into the nineties. While Sir Tufton and his band of Tory rebels were not disgraced, there was nowhere near sufficient to turn the tide. The Whips still ruled effectively across the Tory Benches.

Another issue which showed how members of the Lords could be mobilized by outside forces came in 1986 with the Shops Bill, a Bill designed to allow Sunday Trading unfettered. The Auld Report recommended this to the satisfaction of the Government but for a reason known only to itself, it decided to start it in the Lords, whereas normally Bills which are deemed to be controversial normally start in the Commons. A coalition of interests in which the Churches, Trade Unions and some major retailers combined galvanized communities throughout the land, sufficiently so that the only defeat for a Government Bill at Second Reading was registered for this Bill when it came before the Commons after suffering a defeat by 121 votes to 120 in the Lords.

Thus, the picture emerges during the 1980s and 1990s of a sleeping untapped resource being found and awakened. Most of the sleeping Peers who were awakened went back to sleep again once their special interest passed through the Lords, but from a chamber which sometimes just did not meet on a Monday, which for a long time felt that business after 'the dinner hour' of 7.00 p.m. was infra dig, turned itself into a full four days a week and extra business on a Friday chamber, with votes taking place very often after not only seven o'clock but also after midnight. Without a doubt, this all had much to do with the character of the Labour Benches, in this way. For the years before, say, 1983, there was a broad understanding that, give or take a little, it was the responsibility of the Official Opposition to oppose and pursue, but that, at the end of the day, the Government had the right to expect to get its business through, albeit after a struggle and by giving a few crumbs to the Opposition. But two things happened at Westminster after 1983. First, the nature of the legislation being passed up to the Lords became must more distasteful to not only the Opposition but also to many on both the Crossbenches and on the Government Benches too. Reference has already been made to the Poll Tax issues, and to the legislation to abolish the GLC, but with the increasing and continuous majority for the Conservatives, there came more and more legislation of an illiberal nature. Section 28 of an Education Act 'prohibited the promotion of homosexuality' within schools. This caused great uproar out in the community, not least in universities, and, yet again, hidden stores of potential resentment were stirred up as a result of arrogant legislation.

Within the make-up of the membership of the Lords, other forces were at work. At the same time as the nature of the legislation before their Lordships' House was becoming more and more unpalatable, we saw the rise of the SDP and the eventual emergence of the Liberal Democrat Party. Previously, they had been the old Liberal Benches but in the early 1980s were enlarged when a number of hitherto Labour Peers left Labour Benches and joined the Liberal Benches. Then seen as almost insignificant both for numbers and quality, it was during the 1980s that it grew stronger and now numbers more than fifty members, and includes many of those who left Labour in 1981. The present Leader of the Liberal Democrats in the Lords is Shirley Williams and her Chief Whip is John Roper, both original members of the SDP. Shirley Williams succeeded Bill Rodgers, another of the original 'Gang of Four', and he succeeded Roy Jenkins, yet another of the original Gang. The fourth of the four is David Owen, who went to the Crossbenches when the split between the SDP and the Liberals took place in the late 1980s. As the rise in their fortunes as seen in the country was taking place, their Parliamentary Party saw itself as the element of the Party capable of getting the most limelight and as a consequence became much more ready to join with the Labour Benches in order to score points.

Co-operating for victory

Allied to the increasing militancy of the Liberal Democrat Benches, we saw a stiffening of the resolve on the Labour Benches, this being due in part to the appearance of some who had served in the Commons and had been sent to the Lords specifically to strengthen Labour ranks. At the beginning of the 1980s, Labour ranks consisted of those who had fought the good fight against the Tory Opposition, many of them coming into the Lords as a result of the Life Peerages Act 1958 but bereft of actual experience in Parliament. However, they were seasoned campaigners from such quarters as local government and they were ready to embrace newcomers from the Commons, who arrived with the spur to harry the Tory Government whenever and wherever they could. The groundwork for the sustained attack on the Government lies at the door of the Leader of the Labour Peers, Lord Cledwyn (Hughes) and his Chief Whip, Lord (Tom) Ponsonby. Faced with the dominance of the Tory vote, they concentrated on picking and choosing their moment to strike – unexpectedly – and successfully. They were faced with a most effective Chief Whip, Lord (Bertie) Denham, who, when he retired in 1992, had completed more than thirty years in the Conservative Whips' Office, almost ten of them as Chief Whip. Despite our political differences, Bertie and I are good friends. He was, and is, as straight as a die and never reneged on a promise. A great man.

This is a story of how it was possible that a force (the Labour Peers) with little more than one hundred members could outwit, and at times outgun, the superior forces of Tory Peers who always outnumbered them at least four to one, and at times by almost five to one. Tory ranks always outnumbered Labour in Life Peers, and with the balance of power on the hereditary benches giving the Tories an advantage of four hundred to twenty, it would seem that the ability of anyone to outvote that Tory dominance was illusory. Yet it happened – time and time again. Truly, it ain't what you do, it's the way that you do it – that's what gets results.

It is also a story of the dedication as well as the determination of the Labour Peers Group. Elsewhere, there appears a photograph taken in March 1994. It shows, as far as it goes, those who at that time were alive and well and in the Lords who had in one capacity or another served in a previous Labour Government. More than one third of the Labour Peers strength is shown, and there were notable absences due to a variety or circumstances. There are not only those who had served in the Attlee Government, the Wilson Governments, the Callaghan Government, but remarkably there is shown the Earl of Listowel (Billy) who had served in Churchill's Coalition Government in 1944! Many had done their service in the Commons but a notable number had done so in the Lords. There is the only female Chief

Whip to serve in the Lords, Baroness (Pat) Llewelyn-Davies; there are two Prime Ministers (Harold Wilson and Jim Callaghan); as well as a former Leader of the Lords who started off working in the Conservative Research Department, Lord Pakenham (Frank Longford). It is to those Labour heroes that this story is dedicated and draws heavily on the sad fact that many of them died in harness, as the words used to describe their service are contained in their obituaries and appears elsewhere. The names of those who were Labour Peers in 1979 and survive today appear elsewhere.

The nature of the Labour Peers group

Until the passing of the Life Peerages Act of 1958, all Labour Peers were hereditary, not many of them but some having inherited their titles from their father or grandfather. The ability of a Labour Leader to sent supporters onto the red benches only really began in the period of Harold Wilson and tables elsewhere show that in those early days the supply was restricted. Only with the gross imbalance which became patent in the eighties and nineties was it clear that there was a need to redress that imbalance and this led in the parliaments of Tony Blair in 1997 and 2001 to substantial numbers of new recruits reinforcing Labour ranks, and only when this was allied to the substantial cull of the Hereditary element in the Lords could we begin to see anything like parity between Conservative and Labour benches. Even then, as statistics show elsewhere, Labour even today in 2004 has fewer members of the Lords than the Tories and fewer than the Crossbenches. Labour Peers represent less than 30 per cent of the total membership of the Lords. The very idea that Labour would – or could – call the shots in the Lords was fanciful in the extreme – until after the 1997 General Election when the Government benches were once more occupied by that disparate group we call Labour Peers, but who to me will always remain Bill, or Myer, or Doris, or Nora. They came to the red benches from a variety of routes.

Taking the span from my entry into the Commons, from 1974 to 2004 and now with more than 20 of those years spent in the Lords I can look back and see how both Labour and Conservative Prime Ministers used their opportunities of sending senior members of their Party in the Commons to do service in the Lords. Eddie Shackleton had been a member of the Commons and was made Leader of the Lords by Harold Wilson in 1968 and after the Labour defeat of 1970 continued as Leader of the Labour Peers until the Wilson Government of 1974. He was succeeded by Malcolm Shepherd as Leader from 1974 to 1976. He was succeeded by Fred Peart who was sent up to the Lords and served until 1981. Cledwyn Hughes had become a member of the Lords after 1979, and subsequently served as

Leader of the Labour Peers until he retired in 1992, to be succeeded by Ivor Richard. Four of the above five Labour Leaders in the Lords had come into the job with considerable experience in the Commons.

When Willie Whitelaw became Leader of the Lords in 1983 all previous Tory Leaders of the Lords had been hereditary, and whilst he was succeeded by hereditary John Belstead, subsequently two former Conservative Chief Whips from the Commons, David Waddington and John Wakeham filled that post until there was a reversion to type when hereditary Robert Cranborne was succeeded by hereditary Tom Strathclyde. By the 21st century, Tory Prime Ministers were beginning to recognize the talent coming from the Commons.

From the Trade Unions

As is well known, it was from the bedrock of support from Trade Unions that the Labour Party was born, now more than 100 years ago, and it was through access to the Commons that Trade Unions sought to influence both the Labour Movement and become an integral part of any Parliamentary Labour Party or Labour Government. With the creation of Life Peerages in 1959 came the opportunity for Trade Union nominees to be part of the Labour Peers Group. It has been said that the most powerful Lobby in Parliament is that of the National Farmers Union. It does not directly nominate farmers to sit on either the green or red benches, yet by virtue of its organization and their influence in many rural and farming constituency the NFU wielded power far beyond its nominal strength. As with the NFU, so it is within the Labour Party and Trade Unions. By special arrangements under what is called the Hastings Agreement, Trade Unions are enabled to nominate for vacancies when a seat becomes vacant. Often their nominees are active members of that Union, many of them have parliamentary panels with members of that panel forming those from whom the Union nominee comes. Latterly, however, the practice has grown for panel members to include many without previous experience of that Trade Union, rather their special quality is that they are local, or experienced, or just likely to be selected.

At one time the National Union of Mineworkers had far more sponsored MPs than any other Union, but of late such as the Transport and General Workers, the Public Sector Workers, the General and Municipal Workers and many others see an advantage in sponsoring Labour MPs. There is a cost to the Union, for they are expected to contribute to the expense of running the Constituency Labour Party – not the expenses of the candidate or MP. A glance at the former officials of Trade Unions who served in the Lords while I was there, especially when I was the Chief Whip, will illustrate the strength of the Unions, but also the part trade unionists played during the past thirty years.

We can start with the TUC. Billy Blease was the General Secretary of the Northern Ireland TUC and gives powerful voice from that province. Len Murray (deceased) did the same. There was no more loyal Labour Peer than Harold Collison of the Agricultural Workers, nor Joe Gormley of the Miners. Arthur Bottomley represented Public Sector Workers, while Douglas Houghton represented Inland Revenue workers before entering the Commons and then moving up to the Lords. Derek Gladwin, recently much mourned, was from the 'GMB' while Dennis Howell was prominent in the Clerical Workers Union and Hughie Scanlon of the Engineers (deceased). Vital to the current Labour Group are Tony Clarke (Post Office Workers), Garfield Davies (Shopworkers) Brenda Dean (Print Workers), Muriel Turner (Manufacturing), Keith Brookman (Steelworkers), Hugh Jenkins (Equity), Tony Christopher (Tax Collectors), Bill Jordan, Bill Brett and many others.

For Members of the Commons, going to the Lords is often seen as 'the icing on the cake', a reward for faithful service and, not very often, as a way of extending one's political career. I can only speak from experience, and whilst the confidence one gains in being active in the Commons can often be translated, by and large those who come to the Lords from the Commons tend to be available for advice and guidance as well as acting on the Front Bench holding positions of responsibility. Experience in address-ing either Chamber can be daunting – and experience shows. I can recall Manny Shinwell, on his 100th birthday, having enjoyed accolades paid to him, led by Willie Whitelaw in the Royal Gallery, rising to his feet at the subsequent Question Time and, ignoring the time constraint, proceeding to have the House in stitches as he delivered a tour-de-force – on the benefits of tobacco!

I was there when Richard Attenborough made his maiden speech and addressed The House in beautiful and moving tones. I was there when Bertie Denham, a former Tory Chief Whip moved the Address of thanks to Her Majesty at the end of his illustrious career in the Whips Office which spanned 30 years – a unique record. I was moved to tears as I listened to Brian Morris, my Deputy as Chief Whip, who came to us out of hospital as he was dying to pay tribute to the care and love he had received from those who were nursing him. Yes, all of the above were not from the Commons. They were splendid examples of the rich mix which is the Lords. We often sit deeply impressed by the speech and performance of some who come amongst us with experiences in the Law – besides the late

Pat Llewellyn-Davies

Eddie Shackleton

Eirene White

Nora David

Douglas Houghton

Harold Wilson

Cledwyn Hughes

Denis Healey

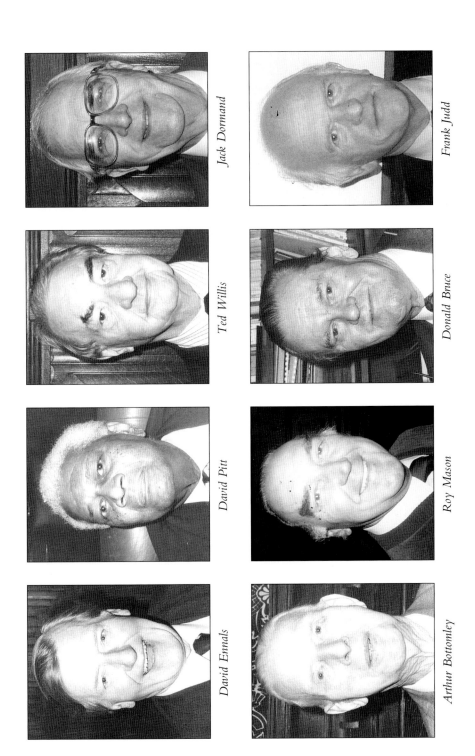

Jack Dormand

Frank Judd

Ted Willis

Donald Bruce

David Pitt

Roy Mason

David Ennals

Arthur Bottomley

89

Merlyn Rees

Derek Gladwin

Dennis Howell

Barbara Castle

Maurice Peston

Patricia Hollis

Ivor Richard

Andrew McIntosh

Betty Boothroyd

Stan Orme

Brenda Dean

Robert Winston

Ann Taylor

Jane Ewart-Biggs

Richard Acton

Ruth Rendell

lamented Leader, Gareth Williams, there is also Robert Alexander who has attained the honour of being Chair of the Bar Council, while eminent practitioners of the law – and the Courts who sit on the Crossbenches – dazzle with their oratory. Who having listened to the brilliant arguments from Victor Mischon can fail to be impressed? And be not moved whenever Donald Soper addressed the House or by Anne Mallalieu with her distinctive voice? Yet it is within the ranks of the Labour Peers that we find the hornyhanded sons of toil John Jacques, Billy Blyton, Roy Mason, Bernard Taylor – all ex-miners, and George Wallace worked at Smithfields. Many Labour Peers left full time schooling at the age of 14 – some went on to achieve high academic honours.

Academia – especially from the eighties and nineties, provided many a welcome recruit to the Labour benches. John Eatwell, Tessa Blackstone, Robert Winston the famed fertility expert, Melvyn Bragg and David Puttnam bring rich experience in the media which gives the Labour ranks depth. But they are the beneficiaries of mainly a Labour Government. That the voice of Labour was heard in the land leading up to the victory in 1997 owes much to those who served selflessly and mostly without reward after the Labour defeat of 1979. Many of them are still there, proud and in the main content to have laboured – and been rewarded simply by sitting on the Government side of the Chamber

Over the years there has been a steady influx into the Labour Peers Group with a prime credential that they have worked for and often within the Co-operative Movement. It is often said that the Labour Movement has three wings – the Labour Party, the Trade Unions and The Co-op. The attachment to the trinity of the working class by the Co-op is fairly said to fluctuate along with the economic buffeting it receives in the market place – or the High Street. Nevertheless the agreement for Co-ops to be treated as equal with Trade Unions in sponsoring candidates running under the 'Labour and Cooperative' Banner was forged as long ago as 1927 when it became patent that for both Labour and Co-operative candidates fighting for the same vote of the working class was counterproductive. Some of those who have gravitated up into the Lords via the Co-op Group have been A.V. Alexander, George Darling, Johnny Jacques, Bert Oram, Frank Beswick – all made Ministers in the Lords. Currently the 'Co-operators' active in the Lords number Alf Morris, John Tomlinson, Wendy Nicol, Glenys Thornton, Garfield Davies (Usdaw), Len Fyfe (ex chair of the CWS) and yours truly. They bring that additional experience of either managing or directing a Co-operative Enterprise, and the Labour Peers Group is all the better for that.

A select band come to the Labour Peers Group with the strong credential of having served as a full-time official of the Labour Party, none more loved and revered that Reg Underhill who rose to be Deputy Leader of the

Group. Three Ex-General Secretaries who continue to serve at present are Larry Whitty, David Triesman and Tom Sawyer. Other national officers include Betty Lockwood, Joyce Gould, Anita Gale and Murray Elder.

Local Government has always figured largely in the affairs of the Labour Party, and so it is fitting that the Peers Group continues to benefit from the services of those who have made outstanding contributions in that sphere. Nora David (still going strong at 90!), Alma Birk, Bill Sefton, Jock Stallard, Andrew McIntosh, Ted Short, Josie Farrington, Patricia Hollis, Lena Jeger, Doris Fisher, Alf Dubs, Bill Molloy, Jack Brooks (Jim Callaghan's Agent).

With especial experience of the European scene have come Barbara Castle, Christine Crawley, John Tomlinson, Angela Billingham and out-standingly two former European Commissioners, Ivor Richard and Stanley Clinton Davis.

Most of those mentioned above were around while the Labour Peers Group was in Opposition and thus carried the burdens outlined elsewhere. Collectively they brought a mix of experience and a lifetime of service and dedication to the Labour cause which is, quite simply unique and unrepeatable. Since 1997, instead of a dribble of new Labour Peers – say 3 or 4 every two years, we have had a steady stream of bright, articulate re-enforcements, A group which was less than 120 in 1997 is now almost 200. But is it a better group? Time will tell!

They also served

One of the impressive things when one becomes a member of the House of Lords is to find that you are sitting amongst the greats, figures who had been giants and had made a lasting impression on the affairs of the nation. One of my memories is of The Shops Bill in 1986. It was designed to bring in Sunday Trading, but would also deprive Shopworkers of basic rights to protect their conditions. I had been part of the team who sought to thwart that. After a particular amendment had been moved, up stood the Earl of Stockton – Harold MacMillan. 'I must say frankly that I do not like this Bill at all. Everything we have built into legislation during the long struggle for the uplifting and benefiting of the masses of our people and every other right should be strictly preserved and if necessary legislatively restated.' Bombshell! I had been working with Tom Denning the High Court Judge and together we sat in the Peers Lobby with Harold MacMillan. Tom suggested a further amendment to delete the word 'cease' and be replaced by the word 'continue' for workers' rights. At the Report Stage this was moved by Tom and seconded by me – and won – by one vote! (Hansard 21///86 Columns 158/160)

Within a few months of my entering the Lords, there was a special reception in the Royal Gallery to honour Manny Shinwell on his one hundredth birthday. Willie Whitelaw was the Leader of the House at the time and he was generous to Manny in every way, marking the event most suitably. That afternoon, there was a question on the Order Paper dealing with tobacco. The questioner was against it. Manny was for it and he rose in his place, not to ask a question but to make a speech, which he proceeded to do. We all roared our appreciation.

When my predecessor, Tom Ponsonby, died, I was moved to write an obituary which was printed in the 'House Magazine' and many remarked that so many comrades departed without his or her death being recorded. Thereafter, I resolved that whenever a colleague from the Labour Benches departed, I would write them an obituary – and I have done just that. Of course, that for Norah Philips was written by her daughter, Gwyneth Dunwoody; that for Fred Peart by Alf Morris; that for Harold Wilson by Enoch Powell; but in all, thanks to the goodwill shown me by the Editor, Patrick Cormack, I have now written more than fifty. And if, in the next few years, I am called upon to write another fifty, I will gladly do so. Most of them will be for men and women who long after others 'retired', they kept going – and the affairs of the nation have been all the better for that. Well done, thou good and faithful servants.

Tom Ponsonby was my Chief Whip when I entered the Lords in 1983. He had succeeded Pat Llewelyn-Davies in 1981. She was a remarkable lady and a superb Chief Whip. Bertie Denham, the Tory Chief Whip, once invited me to be his guest at a special dinner. It was given by the Queen's Bodyguard, of whom he, as Chief Whip, was their Captain. The principal Guests of Honour were Her Majesty The Queen and Prince Philip but all the talk around me was how captivated those illustrious soldiers had been by Pat when she had been their Captain. She was a Cambridge lady and her husband Dick had preceded her into the Lords as a Life Peer. She had been of the era when those who had betrayed their country had been at Cambridge – Blunt, Philby, Burgess and MacLean. She had managed to get almost all of the business through the Lords that had been sent to her and was deeply, deeply respected all round the House.

Tom was one of the few Labour Hereditary Peers. His great grandfather had been Queen Victoria's Private Secretary. He had a style that I could not possibly emulate. He was loved by all the hereditaries and earned the admiration of all the Life Peers. He had a shrinking number of Labour Peers, for it was in his time that the seismic change whereby the SDP was formed took place, and overnight he found that his troops had been dealt an almost mortal blow. At the same time, he had to manage the internal trauma of a change in the leadership of the Labour Peers. A change could be looked upon as one of those things that come along every so often, but this change was not one of them. Fred Peart had been sent up to the Lords

The retirement as Leader of the Lords of Cledwyn Hughes (3rd from left), 1992.
Showing all the then living leaders of the Labour Party past and present: Jim Callaghan,
John Smith, Michael Foot, Harold Wilson and Neil Kinnock

to become Leader by Jim Callaghan but he was never comfortable in that post despite being a very nice man and a huge success as Minister of Agriculture and negotiating splendidly over Common Market issues. In 1979, Cledwyn Hughes came up to the Lords from the Commons and became Fred's Deputy, but it was not very long before there were mutterings regarding Fred's performance in the chamber, and he was approached by senior colleagues and asked to step down in favour of Cledwyn. Whilst in Government, all appointments to the Front Bench, including Leader and Chief Whip, amongst Labour Peers are in the gift of the Prime Minister but it is in the hands of the Labour Peers when in Opposition. Fred refused. There was a contest, Cledwyn won and soon his Deputy was Reg Underhill, the retired National Agent of the Labour Party.

Cledwyn had the difficult task of getting the Labour Peers Group off the floor, where it had been put as a result of the 1979 election. This he did with courage and style in the chamber and, with Tom Ponsonby, selecting a team for the Labour Front Bench which very quickly was giving a good account of itself. Tom and Cledwyn were to march through the 1980s as a duo par excellence. They are still mourned – and remembered.

CHAPTER 8

The distinctive differences

THERE ARE MANY WAYS in which the Commons can outshine the Lords when it comes to performers and there is no question but that the stars in the minds of the public operate in the Commons. Not only by the Prime Minster but others such as the Leaders of all the parties and those who had caught the eye of the electorate by virtue of appearing on television and radio. But there is one aspect of comparison where the Lords shine. They've been there. They've done it. If we are debating aspects of the judiciary, it is almost certain that from all around the benches of the Lords will rise those who have served in a number of ways: ex-Home Secretaries, Lord Chief Justice(s), Chairmen of the Parole Board, Chairs of Special Committees of Inquiry, Bishops and Archbishops. If we are debating aspects of defence, we can listen to not one, not two but, in one debate, four ex-Chiefs of the Imperial Staff! The man who made Sainsbury great can be on his feet when debating retailing, followed by the man who added lustre to Tesco. And to Marks and Spencer! Mr Northern Foods will put in an appearance. If the subject is banking, then we can wheel out the ex-Chairman of every major bank, and now with Lord (Len) Fyfe of Fairfield, we can have the wisdom distilled from his experience at the Co-operative Bank – and Co-operative Insurance too! In other words, the House of Lords demonstrates time and time again that it is served by men and women who have 'made it' in the hard world out there.

There is one aspect of life in which the Lords stands without challenge – service in the Second World War – and in the Great War, as I shall show shortly. In 1990, Margaret Thatcher was instrumental in promoting the War Crimes Act. This was an Act to give the Director of Public Prosecutions the power to put before a British Court of Law any man or woman whom he believed had committed a war crime. His writ at that time ran only insofar as crimes that had been committed in Britain, yet it had been shown that there were residing in Great Britain those who had committed the most dastardly of crimes outside Britain but who were hiding here yet could not be prosecuted. In the Commons, on a free vote, the Bill was passed at all stages with a good majority of three to one, and it duly came to the Lords, when on Second Reading it was defeated. The debate was dramatic, and substantially divided on the following arguments. That the events leading to any prosecution were more than fifty years old, that those accused would now be in their seventies or eighties, that any witnesses would be as old, and that memory would be fallible. How could you get a successful conviction in those circumstances?

On the other hand, murder was murder, the nature of the crimes were horrendous, if all one had to do to escape punishment was to live to a ripe old age and to confuse your accusers, then you could avoid being sentenced. Why rake up the past – for what purpose? The debate was remarkable as much for those taking part as for the arguments they deployed.

From the Crossbenches, we heard the voice of the Chief Rabbi, Lord Jacobovitz. He had lived in Berlin before the war with his family and many of them had perished in the death camps. From those same Benches rose someone who had taken part in the prosecution of the major war criminals at Nuremburg – Lord Hartley Shawcross. He was a senior prosecutor, one of his juniors then had been Elwyn Jones, later to become Lord Chancellor. From the Conservative Benches rose Lord (Alan) Campbell, who had been a prisoner of war at Colditz. On the Liberal Benches sat Lord (George) Mackie, who had flown more than seventy-five times in a bomber and was one of the most decorated members of the Lords. Denis Healey had served with distinction in Italian episodes. Malcolm Shepherd had been at El Alamein. On the Crossbenches there were Lady (Sue) Ryder and her husband, Leonard Cheshire. I have deliberately avoided presenting the arguments they used, for the purpose of this piece is simply to point out that when it comes to experience in this kind of matter, the Commons just cannot equal the experience resting on the red benches of the Lords.

Under the procedures of Parliament, we come across the Parliament Act. When a Bill is sent from the Commons to the Lords and it is rejected at Second Reading, that Bill is dead until the next session. That is what happened with the War Crimes Bill. It was reintroduced in the very next session and was again sent to the Lords with a majority of three to one on a free vote. The same thing happened again. The Bill was rejected at its Second Reading but, this time, it had been sent with the stamp of the Speaker, saying that the Bill was subject to the Parliament Act, which stipulates that when a Bill is rejected at Second Reading for a second time, within twenty-four hours it becomes law by receiving the Royal Assent. Thus, because of the strength of feeling, particularly by those who had been involved in the War, they refused to entertain the Bill, rather than seek amendments to it. Sadly, what they predicted came to pass. Now some twelve years later, despite one or two attempts, no-one has been successfully prosecuted under the Act. I regret this because I voted twice to have the Bill become an Act.

When it was time to commemorate the successful landings in Normandy, which led eventually to the victory in 1945, the task of organizing the whole show fell to the Leader of the Lords at that time, Lord Cranborne. By common consent, he did this brilliantly. He came to me one day and asked if I could supply him with the name of a Labour Peer who had landed on D Day. I was beginning to despair when someone told me to have a word with David Ennals, one time Secretary of State for Social Services. 'Not me' he said, and as I was turning away, he said 'I landed the day before D Day'. He was in the Signals and together with two colleagues, he had landed and had to crawl up the heavily mined beach and snuggle into the sand dunes, there to await the arrival of the fleet and signal back to them what they could see was happening on the beach, and to guide the fire from the ships, and the path for the men, avoiding as much carnage as they could.

He and his team stayed in their dugout for more than seventy-two hours, and David told me that they had saved many disasters from taking place. On 21 June, he had been moving from one spot to another and was passing a bombed out building when he was riddled with a burst of machine gun fire. He fell to the ground and a young German soldier had stood over him and, in perfect English, had said, 'I am very sorry but this is war' and David had replied, 'Don't worry, I understand', and then he passed out. He came to in a chateau near Rennes used by the Germans as a military hospital, where he started to recover from his wounds which left him with a permanent limp and a badly deformed arm. It was there that he was freed by the American forces who swept out of Normandy in August. He represented Labour Peers on 6 June 1994.

Now sweep backwards to the 1914–1918 War. One day, I was explaining to a meeting of the Labour Peers Group that we were making a special effort to catch the Government out on a Bill, and I required every Labour Peer to do their level best to be in their place at about 8.30 p.m. This was not an unusual request but as I sat down, Charlie Leatherland rose to his full height of four feet ten inches. 'I think you should remember that some of us are old soldiers, Ted. You see this limp I have and the bad leg that I have got? I got that on the Somme.' We were all impressed and made suitable noises, whereupon Douglas Houghton said from his seat, 'Yes, Charlie, but you were not at Passchendaele were you?' The hairs stood on the back of my neck. It was a moment worth recording.

Charlie had been a Company Sergeant Major in a machine gun battalion – at the age of eighteen. Douglas had served in the most awful of places. Charlie went on to be a major force when the *Daily Herald* had been a power in the land, and had been a Chairman of Essex County Council. Douglas had gone on from his war service (one of his companions had been Henry Moore, the world famous sculptor) to become the voice of helpfulness during the Second World War with his radio programme 'Can I Help You?' and then on to the Inland Revenue Staff Association, Member of Parliament for Sowerby Bridge, into the Cabinet and Chair of major inquiries into social issues. Here were two men, neither of whom stood more than five feet, gently chiding each other in a room of the House of Lords about which of them had the most illustrious war record. Only in the House of Lords could such a scene be played out as part of a normal day!

Later, I went to see Douglas as he lay dying, in his ninety-seventh year. He had fought the good fight on behalf of man and beast. He was deeply respected. I asked him of his memories of Passchendaele. He closed his eyes and said one word, 'Mud'. Then: 'It was awful. As we went up to the fighting line, we were warned not to fall off the duckboards into the mud. We would not be saved. My best pal, Percy, did that and I could not help him. I left him for dead. In 1924, I was standing in the Strand when a bus passed, and Percy was the conductor. We stopped the traffic as we hugged and kissed. But it was all horrible, horrible.'

Rest in peace, Douglas and Charlie, and all your comrades. We shall remember them. We shall remember them.

Magic moments

During that period before I became the Opposition Chief Whip in the Lords, I cheerfully accepted many a task allotted to me by Tom Ponsonby or in any other way, for I was a glutton for work. In that period, I was the Front Bench spokesperson for Environmental Issues, Planning, Defence, Northern Ireland, and Sport. It was thus that together with my very good friend, Lord Dean of Beswick (Joe Dean) we handled the Football Spectators Bill in 1989/90. During the 1980s, the behaviour of spectators at football matches had deteriorated to such an extent that Margaret Thatcher had called a special meeting at No 10 to see if Government could play a useful part. Hitherto, the wisdom was that these things were best left in the hands of the football clubs and the Police. However, extensive video footage every week showed that inside the grounds, there was a constant running battle between zealots of the opposing teams, leading to mayhem which the Police found difficult to control.

The Government decreed that the answer was a Bill which made it mandatory for spectators to carry an identity card before admittance and this, it was argued, would both deter hooligans but also lead to more speedy arrests, fines or imprisonment. Not for the first time, a Bill borne out of haste and lack of preparation was rushed before Parliament. Clear divisions of opinion both on its necessity and effectiveness soon emerged and although it got through the Commons, when it came to the Lords, it was a different kettle of fish. The Second Reading of the Bill was a classic. In charge of the Bill for the Government was Alexander Hesketh, who later

Giving the Football Spectators' Bill a good kicking. With thanks to Richard Willson and The Times.

© *Richard Willson/*The Times *16.06.1989.*

became the Government Chief Whip. He had impressive sporting credentials, not least because of his connections with the motor racing world but also with the Northampton Football Club.

Everyone in the Chamber had a pedigree of football credentials as long as your arm. We learned that Bob Mellish was the Chairman of the Millwall Supporters Club and that George Wallace was the President of the 'Capital Canaries'. 'The what?' I hear you cry. George Wallace had been the Member of Parliament for Chislehurst in 1945 and worked in the Smithfield Meat Market before that. He went back there after his defeat in 1950 until he was elected as a Member of Parliament for Norwich. The nickname of the Norwich City Football Club is 'The Canaries' and a branch had been formed in London!

The star football supporter, however, was Lord Harmar-Nichols, who had been the Member of Parliament for Peterborough more than once, holding at one time the smallest Parliamentary majority. He lambasted his own Government up hill and down dale, finally leading a successful coalition of interests – and defeated the Government. Pandemonium!

The classic line-up: John Charles, Nat Lofthouse, Tom Finney, Ted Graham (Cambridge Street Juniors), Joe Dean, Jack Kelsey and Ivor Allchurch

The Minister for Sport who had taken the Bill through the Commons was Colin Moynihan and he was not the only one to keep a watchful eye on proceedings in the Lords. National Supporters Groups were regular attenders and Alexander Hesketh gave as good as he got from Joe and me – ably assisted by Lord (John) Harris, the Liberal Democrat Chief Whip, who spoke strongly on the issue, briefed as he was by senior Police Officers. Joe had declared that he was proud to come from Manchester, where he had been the Leader of the Council, and asserted that Manchester had the two finest football clubs in the land – Manchester City and Manchester City Reserves!

The football authorities were against the Bill and they did all they could to give us moral support. They arranged a number of publicity events, one of which will stick in my memory for a long time. Opposite the entrance into the House of Lords is what is called College Green. It is where television cameras interview politicians on all sorts of topics. One day, Joe and I were invited to meet some of those who had been professional footballers. What a line-up! Nat Lofthouse, Ivor Allchurch, Tom Finney, Jack Kelsey – and John Charles! Joe and I had worshipped them all over the previous forty or more years and it was a real pleasure to kick a football about with them and to have photographs taken with them which duly appeared in the national press. After this, Joe and I took them into the Peers' Dining Room for lunch, where they all told us that they had been into the

Commons dining rooms but never into the Lords. That made our day – but more was to follow. As we sat chatting over lunch, Willie Whitelaw came up to me and whispered in my ear that they were all heroes of his, and would I be so kind as to introduce them to him? Would I! And before very long, other senior politicians were queuing up to shake their hands and to wish them – and our opposition to the Bill – every success. Memories are made of this!

Sadly, in one way, it all ended in tragedy. Whilst the Bill was going through the Lords, that terrible event known as the Hillsborough Disaster unfolded. Almost a hundred lives were lost when a crush developed outside and inside the ground before an important match between Liverpool and Nottingham Forest. It was awful, and quite rightly, the Government set up a major inquiry led by that lovely man, Lord (Peter) Taylor, who was the Lord Chief Justice. Before he had time to report on his findings and recommendations, the Government took the wise course of abandoning the Football Spectators Bill.

A victory of sorts, but at what a price. Even worse was to come, for Peter Taylor died very soon thereafter and we still mourn the passing of a lovely man who had too short a time to leave his mark on the judicial system and the Lords. I was even more upset, for Peter was a native of Newcastle-upon-Tyne and he and I had begun to establish a genuine friendship.

Wrong-footing the government

'Am I in time for the surprise vote?'

Everyone knows the reality of life at Westminster. With an overall majority in the Commons (that's why they are the Government), the convention is that it is the duty of the Lords to give the Commons an opportunity to 'think again'. When the Government is defeated in the Lords, that amendment goes to the Commons for consideration. All sorts of things can happen to it there. It can be accepted if that fits in with their plans. It can be rejected but the Commons will put forward another amendment 'in lieu thereof'. The amendment, when it gets back to the Lords, can be amended by the Lords. Of if it is rejected outright, the Government's attempts to make progress are defeated and the Commons is asked to think again. This is what is known in the business as 'ping pong'. But at the end of the day, the convention rules that a Government is entitled to get its business – at what price is the subject of this piece.

Arithmetic being the art of the possible, it does not take much for the astute observer (the Whips) to deduce the outcome of a vote depending on the time of day, the coalitions around the House that can emerge or be worked on, and that indefinable ingredient – the chemistry. There are some issues which transcend party politics and one just knows that an amendment will be passed against the will of the Government because of its powerful appeal and the magic of the advocacy of those who have passion on their sides. If a Government has a majority and Whips to bring it supporters in early in the day – say between 4.00 p.m. and 7.00 p.m. – Oppositions who force votes during that time know that they will be defeated.

As I will show later, the art of the ambush is to time the attendance and vote of your supporters so as to wrong-foot the Government Whips. If you bear in mind that at the end of the day, the Government gets its business through, what the Opposition are doing is to create mischief if not mayhem. It is a good healthy Parliamentary game, which enlivens the scene and keeps Peers on their toes. During my time as Chief Whip, I improved my 'score' but could only do this if I had the collaboration of at least the Liberal Democrat Benches. However, the absolutely vital ingredient in any successful ambush was that of determination from my own supporters. As I would take the voting paper with the successful totals on it indicating a Government defeat, I would glance towards the Labour Benches, where I was met with a sea of thumbs up and grinning faces. That too was one of the purposes of staging surprise votes. With a party in the Commons incapable of defeating the Government, we took it as our job to lift not only Labour morale in the Commons but throughout the country. We did that spectacularly.

The Peer who arrives at Peers' Entrance asking in a loud voice 'Am I in time for the surprise vote?' or the senior Peer who is never seen in the House after 6.00 p.m. but who takes their place at 10.00 p.m. may be a giveaway but they are part of Westminster's rich tapestry. All parties do it, some more often or more successfully than others. So what? What follows are my notes taken immediately after some events. Sometimes the Cowboys won, sometimes the Indians. Happy days!

Changes with a Labour government

There will follow tables showing the comparative strengths within the Lords of the Parties over a period. These clearly show that while both main Parties used the opportunity afforded by the Life Peerages Act 1958 to strengthen their numbers in the Lords, before 1979, there was an overwhelming Conservative presence which did not inhibit successive Tory Leaders from maintaining the proportions of new Peers so that the already heavy number on the Tory Benches simply kept the Tory preponderance as it had always been.

When Labour came to power in 1997, the Peers taking a whip were as follows:

Conservative	481
Labour	116
Liberal Democrat	57
Not taking a whip (crossbenchers)	320

Thus of a total of 974. Labour had less than 12 per cent!

There appear elsewhere extracts from Labour Manifestos leading up to the 1997 landslide victory promised to deal with this situation, and although it is trite to say that everything in a Manifesto has been approved by the electorate, there was a persistent theme throughout the 1990s showing that Labour would not shirk the opportunity whenever it came. The case for abolishing the right of Hereditary Peers to sit and vote in the Lords was made not by Labour but by the actions of the Tory Governments. Tables show that it was only with the aggregate votes of Hereditary Peers that the Government won the day, and that even in a heavily tilted House, a House without Hereditaries would be a sharply different place.

A glance at in what way and how Tony Blair has used his victory will show a ruthlessness and determination applauded by the Labour ranks. The fact that every move to change and make the Lords a different place was bitterly and noisily fought is a matter of record, and the victory of Labour and Liberal Democrat Peers a matter of pride and satisfaction. That the reforms had to come in at least two tranches was the subject of much debate and will take time to be finally resolved, but I am satisfied that the tactic was sound and in accord with the political credo that politics is the art of the possible. It would have been impossible any other way.

In my view, one of the greatest problems facing all Parties over the next period is that of achieving a House of Lords (whatever it may be called) with a better balance of parties and others who are seen both by the electorate as well as those not interested in political affiliation, than it is at present. Certainly, better balanced than it was for more than a hundred years. Tables elsewhere show how a succession of Prime Ministers have seen their role in creating that better balance, or, as some would say, maintaining the current imbalance, for party political reasons.

It has to be remembered that the last attempt to reform the House of Lords prior to that of 1998/99 was in the 1960s, when the proposals were thwarted in the Commons by a combined effort from Michael Foot and Enoch Powell. Tony Blair had to wait not only until 1997 but crucially so that he had a Parliamentary majority in the Commons which would give him not only authority but also muscle to 'get his way'. And whilst there can be arguments about the precise amount of change the electorate would tolerate, in my view, there was no argument about the mood in the country. After the way in which both Margaret Thatcher and John Major dealt with protests at their policies, eighteen years without a serious attempt at reform gave Tony Blair a mandate for change.

A table shows how successive Prime Ministers used their power of patronage from the time of Harold MacMillan – the architect of the Life Peerages Act 1958 – up to the period of December 2000. The table shows that between 1979 and 1997, Tory Prime Ministers created a total of 387 new Peers, 173 of whom took the Tory Whip. In that period, they created 96 new Labour Peers and 69 Crossbenchers. In his first period of office, Tony Blair created 99 new Labour Peers and 30 new Tory Peers, with 32 Crossbenchers. Remember that he inherited a situation in 1997 where there were 481 Peers taking the Tory Whip and only 116 taking the Labour Whip. This imbalance was dealt with by the elimination of almost all of the Hereditary Peers and by reducing the numbers of new Peers made by the parties. 99 Labour and 30 Tory new Peers were created – and that still leaves the Tories with more members of the Lords than Labour!

As the debates during the Reform Bill proceeded, I saw across the Chamber men and women who were fighting for their lives, and I had great sympathy for them. They were decent and honourable and during the twenty years I had known many of them, in a Parliamentary sense, they were friends. I sensed that the loss of the right to sit and vote in the Lords was a grievous blow and for many would change their lives. But I was fighting for the better lives of those who had not been represented in the Lords or even in the Commons for hundreds of years. That could only be done by removing the hereditary right to govern their lives as a right by birth. It had to be done. I was glad I had the chance to vote it through. As they defended their class, I rejoiced as I voted for my class – the working class.

Changes in the total and make-up of the Lords between the General Election of 1997 and 2001 were dramatic, primarily as a result of the Reform Bill of 1998, the main feature being that the total House fell from 1,207 in 1997 down to 679 in 2001, and to 688 by August 2002. By the deal done substantially by the Lord Chancellor and the Leader of the Opposition, Lord Cranborne, the number of Hereditary Peers fell from over 750 down to 75 – giving each party one for ten in an election undertaken by the parties. With further easements, the total of Hereditary Peers after the Reform Bill was passed rose to 92 – a substantial cull from 750!

The drop in totals by more than 500 must have been the most dramatic change in the history of the Second Chamber and goes a long way towards changing the nature of the Lords. A House dominated by those there by right of birth to one where the members will all eventually be Life Peers all in the space of one Parliament took the breath away of many, not least those who lost out in the internal party elections, even though the formula was one jointly proposed by their Leader. The record will show that obstruction and delay was employed at every opportunity but due to the determination of the combined Labour and Liberal Benches, the Bill became an Act in November 1999. Many Peers played their part but the example of the Leader, Margaret Jay, and her Deputy, Gareth Williams, gave their supporters cause for elation. I have in my possession a document of limited circulation. It is a copy of the Act signed by Margaret Beckett, Leader of the Commons, and by Margaret Jay, sent to those who had played more than a small part in the debates on the floor. When I had spoken at Second Reading, it was as speaker 183 out of a total of 192 and at 2.00 a.m. on the second night of the debate!

We turn to the situation of Life Peers. At the election of 2001, there were 193 Labour against 173 Conservative but with the addition of the Hereditary Peers, these figures were Labour 197 to the Conservative 225. Earlier, Tony Blair had stated that the did not wish to see a Second chamber where Labour had more than any other party but at the very least, equality with the main Opposition party – the Conservatives – means that there is still a shortfall of some 28. And if you examine the position of Labour in the House as a whole, you find that Labour has 197 out of a total House of some 679! So where does this talk of swamping the changed House with Labour nominees, or 'Tony's Cronies' come from? It will take some time for the new chemistry of the Lords to be transparent but these are my personal views. There is a tendency for the Conservatives to pull 140/150 when really trying. For Labour, that figure is not far short – say 130. Liberal Democrats muster 40 and Crossbenchers varying numbers between 40 and 50. If the Liberal Democrats poll with Conservative, the Government is defeated but if they poll with Labour, the Government wins. It can fairly be said that the Liberal Democrats tip the balance, and thus are courted assiduously by both main parties.

Front bench and frontline

When I was involved in day-to-day activity in the Lords, both before and after I was Chief Whip, it was easy to forget that I was working with some of the Labour greats. In general, in that period after 1979 and right up to 1997, we had to rely on those who had fought the good fight either in the Commons or in other spheres of public life and, by any reckoning, should have been enjoying a well-deserved retirement. Many is the time I have been chided by friends that, sitting alongside me, was an elderly man (or woman) who appeared to be asleep. I would say to them, if you had a grandfather or mother who was in their eighties and who had been sitting in a warm room after lunch, what would you expect them to be doing? Exactly, and that is why, from time to time, they are caught napping!

The richness of the experience sitting on the Labour Benches during that period was impressive. I want to set out the teams of Labour Peers who gave the Government a run for its money. In Legal Affairs, we had Gerald Gardiner, Elwyn Jones, Victor Mishcon, Elystan Morgan and, latterly, Gareth Williams, Ann Mallalieu and Derry Irvine.

In Economic Affairs, there was Tommy Balogh, Nicky Kaldor, Jack Diamond, Donald Bruce, Harold Lever, and, later, they were reinforced with Maurice Peston, John Eatwell, Charles Williams.

Local government was always well represented and in those early days there was Alma Birk, Nora David, Evelyn Dennington, Doris Fisher, George Pargiter, Tom Ponsonby, Tom Taylor, Bill Sefton, Pat Llewelyn-Davies, Charlie Leatherland, later to be joined by Andrew McIntosh, Patricia Hollis, Joe Dean, Wendy Nicol, Bill Molloy.

When it came to the Media, Labour was well served by such as John Ardwick, Ted Willis, Lena Jeger, Sydney Jacobsen, Ted Castle, Sydney Bernstein, Charlie Leatherland, Alma Birk and, as they faded, they were replaced by the likes of Melvyn Bragg and David Puttnam.

From the ranks of the trade unions, there were George Briginshaw, Alf Allen, Syd Greene, Joe Gormley, Hughie Scanlon, Walter Citrine, Len Murray, Harold Collison, Denis Howell, Cyril Hamnett, and they were reinforced latterly by the likes of Derek Gladwin, Ann Gibson, Garfield Davies, Tony Christopher, Brenda Dean, Keith Brookman. Co-operative interests were represented by George Darling, Frank Beswick, Johnny Jacques, Bert Oram, John Gallacher.

The Health Service was ably advocated by such as David Pitt, Bea Serota, David Ennals and latterly by Robert Winston, and Jill Pitkeathley. Agricultural interests had its champions, John Mackie, Harold Collison, Denis Carter and John Gallacher. Industrial relations could call on the likes of Bill Wedderburn, Bill McCarthy, Muriel Turner and, latterly, David Lea and Derek Gladwin.

The Education brief could call on Michael Stewart, Ted Short, Tessa Blackstone, Maurice Peston, Brian Morris, Nora David and Josie Farrington.

As would be expected, Labour Benches fully represented the regions. Scottish interests were always in the capable hands of Willie Ross, Neil Carmichael, John Kirkhill, Harry Ewing, Myer Galpern and, latterly, Meta Ramsay and John Sewell. Wales had Cledwyn Hughes, Eirene White, Jack Brooks, Gordon Parry and Gwilym Prys-Davies; and Billy Blease always saw that the interests of Northern Ireland were remembered.

As would be expected, the strong anti-nuclear interest was there – Donald Soper, Fenner Brockway, Philip Noel-Baker and, latterly, Hugh Jenkins. The mining interests had their special interests voiced by the likes

The Labour Front Bench, House of Lords, 1995

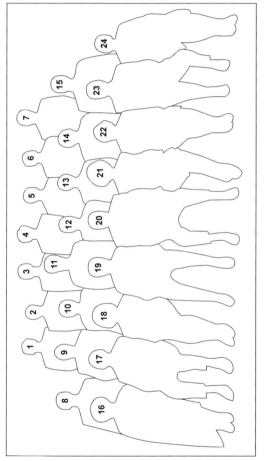

Key to photogtraph

1. Derek Gladwin
2. Neil Carmichael
3. Gareth Williams
4. Alf Dubs
5. Simon Haskel
6. Tony Berkeley
7. John Eatwell
8. Brian Morris
9. Jack Dormand
10. Frank Judd
11. Bernard Donoughue
12. Joe Dean
13. Dennis Carter
14. Stanley Clinton–Davis
15. Ted Graham
16. Brenda Dean
17. Charles Williams
18. Margaret Jay
19. Derry Irvine
20. Ivor Richard
21. Patricia Hollis
22. Jenny Hilton
23. Maurice Peston
24. Joyce Gould

Harold Wilson with me in my office as Opposition Chief Whip

of Bill Blyton, Johnny Jacques, Bernard Taylor, Roy Mason, Joe Gormley and Jack Dormand.

Specialists in Foreign Affairs could be found amongst Tom Brimelow, Hugh Foot, Patrick Gordon-Walker, Frank Judd, Arthur Bottomley and Jane Ewart-Biggs. Experience at a European level found Commissioners Ivor Richard and Stanley Clinton-Davis, augmented latterly by Christine Crawley, Angela Bellingham, Lyndon Harrison and John Tomlinson from the European Parliament. Barbara Castle, as an ex-Leader of the British Group, added this distinction to her many other attributes.

In addition to the above, no review of the strength in depth within the Labour ranks in the Lords over this period would be complete without mentioning some outstanding characters and I do this with great humility. Frank Longford, Douglas Houghton, Malcolm Shepherd, Norah Philips, Barbara Wootton, Edith Summerskill, Jennie Lee, Ernest Shackleton. Hearing Manny Shinwell on his feet in the Chamber on his one hundredth birthday in 1984 is a memory! By their very presence, both Harold Wilson and Jim Callaghan gave great comfort to their colleagues.

Most of those who carried the group into Opposition in 1979 have gone and whilst on the other side of the Chamber gaps in their ranks were readily replenished by succession under the hereditary device, Labour had to wait until 1997 before being adequately replenished, and it is still worth repeating that even in 2002, there are still more Conservative Peers than there are Labour!

Shadow Cabinet

For the seven years I was the Chief Whip, I also served in the Shadow Cabinet and count this as one of the most interesting periods in my Parliamentary life. Ever since I entered the Commons, I was made aware that being elected to the Shadow Cabinet was a benchmark for the popularity of Labour MPs and, as in all popularity contests, these elections produced some exciting times. I got a taste of the electoral sagacity of members of the Parliamentary Labour Party when Harold Wilson dropped his bombshell by resigning in March 1976. There are those who can tell that they were aware of this impending shock – for shock it undoubtedly was – but for me, and most of the others on the backbenches, it was a complete shock. At the time, I was the PPS to Alan Williams, who was the Minister of State at the Department of Prices and Consumer Protection, and I was grateful for this opportunity to work within a Department and thus be involved in Questions and helping the Ministers in the Department. When the news came through of Harold's resignation, we all knew that whoever would succeed him, Parliamentary life for us would never be the same.

The runners were quickly known; Jim Callaghan, Roy Jenkins, Michael Foot, Tony Crosland and Peter Shore. I immediately sought out John Cunningham and joined Jim's team, which was headed up by Merlyn Rees who, at the time, was the Secretary of State for Northern Ireland. Although Michael was ahead on the first ballot, we knew most of the others would come to Jim – and so it proved. I learned to assess the truth of replies from colleagues – especially when I was able to compare some of the answers with other like-minded workers for other candidates! When Jim resigned as Leader, I hitched my efforts to Denis Healey's camp, of which Harry Lambourn was the manager. Harry was the MP for Peckham and a long-time Co-op colleague from the Royal Arsenal Co-op Society. In 1971, when he was the Chairman of the GLC and had the privilege of a box at the Festival Hall, he invited Margaret and me to a concert where we enjoyed the brilliant performances from André Previn and Askanazy. We shared the box with Roy and Jennifer Jenkins and it was on the eve of the historic vote on entering the Common Market.

In shadow cabinet I have served under four Leaders of the Labour Party; Neil Kinnock, John Smith, Margaret Beckett and Tony Blair. It is true to say that they all had distinctive ways of chairing the meetings of the Shadow Cabinet from the languid style of Neil to the brisk style of Tony. My prime role in these meetings was to advise on the weeks – past and future – of the

With Jim Callaghan and Tony Blair arriving at St Mary's, Isles of Scilly, for the funeral of Harold Wilson (behind, Tom Sawyer, Lord Butler and Lord Armstrong)
By kind permission of PA News

Labour Peers Group in the Lords, and I have to say that whenever I was able to report good news, such as a defeat for the Government or a 'near miss', they were always generous in their reception and praise for our efforts. In the Lords, we did not expect to win but when we did, we enjoyed it! Members of the Shadow Cabinet made those moments very enjoyable!

Meeting Her Majesty

'I'd like to meet Lord Graham', said The Queen, and I froze. How was it possible that Her Majesty could wish to meet me? I was at a reception

At Harold Wilson's memorial service in Westminster Abbey, left to right, Norma Major,
John Major, Mary Wilson, Cherie Blair, myself and George Thomas
By kind permission of Express Newspapers

taking place in St James's Palace, which was being held for those involved
in The Prince's Trust charity for which The Prince of Wales had done so
much to assist bright young entrepreneurs to get a start up the commercial
ladder. I felt a tug and turned round to find that Her Majesty was smiling
at me. The clue to the situation lay in the man standing next to her. He
was Major General Richards, whom I had known earlier as the Comman-
dant of the Royal Marines. He was now retired and was the Senior Security
Officer to the Diplomatic Corps. In his conversation with The Queen, it
transpired that she had enquired if there were any present with Royal
Marine connections. Her son, Prince Edward, was undergoing training at
the very depot I had attended almost fifty years earlier, at Lympestone,
Devon, and so I was presented to Her Majesty. I told her that I had been
a trainee at Lympestone in 1943 and had very happy memories of the place
– but not the time!

I next had a conversation with Her Majesty in Buckingham Palace. John
Major was the Prime Minister and he had the splendid thought that those
previously not invited could be invited by The Queen to a Royal
Reception. This took place in that long, lovely room where hang the most
beautiful pictures. Margaret and I had been in conversation with Lord
Huntington-Bass, who, at the time, trained The Queen's horses. He was a

'Labour Greats' – the 43 Labour Peers who in 1994 had served in Labour Governments
By kind permission of John Londei

Key to photograph

1. Earl of Listowel, served in Coalition Government, 1944
2. Lord (Arthur) Bottomley, Commonwealth Secretary
3. Lord (Stanley) Clinton-Davis, EC Commissioner
4. Lord (John) Jacques
5. Baroness (Alma) Birk
6. Lord Merlyn-Rees, Home Secretary, Northern Ireland Secretary
7. Earl of Longford
8. Lord Glenamara (Ted Short)
9. Lord (Fred) Mulley
10. Lord (Denis) Healey, Chancellor
11. Lord (Ivor) Richard, Lords Leader, UN Ambassador, EEC Commissioner
12. Lord (Denis) Howell
13. Lord (Ted) Graham of Edmonton, Chief Whip, House of Lords
14. Baroness (Nora) David
15. Lord (Terry) Boston of Faversham
16. Lord (Joel) Barnett
17. Lord (Harry) Ewing of Kirkford
18. Lord (Jack) Dormand of Easington
19. Lord (Douglas) Jay
20. Lord (Roy) Mason of Barnsley, Defence Secretary, Northern Ireland Secretary
21. Baroness (Bea) Serota
22. Lord (Peter) Archer of Sandwell
23. Lord (Frank) Judd
24. Lord (Jock) Stallard
25. Lord (Eric) Varley
26. Lord Cledwyn of Penrhos, former Leader, House of Lords
27. Lord (Billy) Hughes
28. Lord (David) Strabolgi
29. Lord (Neil) Carmichael of Kelvingrove
30. Baroness (Eirene) White
31. Lord (James) Callaghan of Cardiff, Prime Minister, 1976–79
32. Lord (Wayland) Kennet
33. Lord (Peter) Lovell-Davis
34. Lord (George) Wallace of Coslany
35. Lord (Hugh) Jenkins of Putney, Arts Minister
36. Lord (Malcolm) Shepherd, former Leader, House of Lords
37. Lord (Harold) Wilson of Rievaulx, Prime Minister 1964–70, 1974–76
38. Lord (John) Kirkhill
39. Baroness (Pat) Llewelyn-Davies of Hastoe, Government Chief Whip, 1974–79
40. Lord (Douglas) Houghton of Sowerby, 95
41. Lord (Donald) Bruce of Donnington, PPS to Aneurin Bevan
42. Lord (Will) Howie of Troon
43. Lord (Joe) Dean of Beswick

115

Crossbencher and I got on with him very well. As the Royal Party approached, Her Majesty spotted him and made a beeline for him. He said to her that he had a winner for her at Wolverhampton on the Friday of that week. It was called 'Set the Fashion' and 'Ma'am, it will win'. 'I will be in Wolverhampton to open the all-weather track' she said and Huntington-Bass said 'That is why we have got it ready for you'. Her Majesty turned to me and said, 'Well, Lord Graham, you have a winner and it is straight from the horse's mouth!'

Later that evening, I was waiting for my car to take me home when John Major came bounding down the stairs and, on seeing me, came across and asked me if I had enjoyed the party. 'Very much,' I replied, 'And I can do you a bit of good. The Queen has a horse running at Wolverhampton on Friday called Set the Fashion, and her trainer has just assured her that it will win.' He said that he would be in Sicily on Friday at a summit meeting but would I be so kind as to put £10 to win on it for him? Of course, I said yes, and duly placed his bet. It came third and, thus, John had lost his tenner.

Later, I wrote to him giving him the bad news and asking for my money. He sent it immediately and a note to say that he had been warned of the powers of the Opposition Chief Whip in the Lords! John and I had been friends from the time in the early eighties when we served in the Whips Offices – and a lot of water had flowed under the bridge since then!

The picture

In 1994 after I had been Chief Whip for four years I had written a number of obituaries of colleagues who had made a major contribution to the performance of the Labour Peers Group and I then realized that Labour History was disappearing before my very eyes. I then decided to arrange a photograph in which all those who had served in a Labour Administration as Ministers would be invited to participate. Choosing a date when everyone could be present proved to be impossible, but as you will see, most of them who could attend did so. John Londei is a photographer who excels in taking pictures of large groups, and I am indebted to him for taking such an excellent picture of 'Labour Greats.'

The Labour Peers Group, which emerged after the defeat of 1979, was the product of the first twenty years of the Life Peerages Act 1958. What a cracking assembly of wisdom and experience it was too! Just let me run a few names past you for starters: Alice Bacon; Tommy Balough; Frank Beswick; Alma Birk; Billy Blyton; George Briginshaw; Fenner Brockway; Donald Bruce; Elaine Burton; Ted Castle; Walter Citrine; Harold Collison; Nora David; Harold Davies; Evelyn Dennington; Elwyn Jones; Marcia Falkender; Dora Gaitskell; Gerald Gardiner; Sid Greene; Tony Greenwood;

Cyril Hamnet; John Jacques; Fred Lee; Charlie Leatherland; Jennie Lee; Pat Llewelyn-Davies; Frank Longford; Victor Mishcon; Philip Noel-Baker; Reg Paget; Fred Peart; Tom Ponsonby; Harvey Rhodes; Ritchie Calder; Hughie Scanlon; Bill Sefton; Bea Serota; Ted Short; Malcolm Shepherd; David Strabolgi; Eirene White; George Wigg; Ted Willis; Barbara Wootton; Michael Young.

Of course, there were many more, all having gone through the bruising years of 1974/79 — and survived. They were not to know for how long they would be in Opposition, and when after less than two years, the SDP was formed, some of them left the ranks of Labour and immediately began to seek to undermine the very Party which had given them a place in the House of Lords! Alas, it is exceeding strange how loss of power affects some people, but they left behind a band of brothers — and sisters — who hung on until Tony Blair was able to begin the process whereby the size of the Labour Peers Group grew to something like it had been before 1979 — yet even today it is still smaller than that of the Conservative Party in the Lords! And less than thirty per cent of the total House!

When the picture was taken, those who had soldiered on from 1979 included Billy Listowel, Pat Llewelyn-Davies, George Wallace, Alma Birk, Nora David, John Jacques, Donald Bruce, Eirene White, Frank Pakenham, Terry Boston, Billy Hughes, Bea Serota, David Strabolgi, Douglas Houghton, Will Howie, Ted Short. Sadly, the following on the photograph have since died: Denis Howell, Arthur Bottomley, Billy Listowel, Johnny Jacques, Alma Birk, Frank Longford, Fred Mulley, Douglas Jay, Cledwyn Hughes, Billy Hughes, Neil Carmichael, Eirene White, Malcolm Shepherd, Harold Wilson, Joe Dean, Pat Llewelyn-Davies, Douglas Houghton, Peter Lovell-Davis.

Visiting the Maze

In that period after I entered the Lords and becoming the Chief Whip in 1990, I was a jack of all trades, and one of the posts I filled was that of a spokesman on Northern Ireland. In that capacity, I worked with a real gentleman, Gwilym Prys-Davies, who was the senior spokesman. He was exceedingly diligent and arranged a visit to Northern Ireland for both of us on what could be called a fact-finding mission. As at that time I was the Parliamentary Consultant for the Prison Officers Association, I wanted to visit prisons while he, with his special knowledge and interest in the Health Service, concentrated on those matters.

We were made very welcome and Lord (Charlie) Lisle, the Junior Minister at the Northern Ireland Office, made sure that we saw what we wanted to see. On our first night there, we were entertained at Stormont where we met leading figures in political circles. Next day, we visited the Maze Prison.

Having visited about thirty-two prisons in England and Wales, I was no stranger to a prison atmosphere, but that at the Maze was quite unique. Not long before we arrived, an Assistant Governor had been murdered in his home and the demeanour shown us by both prisoners and prison officers was quite chilling. We were asked if we would like to speak to the prisoners and when we replied, we were asked, 'Which lot first?' Although the fiction that prisoners were not segregated was the firm stance given to the public, we were told that it would have been impossible to maintain any kind of order if they were not segregated, and so they were. We first were taken to the Nationalist compounds and as we walked along, our officer guides told us that they knew we were coming, although they had not been told by them.

We entered a recreational area and were quickly engaged in conversation by prisoners. They told us that as we were Labour politicians, we should be supporting their 'fight for socialism' and they were keen that we should make statements of support for their cause. Of course, we were circumspect and asked our prison officer guides if this was the kind of reception accorded to all visitors. We were told that it was always different. Each of the groups in the Maze was in constant contact from the outside and was told by its contacts outside how to deal with any visitors. On this occasion, they had been told to try and obtain statements from us that could be used in the constant battle going on.

We then went into the segregated part occupied by the Unionists or Protestant prisoners. A different story. Our guide called out who we were and that we would be pleased to hear from them anything they wanted to tell us. Silence. Worse. They turned their backs on us, and we were told that it was clear that they had been told to boycott our visit.

The next prison we visited at Magilligan was completely different. As I understood the situation, at this prison all of the prisoners were towards the end of their sentence and would not lightly jeopardize their end date. Consequently, there was no segregation for the danger of mayhem was far less likely. We had many helpful and understanding conversations with the prisoners who were engaged in a variety of tasks designed to fit them for release and job prospects once they had ended their sentence. We also had valuable conversations with the prison officers over and after lunch. Brave men and women.

When we left Magilligan, we went to Derry where we were received in the Town Hall by the Mayor of Derry. He explained the political situation in graphic detail and described the visit of Tom King in his time as the Secretary of State for Northern Ireland. At that time, the political complexion of the Council was mixed. As Tom King stood on the steps of the Town Hall (where we were standing at the time), Sinn Fein councillors had struck Tom and beat him to the ground. Such an outrage would be unheard of on the mainland but in Northern Ireland, and especially in such a sensitive place as Derry, it was not so unusual. As we left Derry, we were in a long queue of vehicles being searched. We called in at the home of John Hume who was not there but we met his lovely wife and were made to feel very welcome.

We then made our way to an estate on the edge of Derry where, at my request, we visited a Co-operative store and met those active in promoting it. A Catholic priest was prominent and I left in good heart knowing that the Co-operative Idea was working for the people of Derry. In Ireland, the Co-operative Movement has a history of service and the concept of Co-operation in the form of Credit Unions is very strong, and especially in Derry. Agricultural Co-operatives played a useful part and recently, the Consumer Movement had been given a boost by the involvement of the Co-operative Group. Taking the Annual Parliament of the Co-operative Movement – Co-operative Congress – to Belfast in 2002 was an inspiring initiative and both John Hume and John Reid were given rapturous receptions.

I had made an earlier visit to the Province. In 1972, as the National Secretary of the Co-operative Party, I had spent four days there being looked after by Douglas McIlldoon, then a Labour activist who rose to high office in the Civil Service of Northern Ireland. He took me to many places – including a quiet country pub where I had conversations with Nationalist supporters, and to the church presided over by Ian Paisley. He gave the most political speech I heard in Northern Ireland, and commanded that the congregation show their loyalty to the church by participation in a 'silent collection' – one where the only sound would be that of rustling notes! It was also whilst I was there that MacGurk's Bar was the scene of an atrocity when sixteen innocent people were blown to smithereens.

No room – with or without a view

I became the Opposition Chief Whip in 1990 and one of the tasks I inherited was that of finding desks for Labour Peers. Whilst it could be expected that parliamentarians in the Upper Chamber of Parliament would be provided with 'facilities' such as a desk – even a room – the reality was then that many Labour Peers had neither a desk or a room, having to rely on squeezing onto a desk in The Writing Room or a perch in The Library. And with no telephone it was difficult to be taken seriously when this had to be explained to those outside the Lords. It all goes back to 'the old days' when Peers were not expected to attend all that often, and even when they did it would be for a few hours in the afternoon and never later at night. All this changed, of course when, after the Life Peerages Act of 1958, many more than hereditary Peers looked upon the Lords as a place of work, or even a place from which work was generated.

I quickly found that there were those who had been ensconced in the place for a few years, had rightly been given a desk when they were performing official duties such as Ministers or Opposition Spokespersons, but were loath to give them up when that 'stint' was over. Nowadays there has been a sea change, for more than one building near to the Lords has become available, and what with decanting Officers and Staff out of the main building and refurbishing rooms within, the situation has been transformed.

Shortly after becoming Chief Whip I was stopped in a corridor by Jim Callaghan. Having served in his Government of 1976/79 we were firm friends. He reminded me that he had been in the Lords since 1987 and was sharing a room with 5 other colleagues. He was still then much in demand for consultations especially by those from other lands who, when in London wanted to have a chat which could be mutually beneficial – yet he had no room of his own in which to entertain them! I found this astounding and promised that I would see what I could do. The situation was bleak. When I next met the other Chief Whips (the usual channels) I found that the situation was one I had to solve myself, but with no fresh accommodation available I could only do this if I decanted sitting Labour Peers out of a room and gave it to Jim – but I had nowhere else to put the decanted colleagues.

Jim suffered this indignity, barely in silence, but when Margaret Thatcher came to the Lords after the 1992 General Election – and was found a room immediately by the Tory Chief Whip, Alexander Hesketh, he blew his top – and so did I. How had he done it, I asked Alexander. Simple. Taking three Tory Peers out of a room they shared and giving it to the ex-Prime Minister, sending his colleagues to other desks which he had at his disposal. This was perfectly fair and good whipping, but I could not do it.

Salvation came when next I had the opportunity to influence the allocation of a fresh tranche of accommodation. For many, many years it was laid down that the senior officer in the Commons – the Sergeant-at-Arms – should have his living quarters within the Palace. This was so that in any emergency he would be on the spot. Not least because that accommodation was precious, but more because over the years modern means of communication meant that he could still be 'on the job' from living quarters literally just outside the Palace. So, when a new holder of that office was appointed he was allocated living accommodation not inside but outside. If that was good enough for the Commons, why not apply the same principle to the Lords? And so, when a new incumbent to the post of Black Rod was appointed, he too was stripped of his internal rooms and found a very attractive suite of rooms across the road from the Lords. Bingo! The release of this accommodation meant that all Parties in the Lords could lay claim to some of it – and I got two magnificent rooms on the West Front, overlooking the entrance and looking straight into Westminster Abbey – and near a lift!

I had the great pleasure of inviting Jim to view both rooms and to take his pick which he did and from which he now rests in comfort as befitting an ex-Prime Minister. He was delighted.

Postscipt

When I vacated the splendid room I occupied as Opposition Chief Whip on the West Front, Principal floor it was a wrench, but I had saved a tiny room from my allocation to give to a colleague who would not be serving as a Minister in the new Government formed by Tony Blair. I took it, and managed to squeeze another desk into it which I gave to my long-time comrade Garfield Davies, the former top man in the Shopworkers Union. It had previously been Black Rod's Shower Room! It will be some time before Peers will be accorded the dignity and right of working arrangements befitting their role in our parliamentary affairs. That day cannot come soon enough.

CHAPTER 9

The House of Lords in practice

Twentieth-century developments in membership

DURING THE CONSTITUTIONAL CONFLICT between the Lords and Commons in the early years of the twentieth century, Winston Churchill described the House of Lords as a 'one-sided, hereditary, unpurged, unrepresentative, irresponsible, absentee'[1] and as 'filled with old doddering Peers, cute financial magnates, clever wire-pullers, big brewers with bulbous noses. All the enemies of progress are there – weaklings, sleek, smug, comfortable, self-important individuals'[2] while Lloyd George described hereditary Peers as 'dug out of the cellars of the House of Lords, stuff bottled in the Dark Ages, not fit to drink, cobwebby, dusty, muddy, sour'.

The outcome of any division depends upon the number of members voting, as well as the way in which they cast their votes. These basic factors themselves depend upon a number of variables, such as the subject under discussion, the advocacy of certain individuals, the day of the week, and the hour of the day. Any exposition of the political complexion of the House of Lords is invalidated unless it takes into account these factors. When they are taken into account, it becomes apparent that the complete Conservative control evident in 1945, indeed evident into the nineteen sixties, has disappeared; gone are the days when a Conservative Government need have no fear of defeat in the Lords. Indeed, the Lords have in recent years been a source of embarrassment, an irritant, and obstruction to the Conservative Government – as is shown by the more than 150 defeats inflicted upon the Conservative Government in the division lobbies of the House of Lords since 1979. (During the 1988–9 session, the House defeated the Government on twelve occasions, out of 186 divisions in which the Government took a stand.) Today, although an overall Conservative majority is perceived by many to exist, in practice, the Conservative Party lacks an automatic majority over all other groups combined, and, more especially, among active Peers is in a minority – albeit only just – relative to them.

---

[1] Cited in Robert Rhodes James (ed), *Churchill Speaks* (Windward, London, 1981,10).
[2] Ibid.

The House of Lords – in practice

Although much of what appears in this record rests on the subjective application of a partisan mind, we do not have to rely solely on that in order to get a view of the wider picture of how the Lords was operating during the period 1979 to 1997. We are indebted to a work of scholarship *The House of Lords at Work* which was edited by Donald Shell and David Beamish. In their work, they bring together a series of papers prepared by eminent academics and sub-titled it 'A Study based on the 1988–89 session'. At the time, Donald Shell was a Lecturer in the Department of Politics at the University of Belfast; David Beamish is Clerk of the Journals, House of Lords, and Reading Clerk, House of Lords, and a winner in the popular television programme *Mastermind*.

A major contribution in that book is that of Nicholas D.J. Baldwin, Director of Studies at Wroxton College, the British campus of Fairleigh Dickinson University, New Jersey, and his contribution is entitled 'The Membership of the House'.

I have used extensively the tables and surrounding explanations from the book and, in particular, the work of Donald Shell, David Beamish and Nicholas Baldwin to whom I owe a great debt for the clarity of their research which I have freely used to illustrate the thread I wish to weave through this work. *The House of Lords at Work* is perhaps the latest, if not the only, work of an academic nature to appear and deal with the central theme of this story, which, simply told, is to expose the nature of the way in which a central pillar of our parliamentary democracy – the House of Lords – has operated for far too long, has outlived its relevance in a modern day society and should be substantially changed.

Shell has observed – on the basis of an analysis of the period 1974–77 (with Labour in office) and 1979–83 (the early sessions of the Thatcher era) – that:

> 'The proportion of Lords' amendments accepted or rejected by the Commons has varied greatly according to whether the Conservative or Labour Party has been in office . . . One may generalize by saying that when Labour has been in office, it has experienced frequent defeat in the Lords and therefore, as a matter of routine, seeks the cancellation of large number of Lords' amendments in the Commons . . . When the Conservatives are in office, comparatively few amendments are carried in the House against the Government's wishes, though when this does happen, a Conservative Government is much more hesitation about simply asking the Commons to reverse such amendments. This is because their acceptance by the Lords has frequently depended on support by some Conservative Peers, if not on substantial crossbench support, and may well have been foreshadowed by rebellion in the Commons as well.'[3]

---

[3] Shell, *House of Lords*, 146–8.

Therefore, Shell says, 'the pressure to compromise can be considerable'. However, as noted elsewhere in this chapter, and in the next, the 1988–9 session, with a Conservative Government buttressed by a large Commons majority, a willingness to compromise, let alone to bow meekly to Lords defeats, was conspicuous by its absence – even when such defeats stemmed from all-party initiatives.

The Conservative Government lost votes, on average, 12 times a year since 1979. Overwhelmingly, these are in amendments to legislation which invariably are reversed when they are dealt with in the Commons. Contrast this with the average number of Government defeats between 1974–79, of more than 70 every year.

The same fate awaits Conservative victories in the Lords when they reach the Commons – the Labour majority overturns them. But valuable time is wasted.

As the tables show, even with the support of the bulk of the hereditary Peers, the Conservative Government does suffer defeats, but these are brought about only when there is a coalition of oppositions. Basically, this rests firstly on the combined strength of the Labour and Liberal Democrat benches, strengthened on such occasions by most, if not all, of the crossbenchers present.

Even then, it has required the support of some dissident Government supporters, and such Government defeats are often led by a leading Government backbencher, as has happened with increasing frequency in recent years.

This piece is designed to show that the Government wins the overwhelming number of divisions in the Lords solely because it relies on – and calls on – the hundreds of hereditary Peers who owe it their political allegiance. It is proved that without this built-in majority, this Government would be unable to get its business, and that if hereditary Peers were to have their voting rights removed, it would cause a change of seismic proportions in the operation of Parliament as we have known it.

There were 172 Government victories and 12 defeats in divisions during the 1988–89 session. With the votes of Peers by succession excluded, there was an anti-Government majority in 159 divisions, a Government majority in 21, and an equality in 4. This is a built-in bonus for the Government but not every Government – only a Conservative Government.

Statistics relating to the global performance of hereditary Peers in the 1993–94 session are not yet to hand, but the analysis for 1988–89 which translates 172 Government victories down to 21 when the votes of hereditary Peers are excluded is likely to be confirmed.

In other words, if only that one step, to deprive hereditary Peers of a vote, operated now, it would transform Parliamentary arithmetic.

There is almost equality of numbers in Life Peers when one contrasts the Conservatives (147) with Labour and Liberal Democrats (134) and this throws into sharp relief the significant part played in divisions by the crossbenches. The table shows that there are more crossbench Life Peers than Labour, but that when hereditary Peers are taken into account, crossbenchers (275) account for almost all other benches (284) against the Conservative total of 475.

A scrutiny of division lists shows that divergence from party support in the lobbies is not unknown within all three political parties. As the crossbenches do not apply a whip, it follows that members from their benches tend to go into differing lobbies more frequently than do the other benches, except when a member from their midst, invariably with powerful advocacy and persuasive argument, causes the crossbenchers to act with impressive unity.

The way the crossbenches vote can be crucial – and often is.

The House of Lords at work

The Membership of the House

Analysis of Lords as at the beginning of the 1988–9 session not attending during the session

	Hereditary		Created hereditary	Life Peers		Law Lords	Bishops	Total
	M	F		M	F			
Conservative	48	1		2	2			53
Labour	1			4	2			7
Social and Liberal Democrat	5			2				7
Social Democrat								0
Cross Bench	27	1	5	12		2		47
Other	24		2	2				28
Bishops							1	
On leave of absence	143		5	10	4			165
Without writs	76							80
Total	324		12	32		2	1	388

Analysis of Lords as at the beginning of the 1988–9 session attending during the session

	Hereditary		Created hereditary	Life Peers		Law Lords	Bishops	Total
	M	F		M	F			
Conservative	269	4	9	89	13			384
Labour	10		1	80	15			106
Social and Liberal Democrat	23		1	23	2			49
Social Democrat	9			12	2			23
Cross Bench	95	7	2	69	5	18		196
Other	8		2	5				14
Bishops							25	26
Total	414		15	277	37	18	25	797

Political affiliation and peerage category on an average day during the 1988–9 session

Party	Peerage category						
	Hereditary	Created hereditary	Life Peers	Law Lords	Bishops	Total	% of total attendance
Conservative	93	3	51			147	46.6
Labour	6	1	63			70	22.1
Social and Liberal Democrat	11	1	15			27	8.5
Social Democratic Party	4		6			10	3.2
Cross-bench	32	1	21	3		57	18.0
Other	0	0	3			3	1.0
Bishops					2	2	0.7
Total	146	6	159	3	2	316	100.0
% of total attendance	46.1	1.9	50.3	1.0	0.7	100.0	

Note: Figures are based on total attendances recorded during the 1988–9 session, divided by the number of sitting days (153). 0 indicates a figure of less then 0.5, while a blank indicates no attendances by the category in question. Apparent discrepancies in totals and percentages are the result of rounding.

House of Lords: Analysis of composition – 2 April 2001

By party strength

Party	Life Peers	Hereditary: Elected by party	Hereditary: Elected Holders	Hereditary: *Appointed Royal Office Holders	Bishops	Total
Conservative	173	42	9	1		225
Labour	193	2	2			197
Liberal Democrat	57	3	2			62
Crossbench	132	28	2	1		163
Archbishops and Bishops					26	26
Other	6					6
Total	561	75	15	2	26	679

*These are the Duke of Norfolk, The Earl Marshal (Conservative) and The Marquess of Cholmondeley, The Lord Great Chamberlain (Crossbench).
NB Excludes 4 life Peers on leave of absence.

Divisions in the House of Lords

	Divisions	
Session	No of Government defeats[1]	Total no. of divisions
1970–71*	4	196
1971–72	5	168
1972–73	13	80
1973–74**	4	19
1974**	13	21
1974–75	103	119
1975–76	126	146
1976–77	25	45
1977–78	78	96
1978–79	11	21
1979–80*	15	303
1980–81	18	184
1981–82	7	146
1982–83**	5	89
1983–84*	20	237
1984–85	17	145
1985–86	22	250
1986–87**	3	80
1987–88*	17	279

1988–89	12	189
1989–90	20	186
1990–91	17	104
1991–92★★	6	83
1992–93★	19	165
1993–94	16	136
1994–95	7	106
1995–96	10	110
1996–97★★	10	67
1997–98★	39	179
1998–99	31	99
1999–2000	36	192
2000–01★★	2	40
2001–02★	56	172

[1]A Government defeat is defined as a division in which the tellers on the losing side were Government Whips.

★This session was longer than usual: it followed a general election.

★★This session was shorter than usual: it was terminated by a general election.

Source: House of Lords Information Office.

Voting in all divisions, broken down by peerage type (1988–89 session)

Type	Lords voting	Votes cast	Mean	Median	Pro-Govt	Anti-Govt
Hereditary Peers	369	15,154	41.1	22	11,984	3,066
All others	315	16,680	53.0	43	6,963	9,620
Created hereditary Peers	13	550	42.3	31	356	192
Life Peers	283	16,065	56.8	46	6,573	9,397
Law lords	3	28	9.3	5	20	8
Bishops	16	37	2.3	2	14	23
Total	684	31,834	46.5	31	18,947	12,686

Analysis of composition – 1 August 2002

By Party Strength

Party	Life Peers	Hereditary: Elected by party	Hereditary: Elected Holders	Hereditary: *Appointed Royal Office Holders	Bishops	Total
Conservative	170	40**	9			219
Labour	187	2	2			191
Liberal Democrat	60	3	2			65
Crossbench	147	29**	2	1		179
Archbishops and Bishops					26	26
Other***	8					8
Total	572	74	15	1	26	688

NB Excludes 12 Peers: 11 are on leave of absence and 1 (elected hereditary) is bankrupt and cannot attend.

By type

Archbishops and bishops	26
Life Peers under the Appellate Jurisdiction Act 1876	27
Life Peers under the Life Peerages Act 1958 (112 women)	557
Peers under House of Lords Act 1999 (4 women)	91
Total	701

*These are: the Duke of Norfolk, The Earl Marshal (currently on leave of absence) and the Marquess of Cholmondeley, The Lord Great Chamberlain (Crossbench).

**L. Brabazon of Tara was elected as a Conservative but, as the Principal Deputy Chairman of Committees, he now sits on the Crossbenches.

***These are: L. Archer of Weston-super-Mare, *Non-affiliated*; L. Beaumont of Whitley, *Green Party*; L. Elystan-Morgan, *Independent Crossbencher*; L. Fitt, *Independent Socialist*; L. Maginnis of Drumglass, *Ulster Unionist Party*; L. McAlpine of West Green, *Independent Conservative*; L. Stoddart of Swindon, *Independent Labour*; B. Young of Old Scone, *Non-affiliated*.

CHAPTER 10

Prime ministerial peerage creations – July 1958 to 2000

> My Lord Tomnoddy is thirty four,
> The Earl can last but a few years more,
> My Lord in the Peers will take his place,
> Her Majesty's councils his words will grace.
> Office he'll hold and patronage sway,
> Fortunes and lives he will vote away
> And what are his qualifications? One!
> He's the Earl of Fitzdotterel's eldest son
> *(Robert Barnabus Brough, 1828–60)*

As I have acknowledged elsewhere – and do so here – I am indebted to Donald Shell and David Beamish for the invaluable source-material contained in their work *The House of Lords at Work*. It pays special attention to how it does work with particular reference to the Parliamentary year of 1988–9. For this part dealing with how successive Prime Ministers handled the award of Peerages during their period in office is worth quoting – this is said by them in pages 7 and 8:

> Alongside the curtailment of the power of the House, some adjustments have been made in its composition. Traditionally, the House has been an aristocratic chamber, composed of Peers by succession, Peers by creation, and bishops. To be a Peer was by definition to be a man of substance. In the twentieth century that has decisively changed. The aristocracy has declined, and the House of Peers has become more meritocratic and less aristocratic, even a little plebeian and a good deal less plutocratic, certainly as far as the active House is concerned. In large part, this change has been accomplished simply through successive Prime Ministers feeling free to recommend for the award of peerages individuals who were neither rich nor necessarily drawn from the social circles which hitherto had monopolized the peerage.

Later they said:

> Thoughts about the kind of radical surgery which might be performed on the House inhibited action aimed more modestly at modernizing the place. It therefore fell to the Conservatives to pass the only two Acts of Parliament this century which have actually altered the basis of membership of this House.

130

[This was before the passing of the House of Lords Act of 1999.] The first of these was the Life Peerages Act 1958, a simple measure long discussed but which successive governments had shied away from. The 1958 Life Peerages Act permitted the award of peerages which would be held for the lifetime of the recipient only; henceforth membership of the House could be accepted without heirs being threatened with the encumbrance of a peerage! Of greater moment was the fact that no limit was placed on the total of life peerages that could be awarded. Hence, a considerably greater number of peerages could be created than previously without permanently adding to the normal membership of what was already the largest legislative assembly in the world.

The Peerage Act of 1963 allowed Peers by succession to renounce their peerages altogether, though renounced peerages would remain available to be assumed again by heirs.

The Lords' Information Office show that in 1985, the Peers taking the Tory Whip numbered 405. Ten years later – despite the imbalance – this had grown to 477. In 1985, Peers taking the Labour Whip numbered 123, which had declined by 1995 to 114. It didn't even need especial action to achieve this for the 'Right of Succession', whereby the death of a hereditary Peer enabled an automatic replacement, meant for instance that in the three years of 1992/3/4, Tory hereditary Peers were succeeded by 102 replacements. In that same period, Labour benefited by – none!

Harold MacMillan had recognized just how ludicrous the trend had become, and his Life Peerages Act 1958 had thrown out a sort of lifeline but it was only when Labour with the House of Lords Bill 1999 took away the right of most hereditary Peers to sit and vote in the Lords that anything like redress began to take shape. Even so, the Lords' Information Office tell us that in August 2002, after that landmark Act, the total membership of the Lords stood at 688, of which Labour had 191 – less than 28 per cent [see page 111]. In the Second Chamber, or as Her Majesty calls it when opening Parliament 'The Upper House', there were still 219 taking the Tory Whip and 191 the Labour Whip. Crossbenches still retained 179 members. (August 2002 figures)

Perhaps we have moved somewhat since Disraeli said:

> We owe the English Peerage to three sources; the spoilation of the Church; the open and flagrant sale of honours by the elder Stuarts; and the borough-mongering of our own time.
>
> (*Coningsby 1844*)

Tony Blair has been much criticized for proceeding to make new Labour Life Peers ('Tony's Cronies') out of all proportion to an entitlement based on any other criteria, but the fact is that faced with such a mountain to climb, as shown by the above figures, he had little alternative if he was to get his legislative programme through. He has already indicated that he does not wish to wield the power of his patronage for making Peers so loved by almost all of his predecessors. What he has done, and for which he should be applauded, is to narrow the gap between what a Labour Government has historically found when taking office – a Tory dominated House with power to frustrate at will. As a result now the Liberal Democrats hold sway, for their current numbers give them the position that if they back the Government, it wins, but if they side with the Tories, the Government loses.

How successive Prime Ministers have faced up (or not) to the need to make the Upper Chamber more democratic and representative (Labour's Manifesto commitment of 2001) can be seen from the following tables. They make interesting reading!

Peerage creations¹ by Prime Minister in office at time of announcement, July 1958–December 2000

Prime Minister in office	Hereditary		Life		Law²		Total		All	Average annual creation
	M	F	M	F	M	F	M	F		
Macmillan 1958–63	37	–	40	7	6	–	83	7	90	16
Douglas-Home	10	–	14	2	3	–	27	2	29	26
Wilson 1964–70	6	–	121	14	2	–	129	14	143	25
Heath	–	–	37	8	3	–	40	8	48	12
Wilson 1974–76	–	–	69	11	3	–	72	11	83	38
Callaghan	–	–	53	5	2	–	55	5	60	19
Thatcher	4	–	174	27	11	–	189	27	216	18
Major	–	–	131	29	11	–	142	29	171	25
Blair	1 (1)	– (–)	145 (155)	45 (45)	5 (5)	– (–)	151 (161)	45 (45)	196 (206)	51 (54)
All 1958–1998	58 (58)	– (–)	784 (794)	148 (148)	46 (46)	– (–)	888 (898)	148 (148)	1036 (1046)	23 (24)

Notes

1. Excluding Peers created under the Appellate Jurisdiction Act 1876.
2. Peers created under the Appellate Jurisdiction Act 1876.

Figures in brackets include the ten hereditary Peers given life peerages in the honours list published on 2nd November 1999.

Source: House of Lords Information Office.

Peerage creations¹ by age at announcement and Prime Minister in office at time of announcement

Age group	Prime Minister									All 1958–2000	
	Macmillan 1958–63	Douglas-Home	Wilson 1964–70	Heath	Wilson 1974–76	Callaghan	Thatcher	Major	Blair	Number	Per cent
20–29	–	–	–	–	–	–	1	–	– (–)	1 (1)	0 (0)
30–39	2	–	2	1	–	–	–	–	6 (6)	11 (11)	1 (1)
40–49	7	3	7	3	5	6	14	21	29 (29)	95 (95)	10 (10)
50–59	30	8	46	15	26	17	60	49	88 (89)	339 (340)	34 (34)
60–69	33	13	66	23	39	29	102	70	56 (59)	431 (434)	44 (43)
70–79	12	2	17	3	10	5	25	20	12 (12)	106 (106)	11 (11)
80–89	–	–	3	–	–	1	2	–	– (5)	6 (11)	1 (1)
90–99	–	–	–	–	–	–	1	–	– (1)	1 (2)	0 (0)
Total	84	26	141	45	80	58	205	160	191 (201)	990 (1000)	100 (100)

Notes

1. Excluding Peers created under the Appellate Jurisdiction Act 1876.

Figures in brackets include the ten hereditary Peers given life peerages in the honours list published on 2nd November 1999.

Source: House of Lords Information Office.

Peerage creations[1] by party allegiance at creation, type of list, and Prime Minister in power at time of announcement

Party	New Year/ Birthday	Resignation/ Dissolution	Multiple	Ad hoc	Total
(i) Macmillan 1958–63					
Conservative	8	3	6	12	29
Labour	3	1	16	–	20
Liberal/LibDem/SDP	–	–	–	–	–
Independent/crossbench/other	16		10	9	35
All	27	4	32	21	84
(ii) Douglas-Home					
Conservative	4	1	3	3	11
Labour	–	–	9	–	9
Liberal/LibDem/SDP	–	–	–	–	–
Independent/crossbench/other	2	–	3	1	6
All	6	1	15	4	26
(iii) Wilson 1964–70					
Conservative	–	17	2	1	20
Labour	9	25	23	5	62
Liberal/LibDem/SDP	–	3	3	–	6
Independent/crossbench/other	48	–	1	4	53
All	57	45	29	10	141
(iv) Heath					
Conservative	1	–	6	1	8
Labour	–	8	1	–	9
Liberal/LibDem/SDP	–	–	2	–	2
Independent/crossbench/other	9	–	14	3	26
All	10	8	23	4	45
(v) Wilson 1974–76					
Conservative	–	17	3	2	22
Labour	10	21	5	3	39
Liberal/LibDem/SDP	–	4	1	1	6
Independent/crossbench/other	11	2	–	–	13
All	21	44	9	6	80
(vi) Callaghan					
Conservative	1	–	4	–	5
Labour	11	5	11	2	29
Liberal/LibDem/SDP	–	–	1	–	1
Independent/crossbench/other	19	4	–	–	23
All	31	9	16	2	58

(vii) Thatcher					
Conservative	34	19	37	8	98
Labour	6	24	25	1	56
Liberal/LibDem/SDP	4	3	3	–	10
Independent/crossbench/other	34	1	2	4	41
All	78	47	67	13	205
(viii) Major					
Conservative	12	28	30	5	75
Labour	2	13	25	–	40
Liberal/LibDem/SDP	5	4	8	–	17
Independent/crossbench/other	19	4	1	4	28
All	38	49	64	9	160
(xi) Blair (to October 2003)					
Conservative	2	15	18 (25)	1	36 (43)
Labour	2	12	92 (94)	6	112 (114)
Liberal/LibDem/SDP	–	5	30 (30)	–	35 (35)
Independent/crossbench/other	24	2	18* (19)	10	54 (55)
All	28	34	158 (168)	17	237 (247)

Notes

1. Excluding Peers created under the Appellate Jurisdiction Act 1876.

*Including 15 Peers nominated by the Appointments Commission, announced in list of 26th April 2001.

Figures in brackets include the ten hereditary Peers given life peerages in the honours list published on 2nd November 1999.

Source: House of Lords Information Office.

PART IV

Ambushes, Obituaries and Reflections

CHAPTER 11

Ambushes

WHEN I SET OUT to recount and recall the highlights of my time as Opposition Chief Whip there were two aspects which I felt must figure largely – Ambushes and Obituaries. Recalling the planning, staging and ultimately 'delivering' of a successful ambush did more for lifting the morale of the Labour Peers Group than anything I know. In a bleak period when we knew that we had no chance of changing the oppressive policies of the Government, Labour Peers never lost that urge to inflict damage on their political opponents. This was the natural expression of politically savvy men and women who found themselves in a place and with the opportunity to strike back – and my how they loved to do just that! On one occasion told in the following pages this actually meant that they were being asked to come into the House of Lords – surreptitiously – at midnight – hide in tiny rooms – and at the witching hour pop out to stride through the (winning) lobby! Mostly the blows we struck were redressed later in the Commons, but in the period before the 1997 General Election we can claim, modestly, that by holding up Bills and depriving the Government of time to deal with them in the Commons we had an impact on the atmosphere in which that Election was fought. I have selected some of those(written contemporaneously) which convey the mood both of Labour Peers and of others, especially Labour Leaders and the Shadow Cabinet. It was great!

Sometimes you need help!

To achieve a victory against all the odds requires many skills, not least a determination to win. The incentive to do so always lay in the political. The fallout from a defeat for the Conservative Government in the Lords brought huge satisfaction throughout the Labour Party in that period from 1979 to 1997 but it was also a source of great joy and satisfaction to the Liberal Democrat benches in the Lords and elsewhere. There were varying degrees of enthusiasm amongst the Labour ranks due to one of a number of things: what was the point of the exercise? Would a victory really matter? Would we not be just storing up trouble for ourselves when we got into Government? Surely the Government Whips just would not let us win – and then all our subterfuge would be for nothing?

An originator if not the earliest advocate for the ambush or the surprise vote is alive and well and lives in the Whips Office – of the Liberal Democrats. Celia Thomas is the major factotum in that office, keeping their Frontbench on their toes and up-to-date with what is required to be an effective political force. When the thought arose that the weapon of the ambush should be more formally recognized and organized, she was enthusiastic and thanks to Celia that essential ingredient – numbers – came to be more easily attained than hitherto. Celia worked under the direction of two first class Parliamentary 'fixers', first Geoff Tordoff and then John Harris who, as the Liberal Democrat Chief Whips, had the role of discussing with me the when, what and how of the exercise, but it fell to Celia to ensure that Liberal Democrat Peers – those who attended regularly and those who did not – were made fully aware that their presence was not only required but demanded on the fateful day – and time.

For this to be effective, Liberal Democrat Peers had not only to be enthusiastic but had also to respect those who made the appeal to them. In that, I played little part but Celia, Geoff and John worked their group in a highly successful way. I cannot recall a single instance where we lost a vote due to the poor turnout from the Liberal Peers, although there were many times when it was a close run thing! But just think of how a combined force of little more than 150 could beat one that numbers more than 400 – and not forgetting the Crossbenchers – and you can see that every single vote we could garner was crucial.

TWO DEFEATS ON THE COMMITTEE STAGE FOR THE GOVERNMENT ON THE EDUCATION (SCHOOLS) BILL

The two defeats for the Government which took place on Monday 2 March 1992 have such a significance both in essence and in the general folklore of how to engineer a Government defeat, that I deem it appropriate to produce this little resumé of the background.

In the House of Lords, the Government has been able to rely on a majority over all other parties – without really trying – of about 30/40. From 3 p.m. to 7 p.m. any vote is likely to result in a Government total of about 120 and an Opposition total of between 70 and 80. However, it was perceived that whenever the Opposition Parties chose to spring an 'ambush' after supper time, the Government was invariably in difficulty especially on a Monday.

The rationale for Mondays is simple. Monday is the day when Tory Peers coming into London from the country either reach London late, or do not travel at all, whereas Labour Members from out of London invariably reach London by the mid-afternoon. Secondly, Tuesdays are generally reckoned to be out because Tuesday is the only evening in the week when the House

Authorities put on Dinner and the practice has grown up that this is the evening when many Peers – especially Tories – bring in their family and friends for the evening. Wednesdays are out because it is a non-Government day and Thursdays are the poorest nights because invariably Labour Members disappear somewhat quicker than Tories in order to get back to their homes on Thursday evening, whereas many Tories have a second home in London which they use on Thursday evening. The additional reason why Monday is the best night is that even if the Tories are in London, they invariably go out for dinner and as such they are scattered and difficult to bring back to the House for a snap vote.

It emerged about 6 weeks before the event that the Education (Schools) Bill was the Bill that the Government wanted on the Statute Book, above all others, before a General Election. This meant for instance that the Asylum Bill received a lower priority and the Charities Bill was left in a state of limbo between the two Houses. It also meant that this was the last Bill that was available for the Opposition to inflict damage.

Tessa Blackstone, Maurice Peston and I discussed the possibilities. The timetable had a Committee Day on two Mondays – 24 February 1992 and 2 March 1992 – with a Report Stage on Tuesday 10 March 1992. The Third Reading was set down for Monday 16 March, which we knew was quite unrealistic in the light of a 9 April Election. We decided to allow the first Committee Day to go by and to look closely at the issues that could be raised on the second Committee Day. By very astute management of the amendments it was possible to make sure that an amendment of considerable importance was at a time when if it was possible to organize, we could stage an 'ambush'. This was an amendment which ensured that an independent person – someone not associated with the school – would choose the school inspectors and this would be the Chief Inspector of Schools. Even better, it was possible to make sure that an amendment immediately followed which would preserve the powers of local education authorities to inspect their own schools could also be taken.

I asked the Whips to ensure during the week before the vote what response we could expect from our backbenchers and when we met on 27 February, all Whips reported enthusiasm for a surprise vote. In the light of this, I decided to proceed.

I then discussed the whole scenario with Geoff Tordoff, the Liberal Chief Whip, and he assured me that there would be strong support for these 'timed' amendments. The reason why we chose 9 o'clock is that this would appear to very late in the evening and not likely to be a time at which elderly Labour Peers would be willing to attend the House.

The event had to be seen against the previous success. Monday 17 February the Labour Peers had their annual party and by staging an amendment to be called at about 8.15 p.m. it enabled the Labour Peers to leave the party at 8 p.m. and to inflict a defeat on the Government. The business on the Floor of the House at supper time (between 7 p.m. and 8 p.m.) was The Coal Bill. I decided to ask Joe Dean and Bernard Donoughue to stage a vote at about 7.30 p.m. This took place at 7.40 p.m. and the figures were 41 against and 75 for the Government. This did two things. It established in the minds of the Tory Whips that, at what was reckoned to be 'after the voting time', they had a majority in the House of more than 30 and it also established for me that the figure they had was 75. I knew from previous experience that if Labour and Liberal forces voted successfully, we could achieve a total of about 90.

During the day, we had staged two further votes which clearly established that the Government had majorities of 40 and 50, and this together with the coal industry vote created an atmosphere after 8 p.m. in which they were under the impression that there was little danger. All this despite the fact that any scrutiny of the possibilities for an ambush must concentrate on a Monday evening and after supper time. This was confirmed by reported conversations overheard amongst the Tory Whips that 'there would be a vote later' and there will be a vote at about 9 p.m.

By very astute timing the vote was called at 10 minutes past 9 p.m.

The advice given by Geoff Tordoff and me to our supporters was to reach the House *no later than 9 p.m.*, but if indeed they arrived earlier they had to find a means of keeping out of the Chamber. Both Liberal and Labour Whips Offices provided a place where Peers could assemble and by all accounts they were both very full indeed when the Division Bell rang. There is no doubt that the Government were taken substantially, if not wholly, by surprise. The reality is now quite clear and is that unless they are absolutely certain that there is an attempt to beat them, they only can muster – without special effort – about 60/70 Peers. And that is despite the fact that this Bill and this particular issue were crucial to the Government's legislative programme.

The vote of 95 against the Government was made up of Labour 69, Liberal Democrats 21, Crossbenchers 4 and 1 Conservative (Lord Beloff). The Government 67 was made up of 64 Conservatives and 3 Cross-benchers.

Immediately after the result, Earl Baldwin of Bewdley (a Crossbencher) moved the second amendment. I had spoken to him earlier and pressed upon him that in the event of a victory on the first vote, it was absolutely crucial that he moves his amendment as shortly as possible. This he did with commendable brevity.

However, unlike previous occasions, the Government Whips appreciated that we were intent upon a second victory and immediately one could see them moving amongst the Tory backbenchers, urging them to speak on this amendment. The purpose was clear. Many reports came to me that the Tory Whips were on the telephone to their supporters who had failed to turn up and who they thought could get to the Chamber to get here as quickly as possible. It then was transparent that it was the ambition of the Tory Whips to increase their vote in the hope that our majority would fade away.

This was not out of the question, for many of those who had responded to my call did so on the basis that there would be a vote at 9 p.m. and here we were beyond 9.30 p.m. asking them to remain for a second vote. However, the vote was called at 9.45 p.m., largely I believe after the Tory Whips accepted with resignation that they were not going to get their absent supporters in in time. The second vote was won by an even greater majority with 97 supporting the Opposition. Of this 97 there were 70 Labour, (an increase of 1), 19 Liberal Democrats (down 2) and 3 Conservatives (Lord Beloff was accompanied by Lords Hardinge and Teviot). On this occasion we also got the Bishop of Guildford. The Conservative vote was 61, a reduction, and there were only 2 Cross Benchers amongst them. Thus, a famous victory.

Immediately, the news was spread around the Palace of Westminster. One of the first arrivals on the scene was the Secretary of State, Kenneth Clarke. One of the Tory Whips told me that Kenneth Clarke went into the Government Chief Whip's office and said, 'What are you doing to my Bill?', to which the Government Chief Whip, Alexander Hesketh, said 'If you did not send me up such a (expletive deleted) lousy Bill, we wouldn't be in the mess that we are'. The position was immediately seen by the media as a major blow. This had been given away by the Minister, Emily Blatch, who in winding up told the House that if the first amendment was accepted, 'it would tear the heart out of the Bill'.

On the radio the next morning, Kenneth Clarke refused to indicate what action he would take in the light of the defeats. He refused to say that he would not use the Report Stage of the Bill – due on Tuesday 10 March – to reverse the defeats in the House of Lords. He instead immediately castigated the Labour Opposition for denying consumer choice and for being the tool of the Trades Unions. Laughably, he said that the Conservatives were defeated by Labour backwoodsmen, such as Harold Wilson and Marcia Falkender! This from the Party of backwoodsmen in the House of Lords!

The truth, however, emerged during that day. At least 4 Conservatives came to me and after *sotto voce* congratulating me on the victories, said that they had decided to go home and not return simply because they felt that the Bill and the issue were not to their liking.

It is clear that from having more than 130 Government supporters in the early evening and finishing up with 67, that many of those had been prevailed upon to stay only to make their own decisions.

The next piece of business was how the Government would react. Very little information was obtained. The Government business manager asked if I would agree to leaving 'any major row' until the Bill reached the Commons. I told him that I would not agree to facilitate the passage of the Bill into the Commons, let alone anything else, until I was told what the intentions of the Government would be when the Bill reached there. What the Government wanted was agreement to bringing forward the Third Reading from Monday 16 March to possibly Thursday 12 or Friday 13, without giving me any information or guarantee as to what would happen. I told him that no deal could be struck along those lines and that my price for agreeing to truncating the stages of the Bill was the acceptance of the amendments. On Thursday 5 March at 12.30 p.m., the business manager came to me and said he was authorized by the Leader, David Waddington, and the Chief Whip, Alexander Hesketh, to say that if I agreed that the Third Reading would take place on Thursday 12 March that an undertaking would be given that the amendments would be accepted from the Commons. Thus it was a clear unvarnished victory for the Opposition.

Tailpiece

It has to be recorded that out of the episode one or two things emerged which will be a guide to me in the future. First of all, Labour colleagues are willing to respond to a difficult invitation, providing the scene is set and the atmosphere is right. I have nothing but praise for my colleagues. Secondly, the brilliant timing and management of the events on the Floor of the House which were crucial in the victory owe a great deal to Tessa Blackstone, Maurice Peston and Nora David. Third, honourably, David Waddington and Alexander Hesketh both insisted to Kenneth Clarke that they did not wish to reverse the defeats in the Lords and that they wished no action to be taken at the other end. Further, I understand that their recommendation was that the amendments should be accepted. The job of the Lords was to provide the Commons with an opportunity to think again and once the Commons has thought again, that the Lords should accept their decision. Naturally, the Shadow Cabinet were highly delighted and congratulated all Labour Peers.

PORTRAIT OF A PAINFUL MISS

The final day for the Report Stage of the Bill fell on Wednesday 20 October 1993. From previous activity, it was seen for a long time that this was the day when we would be able to deal with – and vote upon – the issues of the British Rail pensioners. The team was led by Stanley Clinton-Davis and the researchers, led by Catherine, had worked very hard and effectively, particularly in liaison with John Peyton (Conservative) and Dick Marsh (Crossbencher), so that the actual matters upon which votes could be forced had been shaped in the best possible way.

Essentially, the line of attack was to be on:

1. The solvency of the Rail Pension Fund as it would exist when the Bill was an Act. This was coupled with the assurances that it would be written on the face of the Bill.
2. The understanding and future responsibilities of the Government which had been enshrined in what had been known as the 'Memorandum of Understanding', an agreement between the Government, the pension trustees and British Rail was under criticism and it was deemed to be crucial that this be enshrined in legislation on the face of the Bill.
3. The question of the future right of pensioners who felt that the terms which were ultimately to be resolved at a high level and which they objected to, could be the subject of an appeal to the House of Lords. This opportunity would come by challenging the Government's intention that the terms of Schedule 10 as far as they would affect the Orders flowing from the Bill, if deemed to be hybrid, would be deemed for the purposes of the Bill, *not to be hybrid*.

Accordingly, the best possible efforts were put into maximizing the attendance of the Opposition Peers. Whilst Labour and the Liberals could work through their Party machine, it was always understood that the extent to which those on the Crossbenches or disaffected supporters of the Government would come into the proper lobby was difficult to assess.

In the event, despite a number of colleagues who would normally attend (Sidney Greene, ex-General Secretary of the NUR had the sad situation that his wife had died the previous week and was being buried on 20 October) and other colleagues who were abroad, etc. nevertheless, the attendance in the House was full.

However, it did seem strange sitting on the Opposition benches that there did not seem to be a big attendance on the Government benches.

The first issue upon which John Peyton led was conceded by the Government. John Peyton had flagged this up just before the debate started and nevertheless it both came as a pleasant surprise and a clear indication that the Government was fighting all the way to avoid defeats. Thus on the first issue that upon which a vote had been taken, the Government could be beaten (would have been beaten), was conceded to us without a division.

The second issue where John Peyton led, supported by Dick Marsh and others, the Government refused to write the sanctity of the Memorandum of Understanding on to the face of the Bill. Thus, the vote took place which resulted as follows.

The Government had 123, the Opposition to the Government was – Labour 89, Conservatives 16, Crossbenchers 22, Liberal Democrats 26 – Total 153. This was a fantastic result and owed everything to the high attendance of Labour Peers. Disappointing, the Liberal Democrat total was below par at 26. The relative strength between Labour and Liberal Democrats in the House is that Labour has almost exactly twice as many Members as Liberal Democrats. Thus by any measure, either two 26s would 55/60, or half of Labour's 89 would be 42/45 – the relative performance meant that Labour had achieved a magnificent figure, whilst that of the Liberal Democrats was poor.

Before the Division took place and without precise knowledge as to what would happen, I sent all of my Whips, and in addition two other non-Whips, to make sure that they went round the House and met all those coming through our Lobby as they left it, with the strict instructions 'Do not leave. Another crucial vote will come soon.'

The next vote was on the 'hybridity' issue. This was moved by Peter Henderson (Lord Henderson of Brompton) and seconded by Jack Simon (Lord Simon of Glaisdale) both Crossbenchers. In retrospect it did not help that between them they took 27 minutes to move and second this motion. As the time moved towards 17.30 a number of things happened. Ivor Richard and Joe Dean left for the Shadow Cabinet. I ensured that when Peter Henderson was on his feet, that they would be alerted to leave the Shadow Cabinet. Peter Henderson got to his feet at 17.41. I immediately asked Shirley Sheppard to ring the Shadow Cabinet room and ask that Ivor and Joe should return. Unfortunately, as will be seen later, this message was not given to them *immediately* and the time taken for them to leave the Shadow Cabinet room and reach the Chamber proved crucial.

The result of the second vote was declared as follows: For the amendment 123, Against the amendment 124 – a Government victory by one vote. The votes for the Opposition were as follows: Labour 78, Conservative 3, Independent Conservative 1, Crossbenches 16, Liberal Democrat 25. An analysis of those figures show that 11 Labour colleagues failed to vote for the second vote, the Conservatives who had voted on the first issue failed to vote on the second issue, the Crossbenchers lost 6 and the Liberal Democrats only lost one.

The sad fact is that the Clerks compared the declared figure, they registered a total of 124 for each of the sides. Whilst the result was given as a victory for the Government by one, in essence it was a tied vote, it would not have affected the result except when one takes into account the following factors:

Of the 11 Labour colleagues who failed to vote on the second vote, having voted on the first one, there had been no request made or given for them to leave. In fact, if as I believe my Whips had, all of them would have been spoken to and urged to remain. However, the sad fact is that if only two of them had waited until 17.45 we would have won. As to Ivor Richard and Joe Dean, it was clear that we needed to take up a situation where a vote is flagged up and the information taken swiftly into the Shadow Cabinet. That would be done.

In having an inquest with Geoff Tordoff afterwards I, of course, offered my apologies for the absences which had either been conspired towards by the missing 'second voters' or by Ivor Richard or Joe Dean. In addition, of course, there were other Labour Front Benchers who had not been present. Geoff, however, was even more angry with the fact that Nancy Seear, his Deputy Leader, had voted on the first vote but not on the second, as well as the fact that many prominent members of his group (Roy Jenkins, Sally Hamwee etc) had missed both votes because they were not available.

Experience has taught me, however, that for every hard luck story on our side of the Chamber, there is a similar hard luck story on the other side. Aggravatingly, this defeat for the Government would have had very serious consequences.

In the Shadow Cabinet that evening, Ivor Richard told the story and whilst colleagues shared his chagrin, John Prescott was very fulsome in his praise for the performance of the Opposition and especially Labour Peers in providing him and his team with a number of valuable bullets to fire when the Bill went back to the Commons.

Postscript

Malcolm Shepherd from his wide experience saw an opportunity of returning to the 'hybridity' issue at Third Reading. This was to take place on Wednesday 27 October and together with Geoff Tordoff, I sought to once more maximize our attendance. Maybe this time the luck would be on our side!

THE ANATOMY OF AN AMBUSH

The opportunities to defeat the Government in what one would call 'normal circumstances' are very limited. Unless the issue is a powerful one and one is able to attract support from virtually the whole of the Crossbenches and some dissident Tories, Labour and the Liberals are always up against a regular – monotonous – total of about 120/140 Tory Peers up to the supper break. It is only after the supper break (ie 8.30 p.m. onwards) that one can detect a lowering of Tory numbers and the prospect of springing a surprise. Hitherto surprises have been sprung but always by asking troops to come in, in force, between the hours of 8.30 p.m. and 10.00 p.m.

Due to the management of the Government business, during primarily the Employment Bill and the Education Bill, it became quite clear that the Government was prepared for the House to sit – often beyond 3.00 a.m in the morning – relying upon the fact that there was no Opposition present and that all they had to keep for 'a House' was about 30 votes.

Annoyance was expressed in more than one quarter and it gradually emerged that if the Government kept up its guard until after 10.00 p.m. then we had to think in terms of an ambush much later than that. Midnight was agreed as the best time.

The first thing that was done was Geoff Tordoff and I asked our Whips to find out how many of our colleagues would be willing to come in for a vote at midnight and stay perhaps a little while after that. Geoff told me after his discussions that he felt confident of producing between 12 and 15. My Whips told me to expect about 50.

We then looked at what we required. During passage of the Education Bill we tested the attendance of the Tories and they kept up a total of between 50 and 60 up to midnight and thereafter they declined rapidly. Thus at midnight the Tories would have in the region of 60 and in order for us to beat them we had to rely on, say 65 plus. Our intelligence told us that we could do that.

The Report Stage of the Education Bill provided a suitable vehicle. Frank Judd, supported by some Liberal Democrats, were asked to consult with their advisors and tell us that they could stage the divisions on important and valuable amendments at about the midnight time and then we would spring the surprise vote. This they were able to assure us they could do on Monday 14 June.

During the week preceding 14 June 1993 the colleagues who had said they would come in were told that the date we would ask them to attend was 14 June at midnight. Was this still all right? One or two people found that this was inconvenient but substantially our 60 plus total held up. Thus we decided 'This would be the day'.

'The Smoke Screen'

If the amendments to be voted on stood out they could be seen as targets for the Government to protect and it was decided to group the amendments we wanted (207b and 207d) within a larger group. They dealt with the laying down for local education authorities of producing a strategy for the special needs which combined both schools in their area under their control and also those under grant maintained status. The other amendment called for a strategy to be provided for nursery provisions.

The plan was that the line which led the required amendments (199a) would be moved by Nora David (Baroness David of Romsey) but not divided upon and the key amendments would be sprung at their appropriate time.

During the day it became clear that the broad strategy was understood by the Government. They could hardly do any other. Any intelligent assessment of if and when the Opposition would strike would concentrate on Monday 14 June. The only thing which they did not know was on what issue and at what time. Although it emerged later that the Government Chief Whip had prevailed upon his Whips to keep as many people as would stay after 8.30 p.m. – even then they did not know the issues nor the precise time.

During the day, the timetable was in and out. Sometimes we were ahead of it, sometimes we were behind, because we had made a calculation of where we should be on what issue at what time. Miraculously (some would say!) we actually arrived at Nora David getting to her feet to move the key amendment (199a) within 7 minutes of our estimate. The idea was that this would be disposed of by about 11 p.m. and then we would strike an hour later. However, due to a series of events, not least the Government Minister taking an extraordinarily long time to reply, it became clear at 11.40 p.m. whilst we were still on this amendment that there was danger in not voting upon it. The simple reason was that colleagues who come in for a 12 o'clock vote want a vote at 12 o'clock and are not particularly concerned at the issue.

I then went to seek Geoff Tordoff to consult with him on where we were. I found him in his room with about a dozen of his colleagues and I was met with a quite short statement. 'Unless we vote on 199a I cannot guarantee to keep my troops for the simple reason we do not know when they will come up and there is a danger in waiting too long'. I had to agree that there was some sense in this logic.

I then went back on to the Front Bench and discussed this reality – that if waited for the proper amendments to vote upon we very well could be short of our total because some people who had come for a 12 o'clock vote would no longer be there. It was agreed that we should do this. Nora David called for a division at 12.05 p.m. and the result was 70 votes with us and 61 for the Government The later analysis showed that Labour produced 48, the Liberals 17 and Crossbenches (including one bishop) 5. It was a very satisfactory forecast of what was required to get the number needed. Both Geoff and I had not approached many of our colleagues on the basis of age and infirmity and thus we had the satisfaction of knowing that those who would have had difficulty in attending were not requested to and those who did attend were taking part in a victory.

Our troops were elated and were immediately told by Geoff and I 'Stay'. Thus the Chamber immediately after the vote showed that the Labour and Liberal troops remained in their places whilst the Conservatives were in some disarray.

There then followed a most interesting hour. For the first part the Minister and Rodney Elton (former Tory Minister) proceeded to filibuster and go exceedingly slow on an innocuous amendment. It was quite clear that this was both to buy time and also to enable some phone calls to be made to see whether troops would come in.

The Government Chief Whip (Lord Hesketh) sent for me. He was extremely upset. His first words to me were that what we had done was unheard of. I told him that it was because I thought that he would not have heard of it that I did it – and it worked. He said that pulling ambushes as late as this was unprecedented. I pointed out that there was no precedent or understanding or agreement by an Opposition with a Government whereby we will behave in a way which is either agreed or predicted. The only weapon that Opposition Parties have, faced with such a massive Government majority, is to adopt guerrilla tactics. His state was due, not to the fact of what we had done, but to the fact that we had done it and won.

I then left the room (at about 12.30 a.m.) and went to see Ivor Richard and explained to him the situation. I then met Mikey Strathmore (Earl Strathmore and Kinghorne) the Deputy Chief Whip, in the corridor and told him 'Would you please immediately see Alexander and tell him I have carefully considered what he has said and it is my intention to divide and win on every amendment in the line which begins 199a'.

I then proceeded to discuss how we would get to the voteable material and there was a loose understanding that we would need to 'not move' some of the amendments which preceded 207b and 207d in order to vote as soon as possible and allow the troops to go home. Whilst we were considering these ploys an amendment was introduced by Lord Campbell of Alloway on the Government side. He laid into the Government very strongly that it was not being fair in operating a 'Code of Practice'. The Minister replying gave nothing and Campbell divided the House.

Sensation! What to do? Very quickly we realized that if, in fact, there was a division and we did not vote on it this would add further confusion to the situation. Thus we voted with Campbell (who was supported as a teller with Peter Henderson from the Crossbenches) and the result of the vote was a defeat of the Government of 68 to 42. Thus, after one hour, we had only lost 2 whilst the Government had lost 19. This quite clearly meant that on any division the Government could be defeated. Both Geoff and I said to our troops 'Stay'. Faced with this situation the Government Chief Whip came in and whispered to the Minister. Consequently when Nora David rose to address the further amendments in the line – before 207b and 207c – the Minister (Emily Blatch, Baroness Blatch of Hinchingbrooke) said 'We will not resist these amendments'.

Then a diversion. An amendment (not in the line) was spoken to by Frank Judd in very strong language and he was backed by Shirley Williams from the Liberal benches.

The Government Chief Whip sent for me even more upset than earlier. What on earth were we doing? I had told him that we intended to vote and win all of the amendments in the line and he was in the process of giving them to us. What we wanted was the substance and what he wanted to avoid was the opprobrium. I then said to him 'Can I have your assurance that when we come to 207b and 207c, and the other 4 amendments that are with them, that they will be conceded?' He said 'Yes.' I then said in that circumstance I would ask Frank Judd not to divide on this amendment. This Frank did and the matter proceeded very satisfactorily with two defeats for the Government and nine amendments, all of some value, being conceded.

Andrew McIntosh told me that Mark Bonham-Carter and the Liberals were upset. Not only had I not consulted with Geoff Tordoff but they had wished to vote on this amendment which Frank withdrew. This puzzled me. I had been told by the Liberals at 11.50 p.m. that unless we voted at 12 o'clock the troops would go and I was now being told at 1.20 a.m. that they were angry that we did not vote again. It's a strange world!

I explained to Shirley Williams and Nancy Seear, who seemed to be jumping up and down, that the 11.50 p.m. conversation had taken place. They were not part of it and were unaware. I then said 'If we have come here tonight with our colleagues and defeated the Government twice, and achieved concessions on 9 amendments, that is indeed a remarkably good haul'.

I then saw Geoff and made my peace and explained to him that in the heat of the hour between 12 o'clock and 1.00 a.m. I just had not been able to get to him either to consult or advise. He quite understood. (I subsequently wrote a letter to him of regret that this had happened and, of course, I have had very amicable conversations with him since.)

In the Bishops Bar between 2.00 a.m. and 3.00 a.m. after the semi-agreement had been reached, the Government Chief Whip seemed to be a more relaxed mood to the extent that before the House went down he had bought drinks for a large number of people, including Geoff Tordoff, Shirley Williams, Mark Bonham-Carter, Nancy Seear and me!

It is easy to regurgitate the events of the time but not so easy to come to conclusions. My first conclusion was that the Government was exposed as being unable to rely on its troops staying beyond midnight. This of course has little to do with the Chief Whip but has much to do with the weariness and the lack of spirit in his troops to stay regardless. I was quite convinced that this would turn out to be a factor in the Government's thinking on how it should deal with the Maastricht Bill and the potential ambush by rebels in the middle of the night. It would just not be allowed to happen.

Secondly, it is clear that colleagues on the Labour and Liberal benches who have been starved of either proper recognition, or to put it another way treated with contempt by Government Ministers, are willing, when the moment is right and the preparation has been done with care to respond and then enjoyed the occasion.

The events were quickly forgotten and the relationships appeared to be back to normal. Subsequently, others sought me out saying that they had heard how the Government had behaved and told me to accept none of it. Whilst Labour was in power in the 1970s there a were a number of occasions where the Conservative Opposition did precisely to the then Labour Government what we had done and, therefore, I should not in any way feel awkward about either the tactic or certainly not the outcome. This was a most acceptable commendation.

THE ONE THAT GOT AWAY

The Railways Bill came to the House of Lords from the Commons in May 1993. It was the major privatization measure during the session. It reached us amid controversy and there was a growing band of disaffected Tory backbenchers in the Commons. The Chairman of the Transport Select Committee was Robert Adley MP for Christchurch. Tragically he died in May. John Prescott, Labour's Transport spokesman had declared that the summer recess would be spent by his team in seeking to damage, if not overturn, the Bill.

In the Lords, there was already a great deal of activity. The outside pressure groups had been active and many Members of the House had expressed unease.

During the Committee Stage of the Bill the Government had suffered a major defeat on the issue of enabling British Rail to bid for the franchise when put out to tender. This had been rejected by the Government in the Commons and was only carried there after the Government had bought off a number of rebels with minor concessions. When it came to the Lords an amendment moved by John Peyton, former Conservative Transport Minister, and seconded by Dick Marsh (Crossbenchers), another former Transport Minister, was successfully moved to insert the right of British Rail to bid for the franchise. On that occasion the vote was 150 to 112. The 150 was made up of 75 Labour, 35 Liberal Democrat, 25 Crossbench (including two former Speakers of the Commons, Lord Weatherill and Viscount Tonypandy) – and 15 Conservative rebels. These included Lord Peyton of Yeovil. This defeat for the Government was seen as of great significance because when that amendment would go back to the Commons there was every prospect that the rebels in the Commons would join against the Government and defeat it. (An indication in August had been that there were at least 16 Conservative backbenchers willing to vote for British Rail when the matter reaches the Commons in October.)

On Wednesday 21 July, it was the 6th day of the Committee Stage of the Bill. This was seen to be less than one week away from the House going into recess. Complicating the progress of the Railways Bill was the Government's overwhelming imperative to secure the passage of the Maastricht Bill. Set down for debate by amendment on that day were two crucial matters. The first dealt with the possible hybridity of orders flowing from the Bill and secondly the issue of satisfactory arrangements for pensions under the Bill.

Geoff Tordoff, the Liberal Chief Whip (and Liberal spokesman on Transport) and I discussed the possibilities. It was noted that on Tuesday 20 July the Third Reading and concluding stages of the Maastricht Bill were due and undoubtedly the Government would have as high a protective shield as possible. It also became known that the additional debate dealing with the Social Chapter would be dealt with on Thursday 22 July. Thus we took the view that – if at all – the Government would be at its weakest in that week on Wednesday 21 July – the day of the Railways Bill.

When we looked back at the vote on the Railways Bill earlier (which we won by 150 to 112) we recognized that although we could rely on Labour, Liberal and possible Crossbench, we could not rely upon the Conservatives. However, with the prospect of anything between 130 and 140 then the Government would really need to be in top form to beat that. Thus both Geoff and I agreed to pull out every single stop on the last major vote before we went into recess. I had examined the list of Members who had *not* voted earlier when we had 75 Labour and it struck me that a great many of those are normally very good attenders and for one reason or another they had missed the vote. Therefore I set my ambition at between 80 and 85 and if the Liberal 35 could be increased to the total it achieved on the Referendum vote (42) we had a very good chance indeed.

In the Whip that week I not only made it three line but gave it also space on our 'Notice Board' and in addition enclosed a separate letter addressed to every single Member of the group which in effect pointed out the enormous damage we could do if we maximised our vote. On top of all of this – and not done before – I also arranged for about 15 of the Labour Peers to be spoken to on the telephone on the afternoon and evening of Tuesday 20 July to reinforce the desire to get a high vote.

On Monday 19 July we had a bit of good luck – and a bit of bad luck. On that day Malcolm Shepherd raised the question of the enormous number of amendments which were set down for Wednesday 21 July. These had been put down by the Government in response to various undertakings and related to the pensions issue. Although they may very well be helpful, Malcolm Shepherd protested that with the complexity of the issue, it was quite impossible for Members, such as himself, who had only received the amendments that morning, to be able to consult and take advice. There then proceeded to be given to him good support from amongst others – Lord Boyd-Carpenter, Lord Campbell of Alloway, Lord Whitelaw, all Conservative, and in addition Lord Simon of Glaisdale (Crossbencher). They pointed out that if the Government proceeded to deal with amendments to Schedule 10 (Pensions) on Wednesday 21 July, they would not only be very unhappy but could very well take action. The Minister undertook 'through the usual channels' to consider this issue and the business proceeded. It was now quite clear that Schedule 10 with its related amendments could not be dealt with on Wednesday 21 July and it would be re-committed to a date in the overspill. This was very good news from a 'delaying tactics' point of view.

However – on Wednesday 21 July at 3 p.m. the Government Chief Whip announced that Schedule 10 and its related amendments would be dealt with in the overspill – and the amendments, whilst spoken to, would not be voted upon. This of course in no way affected the major issue of the afternoon – hybridity. However, I was then told by Tom Taylor of Blackburn that some colleagues around him had expressed the view that in the light of this amendment, there would be no votes that afternoon and he was concerned that some of them may have left. I was astounded at this. Mature politicians should not form their own conclusion but seek advice from the Whips. I immediately sent Tom and other Whips around the House to tell any Labour Members they saw that votes would still take place.

The business proceeded and Geoff Tordoff drew attention to paragraph 1 1(2) of Schedule 10 which said:

If, apart from the provisions of this sub-paragraph, the draft of an instrument containing an order under this schedule would be treated for the purposes of the standing orders of either House of Parliament as a hybrid instrument, it should proceed in that House as if it were not such an instrument.

As Geoff Tordoff said, 'That is Alice in Wonderland writ large. Words mean what I say they mean – if something is hybrid I shall say that it is not hybrid'. He then went on to point out a significant paragraph from the House of Lords Select Committee on Delegated Legislation which when dealing with the Bill and Schedule 10 in particular had said, 'The House may wish to consider whether the obstacles to proper Parliamentary scrutiny and control of delegated legislation, including affirmative resolution in this case provides sufficient Parliamentary control.'

The debate then proceeded and it was vigorous. It lasted until 5.35 p.m. Well within the time limit I had asked colleagues to attend which was from 4.00 p.m. to 6.00p.m. The only exceptional matter was that from the Government backbenches, Lord Peyton declared that he would not be supporting the 'hybridity' amendment on the grounds that this, if carried, would build into the Bill a delay which would affect the payment to pensioners. He also rested his case very heavily on his satisfaction that a so-called 'Memorandum of Agreement' between the Government, British Rail and the pension trustees gave him everything that he wanted. In the event, the vote resulted in the Government winning by 151 to 145.

Inquest

An analysis of the 145 showed Labour 88, Liberal 35, Crossbench 21 and Independent Conservative 1. In my wildest dreams I had not believed that we would induce 88 Labour votes and this was to our great credit. However, the Liberal vote of 35 was very disappointing and Geoff Tordoff had no explanation for it. The Crossbench vote remained solid and the Conservative vote remained with the Government. However, on looking at the issue of whether Labour Members had left the Chamber, I examined those who had 'clocked on' but who had failed to vote and was extremely concerned to find that 9 Labour Peers had been recorded as in attendance but had not voted.

I discussed with Ivor Richard what I should do in this circumstance. I had to bear in mind that the issue was over, we had achieved a magnificent total and although there were people who were recorded as present I did not have any knowledge – at that time – as to whether they had come in late or whether there were genuine reasons as to why they had left early.

Subsequently I spoke to 7 of the 9 and it was as I feared. One member had had to leave because his wife was not well and he had received a phone call saying that she was asking for him. Another had already told me that he had to attend a funeral in Glasgow the next day. He had waited as long as he could before he got a train to Manchester where he had to pick up the rest of his family and then proceed to Glasgow – that night.

Another Member said to me 'I was having dinner with the Queen that night and I waited as long as I could but then I could not keep Her Majesty waiting'. An explanation for this is that the Member had to leave the House to go home and change and thus had left. There were other reasons. One Member had left a meeting in Birmingham on a train that would have got him to the House for 5.00 p.m. but there was a delay on the train at Euston and the traffic from Euston to the House was thick. There were also 4 Liberal Democrats who were recorded as having attended that day but did not vote.

Thus, although I do not say that the Government could have been beaten, I do regret that there was this aggravation. For instance, Lord John Jacques had travelled from Portsmouth in very poor health (his eyesight was failing rapidly) but had responded to the particular cry of the Whip. At the same time, it had to be acknowledged that for the Government to get 150 supporters on a Wednesday, sandwiched between two votes when it received support in excess of 200 each time, was an achievement by the Government Chief Whip. When I discussed this with him he said quite truthfully that no special effort had been made on Wednesday because of the importance of Tuesday and Thursday, 'They simply came in because they didn't want the Government to be let down in the last week', and I had to both agree and acknowledge that this was a good spirit on the Conservative benches.

Postcript

It is clear that the determined efforts of the Opposition Parties had elevated the Railways Bill to a major political matter during the summer and who knows, with an uncertain timetable and with the date of the Queen's Speech still not clear, it may have been possible for further damage to be done. We lived in hope!

BLACK DOG TO THE RESCUE

Patricia Hollis came to see me after the passage of the Second Reading of The Pensions Bill. She explained the bull points for amendments and raised the possibility of arranging what we now call 'an ambush' for she feared that we may not be able to succeed with amendments in the normal way. I readily agreed that, if she could pinpoint an issue which could come up at ambush time, we would do our level best to bring if off. By we I meant The Whips.

She came back to me about 6 February and said that Nancy Seear, with whom she was working closely and well from the Liberal Democrat benches, was equally enthusiastic, and they had together with Clare, our researcher, identified an issue which they were confident could be timed to come up after supper on Monday 20 February. Consideration was given to ensuring that we could avoid bringing in our troops earlier in the day for what would have been important issues. Crucial to this aspect of our timetabling was the fact that amendments relating to War Widows' Pensions were to be scheduled to come up on Tuesday and not Monday as had appeared at first.

Before my Whips meeting on 9 February 1995 I discussed the operation with the Liberal Democrat Chief Whip, John Harris. I explained to him, as he had not managed this operation before, that in my experience we would have to rely on a number of variables. First, experience showed that with nothing untoward the Government could rely on about 60/70 after Supper – we would have to produce 70/80. Of this, on the ratio of Labour producing 2 to 1, the Liberals would be expected to bring in 25/30 and I had to bring in 50/60. He saw no problem in this, always against the caveat that 'on the night' it may be different. Timing. We considered the optimum time and concluded that as early after Supper as possible would be ideal and struck for 8.30 p.m. on Monday 20 February.

The issue identified was related to the future entitlement of women in the light of both sexes now having to work until 65, that the State Earnings Related Pensions (SERPS) would by our amendment be calculated on the best 44 years earnings rather than across the whole working lifetime of 49 years. Timing to arrive at this amendment not too early and not too late was absolutely crucial. The deal was done. Now to test to see if we could get our troops to respond.

On Thursday 9 February I told my Whips of the ploy and told them that for it to be 'on' I had to have from them the best indication of whether their 'flock' would respond. As we now had four relatively new Whips I told them that I would put in writing the method of doing this and accordingly I wrote to them a letter which they had for Monday 13 outlining the best way to ascertain this. In the light of subsequent events this letter assumed an importance no one could have dreamed of!

Each Whip has a section of the Labour Peers to look after. There are approximately 115 Labour Peers. There are about 10 colleagues I never disturb primarily for health reasons. That leaves 105, and there are six Whips, Brian Morris and me. They each have about 15 in their group

$7 \times 15 = 105$. One of my Whips was Dennis Howell and he was off sick so I took the responsibility of contacting his group.

As we met on Thursday 16 February to examine the situation Patricia told me that John Kirkhill had told her that one of the Tories had told him that they knew of our ambush on Monday evening. This was par for the course. We have never arranged an exercise of this kind without someone telling us that we have been rumbled – yet they always fail to take the necessary steps!

The Whips reported their numbers. They all told me that they had between 3 and 4 they had been unable to contact. The total added up to in excess of 60 and I was pleased. I decided to write a special letter to all those I had been told could not come or who had not been contacted asking them, even at this late stage, if they could possibly re-arrange their programme and come on Monday for the surprise vote.

By now the business for the rest of Monday became known and it was seen that some of it could cause delay and make it more difficult to strike at the precise time we wanted. I decided to make the ambush for 8.45 p.m. to allow Patricia a little more leeway to play with the time. This change was crucial as you will see.

I then sent out a letter to be inserted in the Whip to every colleague, save those I had excused for age or infirmity. This letter confirmed what by now they all knew and asking them to arrive in the House at precisely 8.45 p.m. If they were early they were to make their way to the Researchers Room and not appear in the Chamber before the division bell.

At about 10.00 a.m. on Sunday 19 February Brenda Dean rang me and asked if I had seen a piece in the Black Dog column of *The Mail on Sunday*. I said 'no' whereupon she read it to me (it appears on page 175). It gave the game away – one of my letters had found its way into his hands and he had printed it. Calamity! Patricia rang me later. I was out and rang her back in the evening. Understandably she was dismayed. What to do? I told her that I was calling a special Whips' Meeting for 1.45 p.m. on Monday to review the situation. My reaction was to proceed and I would explain to the Whip why. I rang Joyce Gould, Simon Haskel, Derek Gladwin and Alf Dubs. They were shocked. Who was the traitor in our midst? Not to worry I said, we will just have to get on with it. Armed with this knowledge, it seemed highly unlikely that we could pull it off.

When I arrived in my office on Monday morning I began to discuss the hiatus with my secretary, Marianne. She then told me that the letter that had gone astray was not one sent out with the Whip but by virtue of what Black Dog had quoted was from the letter I had sent only to the Whips. I checked this and had to agree. This made it serious in that in one way or another a Whip had allowed a copy of his letter to be sighted and even copied. I went to see John Harris. His immediate remark was that now that the Government were aware of the ambush it had to be called off. He cited members who were travelling in long distances. How can we ask them to do so if we are not going to win?

I then proceeded to tell him that experience shows that even when they suspect an ambush after Supper the Government has a great difficulty in getting its supporters to stay. I was confident Labour Peers would still turn up. How about Liberal Democrats? He then agreed that we should proceed and we would each urge our members to turn up although we both acknowledged that there would be some who would make their own minds up – and not turn up.

I then met my Whips, with Ivor Richard and Patricia. I explained to them that the leaked letter was one only they had received . . . They showed deep concern and there was a general view that in future we should not commit plans to paper, rather use word of mouth and the telephone. I told them that all was not lost. I told them that after making an assessment of their colleagues they could not contact I knew that we would have a good number. The only question was just how successful could the Tory Whips be in getting supporters to stay after Supper?

I then did my final sums. Using my own nous as to what the missing contacts would produce I had the following figures before me at 3.00 p.m.

Joyce Gould–11, Alf Dubs–10, Joe Dean–13, Derek Gladwin–12, Dennis Howell–13, Brian Morris–11, Simon Haskel–11. A total of 81.

During the day all sorts of rumours ran around. Tommy Strathclyde, the Government Chief Whip, chided me asking that now we knew that they knew all about the ambush what were we doing to do? Other Tories especially Ministers were having a great time laughing at the exposure. I told my Whips that they were to contact every Labour Peer and tell them it was still on. During the day Marianne took about six calls from Labour Peers asking if the ambush was still on in the light of what they had read in *The Mail on Sunday*. They were told yes I wanted them there and we still had a good chance of pulling it off.

Timing is the essence in all this. The leaked letter had given 8.30 p.m. for the ambush – in reality I had called it for 8.45 p.m. During the day it was the job of Patricia and her team to speak in order to fill out time and to shut up if we felt we were dragging behind. By her team I meant Muriel Turner, Brenda Dean, Joyce Gould, Simon Haskel and Andrew McIntosh, all of whom had 'speaking parts' who were deeply involved in the plot and who all reacted magnificently to their task. A vote during the afternoon showed that the Government had about 120 supporters and we had less than 80. A vote called by Jock Stallard at 7.20 p.m. revealed that even then, the Government had 99 supporters and a handful who voted against with Jock Stallard. Before Supper, the Government had in excess of 100 supporters in the House.

Suppertime dragged a bit, and by 8.30 p.m. there were signs that some of our members were drifting into the Chamber. They were told to disappear quickly. What I think happened then was this:

1. The Government convinced themselves that now that we knew that they knew about the ambush we would call if off. They took no steps to stop their supporters drifting out. I did a trawl around the dining rooms and whereas I could count about 60 at 8.00 p.m. this had dropped to about 45 by 8.30 p.m.
2. As the magic time of 8.30 p.m. came round, a Tory Whip wandered into the Chamber and guessed that it looked as if the ambush was on. Tommy Strathclyde was sent for by the Minister John Mackay, and after a sharp exchange Tommy left the Chamber. I was satisfied that he then tried to get people to come back, leaving John Mackay to filibuster for as long as he could.
3. Patricia got to our voting amendment at precisely 8.45 p.m. – about 15 minutes later than we would have liked, but in the circumstances a truly great performance. This had meant that a series of amendments were 'not moved' in order to get to the one we wanted. Once she had got to her feet I relaxed. There was nothing more I could do. There was nothing the Government could do. It now depended on how long the Minister could prevaricate, and on the 'stickability' of our troops, who were asked to be there for 8.45 p.m. We were now into that period when they were out of sight and wanting to go home. It always is a sticky period. The trick in these circumstances is not to interrupt the Minister, which helps him. We did not and he could not.

I was told by Roy Mason the next morning that, in the Peers' Guest Room where a number of our colleagues had assembled, the general talk was that it was a waste of time, the Tories had rumbled us and we would be badly beaten. On one of my trawls through the Peers' Dining Room I came across a table at which sat Betty Lockwood, Brenda Dean, Joyce Gould and I think one other. At 8.30 p.m. they were pessimistic and I chided them for not having faith in me!

At 9.15 p.m. the vote was called. I asked Nancy Seear to take our lobby for telling, preferring to tell in the Government Lobby so that I could see who was there. I stood next to Tommy Strathclyde, who said 'You have got your troops here tonight,' and I said 'Yes, we have, and you were given advance warning as to the day and time – what more help do you want?!' He said 'What have you got – 60 or 70?' and I said 'More than that'. He looked pensive!

As we left the voting lobby with his total at 61 I said that he had lost. I just knew that there was no way for us to have less than 80/90. The vote was 61 for the Government and 105 against. This was made up of 80 Labour, 21 Liberal Democrat and 4 Crossbenchers, cultivated by Patricia. Nancy Seear handed the paper to the Chairman amidst great cheers. We did not press any more votes and we concluded a very happy evening. Even though I say it myself, I doubt if there was a single person who believed, as I did, that we could win. Not that we *would* win but that we *could* win. The evening was crowned by the excellent job done by Clare in preparing press releases announcing the victory – before we had it – and by Robert who ensured that the Press got it quickly. I asked him especially to see that a copy went to Black Dog.

Lessons

Security will have to be tightened up so as to avoid the heart stopping leak or any other way in the future which can cause anger and ridicule. This of course invariably comes from those who do little – except snipe if given the opportunity.

In the light of the leak and despite it, it is clear to me that the Government is incapable of persuading their troops to remain after Supper, for a possible ambush. The only way they can do that is if there are big issues of policy which come up after Supper in which case the Whip is cracked. For most of their long suffering troops they have had 15 years of 'standing by' and up with this they will not put – any more.

Our troops will always be willing to respond to an exercise such as this but we have to chose the opportunity with care and I would have thought limit it to no more than twice a year. The Shadow Cabinet enjoyed very much my telling them of the success and the mood of Labour Peers was lifted visibly.

THE LONGEST NIGHT – AND DAY

The Railways Bill received the Royal Assent on Friday 5 November 1993 but it was a close run thing. The Commons were set to consider amendments to the Railways Bill from the Lords on Monday 1 and Tuesday 2 November. The two main points of significance sent back to the Commons from the Lords dealt with the issue of the right of British Rail to bid in the franchizing process and to the Memorandum of Understanding and the protection it enshrined for the future of the British Rail Pension Fund.

With two days there was no clarity or certainty concerning when these issues would be taken. However, during the evening of Monday 1 November, after a handful of amendments had been dealt with, the Leader of the Commons, Tony Newton, announced that a Guillotine Motion would be tabled and this was done on Tuesday evening. It laid down a timetable to conclude the votes on the Lords' amendments so that they would be cleared from the Commons at some time on 2 November so that they could be dealt with in the Lords on 3 November. There were, of course, great arguments and passion and votes, but at the end of 2 November the amendments to the Bill which we had sent to the Commons were returned. Where the Government had rejected the advice of the Lords they had tabled 'amendments in lieu'.

The Members of the Lords most closely involved in the issues were incensed by the action of the Government in the Commons. In respect of the British Rail ability to bid, this had been emasculated to the extent that they would only be allowed to bid when the Regulator was satisfied that there was no other acceptable bid. This was taken with Government statements of a new amendment to provide and encourage Management Buy Outs, but it was clearly seen that the Government intended to outflank the Lords' amendment and that British Rail would be left to pick up any pieces which were not attractive to others.

The weekend before, Geoff Tordoff and I had realized that the kind of situation which had emerged to face the Lords, Wednesday 3 November was the last opportunity to inflict damage on the Bill. We both agreed that no matter what happened to the Commons' amendments in the Lords, if we were successful in sending them back to the Commons, we would not thereafter be involved in 'Parliamentary ping-pong' by sending amendments backwards and forwards down the corridor.

As a consequence we maximized the attendance that we could achieve. At the end of this piece I have indicated the attendances and voting, but we both agreed that was our last great opportunity.

The attack on the Government in the Lords was led by Dick Marsh. He was feeling somewhat chastened because on the previous Wednesday 27 October we had lost votes by one and both he and John Peyton were absent. In his attack on the Government he was scathing and really excelled himself. The support for his stance came from all round the House. The Minister – Lord Caithness – tried to point out that this was not the way it was. British Rail would have a part to play, etc etc. The House was not amused. The matters were pushed to a vote and the Government lost by 10 (170 to 160). Of immediate significance here was that the Government had mustered 160. Almost without exception they stood alone. The other benches in the House, plus a significant number of Conservatives, had gone into the lobby against them. Normally, without assistance from anywhere else, the Government would supply about 130 of its own members. It is clear that an effort was made and I think they were entitled to believe that if they could muster 160 they would win.

However, they were unable to anticipate just how strong and how supportive the Whipping opposite them had been. There is of course no Whipping of the Crossbenchers but the Crossbenchers really excelled themselves producing 39 votes against the Government – a quite exceptional total in my experience.

There were two other amendments slightly related and could certainly be seen as consequential and tactically the Government should have accepted those. However, the Minister (with the Leader of the House sitting next to him) objected when the issues were put and thus the Government forced votes 2 and 3 which they lost by 6 and then by 2. The picture was emerging. The Government had lost three votes by 10, 6 and 2. This (after analysis) was due to those who inevitably kid themselves that one vote is enough and then depart. Thus the Government were defeated three times when it need only have been once.

Between the third and just before Muriel Turner had moved an amendment to insist on the Lords' amendment in respect of protecting the Pension Funds, the Government Chief Whip told me that when the Business was ended, it was being proposed that the House should adjourn for one hour during pleasure, whilst consideration would be given to the next stages in the Bill. I said to him 'The next stages (Consideration of Commons Amendments) will be when we receive the amendments from the Commons and we will be dealing with those tomorrow'. His response to me was 'Let us have the Statement and our conversations'. The fourth vote took place which the Government won by 13 votes. My advice to my Whips, who had gone through the lobby early, was to thank our colleagues for their attendance, their magnificent support, and to say that they were not required further that evening. The Leader of the House then moved that the House adjourn during pleasure and return to the Chamber at 7 p.m.

When I was in the Opposition Whips Office, Barbara Castle came in to me and said 'Ted, are you sure you do not require us any more? I have overheard a conversation in the Ladies lavatory where two Tory ladies were talking and they said that they were required to be in the Chamber at 7 o'clock and for other business later that evening.' I told Barbara (who was with Ann Mallalieu) that this was completely new to me, there was no agreement that we would proceed with the Commons reception of the

Lords' amendments that evening, and as far as I was concerned there was no need to stay. Ivor Richard and I, accompanied by Geoff Tordoff, then went into the room of the Leader of the House, John Wakeham. He said, 'When the matters are dealt with in the Commons they will be brought back here and we will dispose of the amendments this evening'. Ivor and I expressed our incredulity and this was matched by that of Geoff Tordoff. We all indicated that whilst there was not an agreement that the business would be dealt with on Thursday afternoon, it was a natural assumption, and never at any stage had the suggestion that the House would deal with the Commons' amendments later that evening been raised. In answer to a question from Ivor Richard as to why the business could not wait until Thursday afternoon, he was told that this was complicated by the absence of members of the Royal Family to receive an audience of Privy Councillors, in order to progress the matters. When it was pointed out to John Wakeham that the Queen was back in the country later that evening he said nothing. We asked him what was the timescale this evening. He said that the Commons would dispose of the Lords' amendments by 10 o'clock and he would go and suggest to the House, when it reassembled at 7 o'clock, that the Lords should re-assemble at 11 p.m. All of this, of course was done, without the agreement of the Opposition Parties.

When I left the Leader's Room, I immediately asked my Whips to see if there were any Labour colleagues about and to ask them to be in the Chamber at 7 p.m. to see what was going to transpire. The House re-assembled at 7 p.m. and the Conservative benches were very full indeed. There was a good representation on the Opposition benches (Labour and Liberal, although the Crossbenches were very sparse indeed). The Leader of the House said that he felt that it was 'for the convenience of the House' that we should sit and receive the messages from the Commons and dispose of the matter that evening. Ivor Richard, followed by Geoff Tordoff, ridiculed 'that this was for the convenience of the House'. They both very strongly made the point that it was purely for the convenience of the Government and its ploy in springing this at the very last moment was to be deplored. Conservative Members protested at the allegation that they had been told to remain behind. As one of them said 'we were advised to be here to see the concluding stages of the Railways Bill and if that means that we have to stay here until the end of the day – so be it'. It became clear to me from observing the situation, and using my own intelligence, that the defeats by the Government had not been anticipated. They had assumed that the Government would beat off the attacks in the Lords and that the business would end them. Only when the Government realized that they were involved in a further stage of the Bill did they react and in panic. Remember that the intention for the House to convene at 7 p.m. was only indicated to me between the third and fourth votes.

The interesting point is that when Ivor Richard moved, as an amendment to the Leader's Motion, 'That the House be reconvened at 11 p.m.' Ivor moved an amendment 'That this House stand adjourned until 3 p.m. on Thursday'. This amendment was only defeated by 71 to 61 and as I was a teller in the lobby for the amendment, I can tell you that there were at least 7 or 8 – even more – Conservatives who had been sitting behind the Leader of the House, who went into the lobby against him. In retrospect and hindsight, if we had managed either to retain more people or alternatively not acquiesce in their leaving, the matter could very well have ended in chaos then. The chaos was to come later.

As soon as the issue was disposed of in the Lords, a number of us met in my office. The consideration was given as to how we would deal with the amendments when they came back. However, it was quickly seen that if the amendments did not leave the Commons, so that they were not available at 11 p.m., then the House could not proceed. Both Geoff Tordoff and I immediately made tracks to the Commons. I do not know what Geoff did – except he was party to the most significant wrecking ploy of all. For my part, I spoke both to Derek Foster (Labour Chief Whip) and Don Dixon (Labour Deputy Chief Whip) and told them of the situation, advising them that if the matters were not out of the Commons and back to us by 11 p.m. the Government would once more be seen to be caught flat footed. I was told that there were four votes and that the voting would start at 8.36 p.m. in accordance to the Commons timetable. I left to my colleagues how they would deploy the various opportunities that might arise. It emerged that by using a number of ploys, voting on the issues was extended to such an extent that the Commons still had the matter in hand at 11 p.m., when the Leader of the House rose. John Wakeham made an announcement to the effect that he was asking for the House to be reconvened at 11.30 p.m. Of significance, however, was his rider, 'if the message from the Commons is not then received, that the House stand adjourned until Thursday November 3rd.' Ivor Richard immediately asked him what had changed between the 6 o'clock meeting, when this could not be tolerated, and the fact that it was now part of the Government's strategy. To this of course there was no reply. Between 11 p.m. and 11.30 p.m. I then made enquiries in the Commons. When the Commons dispose of amendments from the Lords there needs to sit 'the Reasons Committee'. This is a committee of five, made up of three from the Government and two from the Opposition, and its purpose is to agree on the reasons why the Commons have rejected the Lords' amendments. During the debates in the Commons John Prescott had announced that he was so disgusted with the procedure that he had resigned from the Reasons Committee. His place was taken by Alex Carlile, a senior Liberal Democrat spokesman on Employment. He proved to be the winning card.

When the Reasons Committee met after 10 p.m. he was able, together with the assistance of Brian Wilson (Labour), to stretch the time out so that the Reasons Committee took more than one hour and a half to come to their conclusions. By this time, at 11.30 p.m. John Wakeham had to abandon the ploy in the Lords and agreed to meet next day.

Next day it was further chaos when the Reasons Committee reported to the Lords. The reasons drawn up by the Commons (of course wholly dictated by the three Conservative Members), led by the Minister of Transport (John MacGregor) were seen to be unacceptable. Geoff Tordoff immediately put down a motion which accepted reasons 1 and 2 but rejected the reasons for the third. He had of course a powerful case and at any other time, at almost any other circumstance, we would have protested vigorously and voted. However, when I was advised of Geoff's action (he had come to see me but I was not available) I immediately went to see him but he was not available. Celia Thomas (his secretary) said that he was busy writing his speech. I asked her whether he intended to vote and she said that he was uncertain. I reminded her and asked her to tell Geoff our understanding was, that having taken soundings, it would not be wise to vote again.

I then saw Ivor, who had had a conversation with Geoff and with Muriel Turner, with whom Geoff had consulted. Muriel was all for voting again. Ivor told me that he had had a conversation with John Smith and whilst John was content to leave the matter in the hands of the Lords, he had wondered whether it was possible to vote for the very good reason that Labour colleagues had got their spirits up due to the shenanigans of the Government. Ivor told me that the conversation had concluded by an agreement that it would not be wise to proceed with any votes that afternoon.

When the House reassembled and during Question Time Geoff came into the Chamber and I immediately went out with him and said 'Geoff, what are your intentions in respect of your amendment?' He told me that he had no intention of pressing it to a vote but he felt that the strongest possible protest should be made. I was relieved to hear this because I had told Celia to tell him that, if he did push it to a vote, it would be my intention to keep Labour colleagues out of the lobby.

Geoff then proceeded to make an excellent case for his amendment, to such an extent that there was clear grounds for believing that he intended to push it to a vote. Patricia Hollis, who was sitting next to me on the Front Bench, said 'He is going to press it to a vote and we should go into the lobby with him'. I said to Patricia 'He is not going to push it to a vote and if he does then our Front Bench at least will not be voting'. After a masterly performance of walking the tightrope Geoff told the House that he had come to the conclusion that nothing that the House of Lords did would make any impression whatsoever on the Commons. The Government quite clearly was not prepared to give the Lords any credence whatsoever and in these circumstances he felt it was pointless once more to send the amendment back to the Commons and he withdrew it. There was a general sense of disappointment around the House but that is how the matter concluded.

A number of colleagues came to me afterwards expressing disappointment that we had not supported a vote: I had to say to them in terms thus – 'My job as the Chief Whip is to defeat the Government as often as I can on any issues that I can'. You have only to reflect on the totality of the Railways Bill to realize just how successful we had all been at this. The Government and its supporters were in absolute disarray and depression due to the bad management, of both the Bill and the House, by the Government.

Before Geoff Tordoff stood up we knew the following. That John Peyton had publicly announced that he would not support any votes. This could diminish our total by 10/12. Dick Marsh had said exactly the same. This could further diminish our vote by anything up to 25/30. I also knew there were many of my own colleagues who would have been very unhappy indeed if we had supported a vote in the lobby because they were strongly of the view that at the end of the day, which this was, the elected House should prevail and to simply push matters back – or seem to be attempting to, push matters back (down the corridor) was not good either for the Labour Party or for the House of Lords. Thus I had to contemplate leading my troops into a lobby and being defeated. Not only would they have been defeated (my judgement) but we would then have been unable to resist the charge then, or later, that we were determined to try to assert the will of the unelected Lords over the elected Commons, even though the issues had been dealt with three times between both Houses.

I am bound to say that those colleagues with whom I had these conversations, whilst still unhappy, acknowledged the sense of what I was saying even though they may themselves have acted differently.

SWEET AND SOUR

The Deregulation and Contracting Out Bill is one which is divided up into clear portions. The Government is determined not to suffer any defeats. When I looked at the situation for the week commencing Monday 4 July

1994, I saw this possibility. On Tuesday 5 July 1994, there was bound to be a heavy Government Whip to defend the Criminal Justice Bill because issues were coming up that I knew they would want to protect. The same thing applied on Thursday, whilst on Wednesday we had this day for the Deregulation Bill. It so transpired that it dealt with transport issues and there was the prospect therefore of inflicting defeats on this day. I discussed this matter with Geoff Tordoff, Liberal Chief Whip, and we both agreed that there was a possibility. We recognized that it would require an 'ambush' of the old fashioned kind, ie to lull the Government into a sense of false security and then produce our troops when they were not expected. We both agreed that we would sound out our troops and then consult. On the Thursday before the Wednesday voting date, we met in the morning and agreed that the vibes were good for a vote that we would seek to force after supper.

My Whips had told me that there was a good spirit – especially as we were beating the Government on a regular basis, and this had given a good boost to morale. However, a potential serious situation was revealed when I reported our ploy to the meeting of the Front Bench. Charles Williams told us that he understood that Lord Campbell of Croy had booked the Cholmondeley Room for a party to celebrate his 75th birthday and there were bound to be many Tory Peers present. I enquired and that party was due from 6.30 p.m. to 8.30 p.m. I therefore discussed with Geoff Tordoff and we decided to call our surprise vote for 8.45 p.m. in the hope that with the Tories clearing off, if not completely gone, our troops would arrive after they had gone and surprise the Government Front Bench.

During the day Lena Jeger said that she had been told by one of the Tories that they knew there was going to be an ambush between 8.30 p.m. and 9.00 p.m. In the certain knowledge that if this was true, and with the Tory presence in the Cholmondeley Room, I was asked by more than one colleague whether I was going to persist with the ambush. I told them that there was no question of calling if off on the basis that information we had been given may or may not be true. All I knew from my trawl is that I had received promises from 67 Labour Peers. Geoff was less certain, but he felt that he might be in the high 20s. Thus, with the prospect of a vote between 85 and 90, the Government would had had to do exceptionally well to produce more than 90 at 9 p.m. in the evening.

The timetable on the day went exceedingly well, although there was a scare when Jack Simons (Lord Simons of Glaisdale, a Crossbencher) complained at the inordinate number of amendments which had been tabled late. This had been done of course to provide 'padding' so that the time could be strung out or drawn in like a piece of elastic.

At the break, which was at 7.10 p.m. Dennis Howell, Stanley Clinton-David, Geoff Tordoff and I met to discuss the situation in my office. We agreed that our timetable now looked exceedingly good. Stanley would call a Division at exactly 8.45 p.m. If we lost the vote, we would send our troops home, but if we won then we would persist in trying to catch another victory on an amendment dealing with seat belts in mini-buses. This was down on the Marshalled List and on the groupings at 197b.

The plan worked well. At 8.45 p.m. a Division was called and we won the Division by 90 to 50. This was a spectacular Division, catching the Government completely unawares. However, instead of proceeding to the other Division, Stanley called a Division on an intervening amendment. This we won by the same margin. By then some of our troops were saying 'We were asked to come in here to vote at 8.45 p.m. and it is now 9.00 p.m. and we have voted twice'. My answer to them was 'Yes, but if in fact you unusually have a House in which we have a majority of 40, it would be madness not to capitalize'. So we pressed on with the next amendment. This was 197b.

Unfortunately, Stanley, who was calling the numbers when the Chairman called 197b, said 'Not Moved'. The Chairman then proceeded to 197c. Dennis Howell got to the Despatch Box and began speaking on the matter relating to 197b. The Government Chief Whip rose and pointed out that 197b had already gone. Pandemonium. It was then revealed that Stanley was working off a Marshalled List which had been superseded and in actual fact he had in his hands two Marshalled Lists, one of which showed the important amendment as 197c and another as 197b. Dennis Howell sought to proceed, but the Government Chief Whip moved quite firmly 'that the speaker be no longer heard'. Move the adjournment of the House. Move the motion. Withdraw the motion. Send our troops home and keep talking. There was a real dilemma on how we could get out of the hole. I called Maurice Peston and Geoff Tordoff out into the Princes Chamber and we resolved that the only way out was to get Stanley to withdraw the manuscript amendment and at least that would make progress so that we could bring back 197b on another day. However, when I returned to the Chamber, Dennis Howell had already done this and the matter was concluded.

Of course in retrospect there was a series of points which, different decisions being taken, would have avoided the sourness at the end of the evening. This included the failure of Stanley to handle 197b at the appropriate time and the unwillingness to call off the matter when we could. It was further compounded by me pursuing the 'manuscript amendment' route until we were in a corner.

The next day, however, I was both pleasantly and gratefully surprised by the goodwill of colleagues who almost to a man, whilst acknowledging that we had been ousted at the end, nevertheless, put the two victories in perspective and at the end of the day some valuable lessons were learned. The main one for me is that when you find yourself in a hole you stop digging!

IT HAS NEVER BEEN DONE BEFORE . . . AND NOT LIKELY TO BE DONE AGAIN!

The Labour Supply day was set down for 1 December 1993. This was immediately seen to be the day following the Budget and it was decided to concentrate on an economic and social theme so that the Labour speakers could pick up on the themes coming out of the Budget. The Labour group endorsed this suggestion and gave the Co-ordinating Committee authority to dot the i's and cross the t's of the title at a meeting which was called for 24 November – the last possible day to put down the title.

At this meeting the Leader of the Labour Peers, Ivor Richard thought it would be a good idea to use the debate to do something which had never been done before – to put down a motion which said, 'That this House has no confidence in the policies of Her Majesty's Government'. He explained to the Co-ordinating Committee that it would be opportune on the day after the Budget and in effect to start off the new session, to make it plain that Labour Peers were not going to acquiesce in letting the Government have its own way.

I am bound to say that although this was seen as a good idea, there were some caveats entered as to the wisdom of so doing. Nevertheless, the decision of the Co-ordinating Committee to table the motion was taken.

Before tabling the motion, I went to see Geoff Tordoff, the Liberal Chief Whip. He was not in his room but I told Celia Thomas, his main administrator, what we had in mind. She promised to tell this to Geoff. When the House met that afternoon at 2.30 p.m. Geoff came into the Chamber and I immediately told him what we had in mind and asked for their support. He told me that he would give us their support and that was that I then advised the Labour Chief Whip in the Commons, Derek Foster, and also the Leader's office in the Commons by speaking to Murray Elder, John Smith's political chief. Subsequently, the matter was reported to the Shadow Cabinet. Ivor explained the background, pointing out that there could not possibly be any chance of winning a vote but nevertheless it seemed to him to be a good idea. John Smith said that he agreed and wished us well.

Prior to putting down the motion I had discussed it with the Clerk of the Parliaments and whilst of course making no comment on the wisdom, or otherwise, of doing so, he said that whilst it was difficult to find a precedent, as far as he was concerned it was in order. The only thing he said was whether we had considered tabling a reasoned amendment to the Queen's Speech which was due to conclude on the Thursday – two days later. I told him that we had considered this but that we wanted to have this particular motion to begin the new session.

When I reported the matter to the secretary to the Government Chief Whip he, of course, expressed surprise and wondered whether this was a wise thing to do. I had to tell him that we had considered these matters but that we intended to proceed.

On Thursday 26 November, the matter was reported to the Front Bench meeting when Ivor explained the matter. There was general approval but voices were raised as to the wisdom of the matter. It was the same in the full meeting of the group of Labour Peers later that afternoon. Thus, although the die had been cast, there were colleagues who had explained that, not only were they unhappy with the motion, but because of the shortness of notice, they would find it exceedingly difficult to attend.

I set in motion my normal methods of ensuring a maximum attendance. Not only was the matter brought up at the Party meeting but all of my Whips were instructed to contact all of their Members and ask them to respond to a vote on Wednesday evening. In addition, the notice board drew attention to the motion and a special letter appeared inside the Whip. As well as all these steps about 40 Members who needed a reminder were telephoned on Friday morning 26 November.

I knew that Geoff Tordoff would not be about the House that week because he was off to New Zealand and in fact departed in the latter part of the previous Thursday. Nevertheless he had told me that I should contact his Deputy, Lucius Falkland, (The Viscount Falkland) on any matters that needed to be resolved. I saw Lucius during the day on the Monday and said to him 'I am assuming that you are pulling out all the stops to get a good vote on Wednesday?'. Lucius replied to me that he was doing his best although he was not too sure whether we would get the maximum attendance. Nothing in these conversations led me to believe what subsequently transpired.

The next consideration was the length of the debate. We had always taken the view that debates should be timed even though this might restrict the number of speakers and I instructed the business manager that we wished the debate to be timed for 5 hours. Subsequently a problem arose. It became clear that a Statement would be made in the House of Commons by Peter Lilley on changes in Social Security benefits and that this would be offered to us on 1 December. Consideration took place as to whether we should take it during the debate or at the end. I came to the view that it was more important to be precise when the vote should take place –

8 p.m. – and that we would be in difficulty if we were unable to be precise on the time of the vote due to being unable to forecast the length of time taken out of the debate time (but added later) by the Statement. I told the business manager we intended to have the Statement taken at the end of the debate.

On Tuesday 30 November the business manager came to me and said that when this had been put to the Liberals and the Government Chief Whip they were both firmly of the view that the Statement should be taken when available – at about 4 p.m. The house would not understand having to wait until the end of the day, etc etc. Reluctantly, I came to the view that we would not make any friends by leaving the Statement to the end and we agreed that the Statement should be made during the day. Of course, this then meant that the vote would be stretched to approximately 9 p.m. instead of 8 p.m. – but this was not of my doing.

On the morning of the debate, this list showed that there were 48 speakers down to speak as well as the movers of the motion. I prevailed upon three of my colleagues to have their names taken off and thus by this means every speaker was allocated 5 minutes and the Frontbenchers and those who wound up were given an appropriate total.

To the debate. Ivor Richard opened the debate and took the issue head on as to the appropriateness of it. He argued that it was the job of the Opposition from time to time to challenge the policies of the Government and this was our chosen way of doing it. John Wakeham, the Leader of the House, on behalf of the Government pointed out that there had been opportunities to do this during the Queen's Speech, that this step was very rare, and then proceeded to defend the Government. A vigorous debate took place.

Whilst sitting on the Front Bench waiting for the wind-up speakers, I deduced that there was some time in hand and I went to Nancy Seear, who was the only Liberal spokesman set down in the lists and said to her 'Nancy, there is some time in hand and you have some of it to use as you wish.' She then said to me, 'I do not need any extra time. I think the motion is an awful motion and should never have been put down.' I was somewhat taken aback by this reaction and became uneasy when I reflected that not only had no Liberals spoken in the debate but there did not appear to be many Liberals around the House. I then went back to Ivor and told him about this and we both realized that there was something wrong – but we did not know what.

During her speech, Nancy Seear laid about not only the Government but also the Labour Party. At one stage she said 'Whilst there is an official Opposition we on these benches are the unofficial Opposition. We have no confidence in the policies of Her Majesty's Government – neither have we any confidence in the policies of Her Majesty's Official Opposition.' As Hansard records, it says 'Noble Lords – Oh!'.

When she sat down, Ivor asked me to find out from her whether the Liberals were going to support the motion. When I put this question directly to her, Nancy Seear simply shrugged her shoulders and did not say anything at all. When the vote was called at 8.48 p.m. the Conservative benches were absolutely packed to overflowing, whilst the Labour benches were reasonably full, there was just a handful of Crossbenchers, and the same on the Liberal benches. The vote resulted as follows – for the motion of no confidence in the policies of the Government – there voted 95 – consisting of Labour 79, Liberal 13, Crossbenches 3. Against the motion, Conservative 276, Crossbenches 6. Of course the Conservatives were elated but our side, whilst angry with the Liberal reaction, were also conscious that we had polled well. Early in the day at the press conference that Ivor and I regularly called I had indicated that my forecast would be 100 minus. In other words 95 to 100 for the motion and 200 + against the motion, in the knowledge that the Conservatives were bound to bring out as many people as they could. I had a drink with Ivor and went into the Bishop's Bar with him, when there was some reaction but not much. Nancy Seear and one or two Liberals were sitting having a drink but they passed out of the room without making any comment to us at all.

In the light of the poor turnout by the Liberals, I decided to see Lucius Falkland and ask for an explanation. When I went down to his room, he had not arrived, but I spoke to Celia Thomas. Celia explained a range of reasons why people had been unable to attend and I quite understood this, but I said to her 'In the light of all that, Celia, it is difficult to understand only 13 Liberals attended, whilst with the same range of difficulties, Labour produced 79.' To which she replied 'Ah yes, but it was your motion and it was not ours.' I asked if Lucius could see me as soon as he was free. He came to see me and he then said 'I am afraid that there has been a misunderstanding and in discussing the matter with Celia I believe that we have got the answer. When Geoff Tordoff reported the matter to our Party meeting last Thursday the view of the group was that the motion was ill timed and ill advised and that we would not have a Whip on it at all.' I expressed my astonishment because, although that reaction would have not been welcome, nevertheless, I did not understand what had happened.

Lucius then explained 'It appears to us that Geoff failed to convey this to you and he left for New Zealand with all of us thinking that he had told you that the Liberals were not in effect taking part in the debate. When you had asked me on Monday to 'pull out all the stops' I said I would do my best in the mistaken belief that you already knew that we were not Whipped and would not be partaking in the debate fully.' Of course, he expressed regret for the misunderstanding but then explained he had tried to do his best but there was real difficulty in persuading his Members to come in and support something that they genuinely believed had been misguided.

I told Lucius that I could well understand that this was the explanation for the poor attendance of Liberals but I had to tell him that the words used by Nancy Seear had done harm to relationships and that this was not the way for the two Parties to work together. I acknowledged that more time should be given but that I felt sure that my colleagues would take a dim view of both the attitude of the Liberal Party and in particular the words used by Nancy Seear.

At the meeting of the Front Bench I gave the explanation and the Front Bench were satisfied. In the inquest, Maurice Peston said that although he had in the previous week expressed his view that it was a wrong action to do and that he would not be in attendance, nevertheless, having heard Ivor Richard make his speech, he had not only changed his plans and in effect attended and voted, but that he had also now concluded that it was a wise thing to do. At the meeting of the Party later, something comparable took place.

I took the view that it was – in retrospect – not the way in which we should have dealt with the issue. At the end of the day it is true that we acquitted ourselves well by both putting up excellent cases and a satisfactory vote, but it was one of the few times in my period of being Chief Whip now for nearly three and a half years when I have felt that either we had shot ourselves in the foot or that we had been wrong footed by the Government. That was not the way to do things!

Ivor and I agreed that this was the appropriate time when together we should discuss with John Wakeham (Leader of the House) and Nick Ullswater, the Government Chief Whip, the best way in which to maintain good relations, especially after the manner in which the Government had treated us and the House over the concluding stages of the Railways Bill. Therefore on Thursday 2 December I asked the business manager if he would convey to John Wakeham and Nick Ullswater our wish that an early meeting take place in order to clear the air in respect of the' usual channels'.

Postscript

Subsequent publicity has not been all one way. Attached to this piece are two items which (a) reveal the annoyance we created amongst the Conservative benches and (b) the manner in which the seriousness of the motion was treated by the press. In addition, Ivor Richard appeared on 'The Week in Westminster' on the following Saturday and in an interview with

Peter Riddell gave a vigorous defence of the tactic and the outcome especially as it illustrated that, whereas Opposition Parties would always be able to produce in the region of 100 votes when they pulled out all the stops, the Conservative Government was able to whistle up 150 votes literally at the drop of a hat. These were bound to be factors taken into account when one considers the anti-democratic nature of the House of Lords.

★   ★   ★

NEWSPAPER EXTRACTS

BLUFF AND COUNTER-BLUFF – STEADY THE BUFFS!

Shh! This is the plan

Dog hates to be a killjoy. But I cannot resist divulging a 'strictly private and confidential' letter to Labour Peers from Chief Whip, Lord Graham of Edmonton.

Their Lordships are instructed to sneak into the House tomorrow to ambush the Government.

Stressing secrecy, Lord Graham gloats: 'We plan to call a division at 8.30 p.m. If Members are already in the building, please keep out of the Chamber.' Those arriving early are to hide in the second-floor researchers' room while Tories toddle off to dinner.

Lord Graham ends: 'Good luck!'

Oh dear, I hope he did not waste too much time on the stratagem.

Mail on Sunday

GOVERNMENT DEFEATED IN LORDS OVER PENSIONS RULE

The government was defeated last night as the Lords backed a move to base the state earnings-related pension on the best 44 years' earnings rather than the 49 years proposed by the government.

The amendment, during the committee stage of the Pensions Bill, was carried by a majority of 44. The government will now have to decide whether to reverse the vote when the measure returns to the Commons.

It also emerged during the debate on the bill, which equalizes the state pension age at 65 for men and women, that the government is considering changing the law to allow pension rights to be taken into account in divorce settlements in England and Wales.

Labour's Baroness Hollis said after the debate: 'Women's employment is almost always interrupted by family responsibilities. Men's employment can be interrupted for a number of reasons. The government is trying to deny a full state earnings-related pension to most women and to some vulnerable men by its insistence that after equalization at 65 women and men will both have to make contributions over 49 years to qualify.'

Mr Alex Carlile, Liberal Democrat social security spokesman, said the defeat 'will give more low-paid workers, women and those with broken working patterns a chance to qualify for a full state pension when they retire.'

Lord Mackay of Ardbrecknish, social security minister, told Peers during the debate that the 44-year option would 'raise expenditure in the long term in a poorly targeted way – high-earning men would benefit as well as low-earning women.'

Earlier, Lord Mackay told the Lords that the government was considering whether to amend the Matrimonial Causes Act to bring England and Wales into line with Scotland, where pension rights could be taken into account in divorce.

The government would also consider whether there should be power for ministers to 'prescribe a method of valuing pensions on divorce,' he said.

Peers also rejected, by 53 votes, cross-party demands for pensions of all UK citizens in retirement overseas to be unfrozen.

Financial Times, 21 February 1995

LORDS OVERTURN BILL ON SCHOOL INSPECTORS

Time runs out for Conservatives' privatization plan

The Government's controversial plans to privatize the schools' inspectorate were on the verge of collapse last night after Peers inflicted two defeats which ministers admitted tore the heart out of the bill.

The first of two amendments by the Peers to the Education (Schools) Bill, came when they removed the proposed right of schools governing bodies to choose their own inspectors.

Despite pleas from Baroness Blatch, the Environment Minister, that the amendment would 'tear the heart out' of the bill, Peers passed the measure by 95 votes to 67.

Soon after, they voted 97 to 63 to reject the bill's provisions to remove from local authorities the right of entry to inspect the schools they maintain.

Instead, they gave Her Majesty's Inspectorate the right to inspect schools over and above the normal cyclical visits.

Jack Straw, the Shadow Education Secretary, said the effect of the amendments was to turn a Conservative bill into a Labour one.

He said: 'This legislation was a piece of wreckage anyway . . . now it's well on the way to being sunk.'

Matthew Taylor, the Liberal Democrats' education spokesman, said: 'These votes mean a very bad night for the Conservatives and a very good night for education.'

With time running out before the election, Tory business managers can reverse the defeats only at the Lords report stage next Tuesday, Budget Day.

Kenneth Clarke, the Education Secretary, said: 'We will have to decide what to do. If the bill is of a form consistent with the Parent's Charter, we will take it through the Commons. If it is not, we will try to amend it.'

The Lords' amendments do not alter the Government's proposals on school inspections completely. There is still scope for inspection teams to be set up outside the local education authority system, and Her Majesty's Inspectorate still faces staff cuts.

The plans to privatize school inspections were dented last week by the decision of leading management consultants not to bid to set up inspection teams. They said they had serious reservations about the feasibility of the scheme and quibbled at the amount of money the Government was allowing for inspections.

The Government last week conceded that Her Majesty's Inspectorate should have a veto in the choosing of private inspectors.

The Schools Bill's Third Reading in the Lords is set for March 16.

The Guardian

CLARKE WAS AMBUSHED BY CLAIMS OF CLUBLAND

Kenneth Clarke may have been ambushed in the Lords on Monday night, but he sounded anything but mortally wounded yesterday. The Education Secretary was back on his feet and aiming his fire at the unions, blaming them for the amendments that 'tore the heart' from his Schools Bill.

The unions, it is true, have been active in opposing the bill. But Mr Clarke might have looked a little closer to home for his scapegoat: to the Tory Peers who failed to turn out for the vital votes. They disappeared to their homes, their clubs, their restaurants, after the first division – and then the opposition forces sprang their trap.

The absence of Tory Peers has played into the opposition's hands before. A Tory Whip once complained to Margaret Thatcher, after a handbagging over a Lords defeat, that he was powerless. 'After 7 p.m. they all got off to White's and I can't get them back.' A new restaurant was subsequently opened in the Lords to tempt Peers away from club-land – but on Monday night it failed.

The Tory Whips were enjoying the support of more than 100 Peers rallying to a two-line whip in the votes held before 7 p.m. However, the first of the two defeats, at 9.11 p.m, saw only 67 Peers trooping into the lobby, while 96 filed in to vote for the opposition. Had the government Whips known what was up, they might have made a better fist of keeping their troops on guard, but the opposition had prepared its ambush subtly.

Labour and Liberal Peers were instructed to arrive for the crucial votes at 9 p.m. – but not to tell anyone. Celia Thomas, unofficial manager of the 60 Liberal Democrat Peers, served her supporters wine in her office until the division bells sounded. While they did not actually hide in cupboards, the 'ambushers' maintained a low profile for fear of tipping off the Tory Whips. Some left at about 7 p.m., only to return later.

These tactics clinched success but the truth is that they would have availed nothing had it not been for the failure of the government to convince the Lords of its case. There are 455 Tory Peers in the Lords, a net increase of 35 since 1979. Labour boasts only 116 Peers, a net fall of 27. Many Labour and Liberal Democrat Peers are in their 80s and 90s.

Faced by this weight of numbers, the opposition can only defeat the Tories if it unites against the government and attracts the support of non-partisan crossbench Peers. The unity of the opposition on Monday was ensured by the co-operation of two experienced Whips, the affable Lord Graham of Edmonton, a former Co-op sponsored MP for Labour, and Lord Tordoff, of the Liberal Democrats. By contrast, the Tory Whip, Lord Hesketh, is relatively inexperienced, having only recently succeeded the legendary 'Bertie' Denham.

Lady Blatch, handling the bill for the Tories, thought she had headed off defeat with minor concessions on the bill. In fact, she merely reinforced the complacency of her Whips, who were confident that its opponents had been appeased.

Even this would not have mattered had the notion that schools should appoint their own inspectors been convincing, but to many Peers it sounded rather akin to suggesting that batsmen choose their own umpires.

Since the proposal was not included in the government's election manifesto, Tory Peers did not feel obliged to back it and the opposition felt no inhibitions about fighting it.

The unions and local authority associations had also vociferously opposed the schools bill. On February 18, six teaching union general secretaries wrote to every Peer, protesting about provisions that would deny education authorities the right to send in inspectors, and about plans for governing bodies to appoint inspectors.

However, even union officials closely involved in the campaign were disinclined to claim the credit for the government defeat. 'I wish we were that powerful', Olive Forsyth of the National Union of Teachers said.

In the end, the legislation's defeat owed far less to their powers of persuasion than to the behaviour of the Peers. Other than the payroll vote of ministers and others, fewer than 40 other Tory Peers were still in the Palace of Westminster by 9 p.m. The ambush was ripe for springing.

The Times

CHAPTER 12

Obituaries

I N THE PERIOD FROM 1990 to about 2002 I wrote more than 60 Obituaries of Labour Peers. This came about when the then Opposition Chief Whip, Tom Ponsonby, asked me to write one for a comrade who had just died. I did so. Not only Tom but others all round the Lords told me how much they appreciated it, and from then on I determined that I would write one for every Labour Peer who died – and I have done just that. I took the view that in addition to what is written by the National and local papers, the family would appreciate 'a view from his colleagues'. I was always able to weave in references to how I had known them – and was proud to say so. Sometimes there were good years when few comrades departed, but in others there were many. In a five-week period at the end of 2003 the Labour Peers Group lost 8 colleagues. It is not possible to include them all so I have had to leave many out, but have included those I feel would be of interest to the reader. 'They shall not grow old, as we who are left grow old, at the going down of the sun, and in the morning, we shall remember them. We shall remember them.' I am grateful to the Chairman of *The House Magazine*, Sir Patrick Cormack, for his permission to reproduce them here.

Lord Ardwick 1910–94

Just as in the Commons, Members are often grouped in the year they entered (the 1974 intake was a very good one!) so it is in the Lords. Of course, all sides of the Chamber will have their own benchmarks, but for Labour the 1970 intake was pretty impressive with, amongst others, John Beavan, who had just completed a tempestuous period as one of the busiest men in Fleet Street. Labour seems to have had a penchant for ennobling newspapermen (and women). Besides John there was also Sydney Jacobson, Ted Castle, Hugh Cudlipp, and, before the seventies were out, Alma Birk and Lena Jeger combined to give the Labour benches a distinctive 'Fleet Street' hue.

John Beavan reached almost the top at a comparatively early age after stints on both Manchester evening papers – the *Chronicle* and the *News* – and then lured to London for posts on the *Evening Standard* until finally he was to make his mark journalistically with *The Guardian*, becoming its London editor. After a short spell away from Fleet Street he was to return

179

and assume the editorship of Labour's paper, *The Daily Herald*, in the early sixties – but he was not allowed sufficient time to make his mark before ending his Fleet Street life in style as the political adviser to the Mirror Group. Thus, when Harold Wilson was to put him in the Lords to be a spokesman for newspapermen and women, he transmogrified easily onto the red benches in the Upper House, where he spent, most profitably, the last 24 years of his life.

Unlike some who look upon reaching that illustrious place as some kind of 'God's Waiting Room' – a term coined by another of Labour's men of letters, Ted Willis – John grasped its opportunities with both hands, and before long he was in the swim, and swimming very strongly. He was always an interesting, sometimes compelling, speaker, always with notes typed by himself (what else for a newspaperman?) and delivered in a strong voice, with emphasis for effect sprinkled liberally within it. He never waffled, and in my experience was a Chief Whip's dream. He was always willing, nay, anxious to speak in any debate, and if I asked him, his name would be put down immediately. But his other endearing trait – for a Chief Whip – was that he never complained if I asked him to either withdraw or to 'keep it short' in the interests of either getting a vote or to wrap it all up a decent time.

John came from a family steeped in the mores of the Labour Movement, his mother carrying a great reputation as Alderman Emily Beavan on the Manchester City Council. She was prominent in the Women's Co-operative Guild and it was through that avenue that so many of Labour's bright sparks were given encouragement and support in their task of fighting the good fight for Socialism. The Guild was a force then, more so than it is today. George Thomas, the former Speaker, often told me that his mother was a stalwart of the Guild in South Wales, and that the dividend was vital to the family's wealth. Baroness Fisher of Rednal (Doris in an early life) has the unique distinction of having been a National President of the Guild.

Manchester, and proud of it, was John. Like many others he took in his title the name of the place he grew up in and thus, changed from John Beavan to Lord Ardwick of Barnes – the place in which he lived happily later. John was always passionately pro-European and a defender of both membership and enlargement of the EEC. He told the House last year during the great debates on Maastricht that it was in 1948, when covering a Congress in The Hague for the *Manchester Guardian*, that he heard Bertrand Russell say over dinner that the Russians could be at the channel ports whenever they wished. He not only talked about it, he was tireless in his support for the concept of European Unity. Within the Labour Party, like others, he had to suffer derision often as the line of the party changed over the years, but he never wavered in his beliefs.

He was an early advocate of televising the proceedings of the Lords, and he enjoyed immensely the rising prestige given to the Upper House as a result of television. Much later, and largely as the result of his initiative, the Commons decided that it was too much of a good thing to be left to the Lords.

He kept up links with the press and proved invaluable as a conduit for Labour Peers into Fleet Street. He had an honoured place at the weekly press conference held by the Labour leadership and was greatly respected by those who reported politics and Westminster. He was the kind of Life Peer who gave the House of Lords a good name and accepted with open arms the opportunities it gave him. His colleagues sent him to represent them in the European Parliament from 1975 to 1979 before direct elections, and to the North Atlantic Assembly, where he developed valuable expertise in the field of defence, which he deployed with great effect in debates. He was elected to, and served, as the Chairman of the Labour Peers' backbench committee for many years. He used his regular contributions in *The House Magazine* with wit, panache and charm.

With his wife Gladys and daughter Jennifer he supported Labour's social functions with gusto. He was a lovely man and one who lived and enjoyed his life to the very end. He will be missed in many places, but especially amongst his colleagues in the Labour Peers Group who mourn the passing of a great man.

The House Magazine, October 17, 1994

Baroness Bacon

Alice Bacon was the daughter of a miner who was a county councillor so it is no surprise that she stepped into the gamut of public life that makes up the Labour Movement with ease and panache. That she served at the highest level with distinction and success brings a glow of remembered satisfaction to her many friends throughout that Labour Movement – and beyond. She was the product of Normanton Girls' School and Stockwell Training College and subsequently became a headmistress. Years later she was to become a Minister of State at the Department of Education and Science.

It is more than 50 years since she became a member of the National Executive Committee of the Labour Party where she served for more than 30 years, becoming chairman in 1950. She made her mark in the Commons when she became one of the Leeds MPs in 1945 and held her seat until retirement 25 years later. She was a Minister of State at the Home Office in Harold Wilson's first administration and when she retired from the Commons she came to the Lords in 1970 and served as a member of the North Atlantic Assembly from 1974 to 1980.

Alice was as straight as a die. She was the mistress of her brief and had an enviable reputation as a committee person. Not every parliamentarian relished the special kind of qualities required to be a good 'committee person'.

Alice was a formidable conference performer. She was not only a safe pair of hands, utterly reliable in presenting the case for the NEC, but by her sheer personality she drew votes for her case by the ballot boxful. Brisk is a word to describe her approach, yet she also laughed easily. 'She was a canny crack' – a good talker in Tyneside vernacular. She was very much at home with all elements within the Labour Movement and a fine ambassador for Leeds, for her party and for Parliament.

Alice Bacon was looked upon as a typical Yorkshire lass who stood no nonsense within any committee on which she served. She was of that generation within the Labour Movement who had been brought up to fight for their class. She was a 'bonny' fighter who visibly enjoyed a good argument. Old-fashioned may be another word to describe her qualities, but they proved to be the backbone of Labour's successful struggle to assert itself as a party of government under Clem Attlee and Harold Wilson. Ill health prevented her from being a regular attender in the Lords in her last years, but she never was long out of touch, for her many friends, especially those who lived in Yorkshire, brought her Westminster news from both Houses. I think especially of Walter Harrison, former MP for Wakefield and Labour Deputy Chief Whip during the 1970s, and of Merlyn Rees who served with Alice in Leeds, the Commons and the Lords.

Alice was dedicated in everything she did. There were no half measures for Alice. She never flinched from confrontation – some would say she even relished it, especially in her running battles with the extreme left both within and out with the party and the machine. An 'in fighter' is a good description of her record, and she resented being labelled anything less. When she was once described as a 'kindly Yorkshire woman' she bridled. 'There is nothing wrong with the Yorkshire bit, and nothing wrong with me being kind. But kindly tends to sound a bit wet.' Her attitude to life was summed up by her when she received her peerage. 'I have never been a part-time MP, or come to that, even a full-time MP. I have always been an over-time MP.'

Remembering Alice brings a warm glow to all her friends. She was a lovely lady and we will miss her.

The House Magazine, 5 and 14 April 1993

Rt Hon Lord Bottomley OBE 1907–1995

From 1945 to 1995, Arthur Bottomley was a Westminster parliamentarian except for two short spells totalling less than four years. This magnificent record of public service came to a sad end with his death in Chingford Hospital, where he died peacefully after heart failure. Aged 88 when he died, he was looked after by his devoted wife Bess, who had been his life companion since they were married in 1936.

Until his later years, Arthur was the picture of ruddy health and his creased face, which wrinkled around the eyes when he smiled, was a beloved feature at Westminster. He and his wife had settled in Walthamstow and Arthur was made the Chairman of the Emergency Committee and the ARP Controller for Walthamstow during the war. Fittingly he was made Mayor of Walthamstow in 1945 and thus was involved in those days of thanksgiving.

Entering the Commons for the first time in 1945 to represent Chatham, he did so until the 1959 election, only to re-enter the Commons again – this time for Middlesbrough in 1962 which he represented until the 1983 General Election. By then he had enjoyed a career of spectacular success and, like so many others, took his title of Lord Bottomley of Middlesbrough out of regard for the people of Teesside who loved him for his ebullient and passionate defence of their interest.

Arthur was a Harold Wilson man from beginning to end, and many of us saw the swift deterioration in Arthur with the death of his dear friend Harold earlier this year. His earlier mentor had been Clem Attlee who had made him Parliamentary Under Secretary of State for the Dominions and then Secretary of State for Overseas Aid in that first postwar Government. It was whilst he served Harold Wilson as Secretary of State for Commonwealth Relations that he was seen at Harold's side during the tortuous negotiations with Ian Smith in Rhodesia, as well as on board HMS *Fearless*.

He was especially proud of the fact that he was awarded the Freedom of Chatham, Middlesbrough and the City of London. He was one of a diminishing band who came to the Lords from the Commons – he never left for home until he had been told personally that 'the Whip is off' – then he scarpered! He was active in the affairs of Toynbee Hall for many years.

Arthur Bottomley led a full and active public life until struck down by illness towards the end of his life. He was ready to go. When I visited him in hospital in October he said to me 'I'd like you to pick the pears off my tree' and when I asked him if I should save some for him he said with that knowing twinkle in his eyes 'I won't be needing any of them'.

The House Magazine, 13 November 1995

Baroness Birk of Regents Park 1919–1996

Alma Birk came to be recognized as one of a select band of woman Labour Peers sent to the House of Lords by Harold Wilson and Jim Callaghan who found in that place the ideal forum for them to develop and prosper politically in service to the Party they had served for many years before. When Alma Birk arrived in the House of Lords in 1967 she had already fought three General Elections, been leader of the Labour Group on Mrs Thatcher's local council – Finchley – had risen to the highest posts in local government and served as a Magistrate, a service which eventually totalled more than 30 years on the Highgate Bench. All this while bringing up a son and a daughter, no doubt with the sterling support of her husband Ellis. Her sparkling service in Labour administrations had yet to begin. She had by then (1967) demonstrated her indefatigable energy and hunger for hard work. She told me 'I was always torn between my children and my political lifestyle, but I was lucky because my husband Ellis who was a solicitor was ahead of his time and was always willing to help out and was enormously supportive.'

Although she told me that it came as a bolt out of the blue when Harold Wilson sent for her to tell her he was sending her to the House of Lords she was well fitted for that new role. In the Lords she swiftly rose and by the time Labour left office in 1979 she had progressed through the ranks being successively a Baroness-in-waiting (Whip), Parliamentary Under Secretary at the Department of the Environment and Minister of State at the Privy Council Office dealing with Economic Affairs in the Lords. She once told me that she was interested in all the arts and went to plays, ballet, concerts and art exhibitions. 'My own particular love is the theatre, and I often wonder whether my early desire to go into politics showed I was an actress manqué.'

Her favourite subject as school was history and she remembers that one day she was writing an essay on Charles Dickens which turned into a comparison between social conditions then and now. 'I felt then that I must do something to try and improve conditions and so I joined the Labour Party. Yet I sometimes look around today and think how far have we really come? You still see people sleeping under the arches and in shop doorways. It saddens me enormously to see how our infrastructure is being run down, how grotty our streets look and in spite of more funds being made available recently, how the Arts and Museums are starved of resources by a philistine Government'. She fought three parliamentary elections: Ruislip and Norwood in 1950, Portsmouth West in 1951 and again in 1955.

Portsmouth can be proud of Alma. The city was not only the birth place of a Prime Minister Jim Callaghan, it also gave the Labour ranks in the Lords at least three invaluable colleagues, Donald Bruce, John Jacques and Frank Judd. When I was in that city not long ago I got talking to some Co-operative Women's Guild members about the good old days. One of them Jessie Worrall told me of the great day they had when 'that marvellous and beautiful redhead would come down and held an audience outside the Dockyard Gate in thrall as she lashed the Tories and urged us on to fight, fight, fight.' 'I didn't know that Barbara Castle had been busy down here,' I said. 'Not Barbara, that was our Alma, she was a terrier and we all loved her and followed her in her great fights here.'

Although she fell on sad times of late, it is memories like that held by Jessie Worrall which warmed the hearts of all who were fortunate to know – and love – this remarkable woman.

Rt Hon Baroness Castle of Blackburn 1910–2002

If one judged the eminence of a politician by the column inches devoted to them in the obituaries, Baroness Castle of Blackburn was indeed a giantess amongst us. To those of us who had the pleasure and the privilege of working with her in one of her many guises over the years she was all that – and more. There are colleagues in the Lords who had the opportunity of serving with her in Cabinet in both Houses, on 'the stump', and in many hectic corners and committees of one sort or another invariably connected with the love of her life politics and the pursuit of socialism.

She was a heroine then to women in the Labour movement. When I met her for the first time at a Labour Party conference after she was in her first cabinet post as Secretary of Overseas Development, I told her 'I know your brother.' She did not hesitate to come out to Enfield. It was the largest meeting I ever organized!

Barbara married Ted (later Lord) Castle who was devoted to her and when he died after a very happy life with her, she missed his solid support and constant encouragement.

The list of achievements stands as a litany of benefits to mankind – and especially to womankind. On top of the Offices of State that she held – and cabinet posts she filled – were Secretary of State for Employment, Health and Social Services, Transport and Overseas Development. All of these were under the premiership of her long time political ally, Harold Wilson. She was in the midst of being Secretary of State for Health and Social Security in April 1976 when Harold resigned and was succeeded by Jim Callaghan. Not the most congenial of companions, she was sacked immediately.

When she went to the newly formed Department of Overseas Development with no record of what it was for, she told her civil servants that it was all in a Fabian pamphlet she had written in opposition. And so it was, and it came to pass – just like that.

There are those of us who are delighted to be invited to address one fringe meeting at Party Conference, but Barbara often addressed two at lunchtime and three in the evening – every day! One of my abiding memories is of seeing Barbara battling against the elements along the front at Brighton or Blackpool – even Scarborough – dashing from one meeting to another. 'Can't stop – I'm late already!' came the familiar cry. But she was always worth waiting for.

The House Magazine, 13 May 2002

Rt Hon Lord Cledwyn of Penrhos CH 1916–2001

Cledwyn (Cled) had graced the Palace of Westminster for 50 years, and before that had been a force in the community from which he sprang, serving as both an elected county councillor and a senior local civil servant. His entry into Westminster politics had been far from smooth, taking three contests before he was successful in 1951. He went on to represent that seat until he went to the Lords – and those of us who knew him recognized that in reality he never stopped representing the people of Anglesey.

Undoubtedly the most traumatic period for Cledwyn was when, as Secretary of State for Wales, he had to preside over the horror of the Aberfan disaster in 1966. He was in North Wales when the news of the disaster came and he immediately flew to Aberfan, joining the Prime Minister Harold Wilson, who said 'Cledwyn Hughes has military-type powers'. Cledwyn immediately cancelled a five-day visit to Northern Ireland and never left the area for a week. During this period he assisted the Queen, Prince Philip and the Prince of Wales to understand the full horror of the incident. He was to work on the investiture of Prince Charles as the Prince of Wales only for Harold Wilson to move him to become Secretary of State for Agriculture before the event. Prince Charles was one of many who expressed their concern on learning of the illness which presaged his death. He saw the rise of a militant tendency within the PLP and he successfully challenged Ian Mikardo for the chairmanship of the PLP. This gave him a pivotal position in the period 1974 to 1979, for he was a most effective conduit between the Prime Minister and the PLP. He was always able to receive the confidences of colleagues and to respect them.

When he went to the Lords after the 1979 general election it was to assume the office of deputy leader of the Labour Peers Group, and in 1982 he succeeded Fred Peart as Leader. This coincided with the departure of an outstanding Labour Chief Whip, Pat Llewelyn-Davies, and her replacement by Tom Ponsonby. Together they proved more than a match for any duo in office on the government benches. He was succeeded as Leader of the Opposition by Ivor Richard, but not before he had stamped his leadership on the Lords through impressive performances at the despatch box.

A withdrawal from frontbench duties after more than 30 years meant that he could devote himself to other matters. He became a member of the

Scrutiny Committee, charged with vetting nominees for honours and he did this for almost 10 years. He was able to devote time to his beloved University of Wales where he was the Pro-Chancellor. He never wasted an opportunity to champion the cause of Wales and the Welsh, whether the Order Paper allowed it or not, and the House hugely enjoyed his many successful attempts to get the affairs of the Principality noticed. He was proud of the fact that he received many honorary degrees and the freedom of towns and cities, none more so than that the City of Cardiff which he accepted a few weeks before his death.

Cledwyn was proud of his Welsh ancestry, his roots and his forebears. He leaves us as the senior statesman for and of Wales, a Companion of Honour and a druid, but above all, as a much loved colleague who brightened our days, and whose passing makes our days darker but leaves our hopes undimmed. Our thoughts are with his wife Jean and with Ann and Harri.

The House Magazine, 5 March 2001

Lord Dean of Beswick 1922–1999

Lord Dean of Beswick was never Lord Dean of Beswick around Westminster. He was always Joe, and in a time when characters were few and far between Joe was without a doubt a character. He came into the Commons at the same election that I did – in February 1974 – and we left the Commons for the Lords at the same time – after the 1983 election. We shared a possibly unique record, for both Joe and I served in Whips' offices, in the Commons in both government and opposition, and when we came up to the Lords we both served for more than 13 years making almost 20 years as Whips. Whilst he rose to become the pairing Whip in Opposition in the Commons, I went on to become Opposition Chief Whip in the Lords. I had no finer colleague in the whole of my parliamentary career. We had met before entering parliament for his role undoubtedly was local government and Joe rose to become the leader of Manchester City Council at the same time as I was leader of the London Borough of Enfield in the 1960s.

Joe possessed one of the best memories for sporting detail I ever came across. We shared a love both of boxing as well as football. I happened to be in Manchester in September 1944 and found my way to Belle Vue where I saw Jack London beat Freddie Mills for the vacant Heavyweight Championship of Britain. Joe then took me down memory lane by describing the fights he had seen there before the war and Jackie Brown, a world champion, always came to the fore as one of his heroes. When I told him that I had managed to be at White Hart Lane to see Bruce Woodcock take the title from Jack London he was able to remind me of every other fight on the bill! It was the same with football, for every great era for Manchester City he was able to recite the whole of the team right through the years and until the end was a great supporter for boxing, football and rugby, being a member of the appropriate parliamentary group.

He always enjoyed the annual dinner – he even enjoyed the one where the guest of honour was Alex Ferguson. There are many a member of both Commons and Lords who have cause to be grateful to Joe for ensuring that tickets for events were forthcoming.

One of the first ports of call for any new Labour Peers was to be directed to Joe in order to be told the facts of life as seen from the shop floor, a place Joe had occupied for many years ago in that forcing ground for trade unionism, engineering and Trafford Park. He was a lifelong member of the old AEU and a contemporary of Hughie Scanlon who introduced Joe when he came to the Lords.

Joe was an emotional man. I will never forget the passion he brought to the debates in the Lords following the IRA bombing of central Manchester. When Joe was aroused there was no finer orator in either chamber or in any forum. He was a good man to have on your side and woe betide you if he wasn't.

He leaves behind him a record of achievement for the people he served and from which he sprang, of which we could all take intense satisfaction. He was good company and his Labour colleagues mourn the passing of a good man who served us all well.

The House Magazine, 15 March 1999

Lord Ennals of Norwich 1922–1995

Those of us who have known and admired David Ennals over the years were not completely surprised when just a few weeks ago, he announced to the world that he had inoperable cancer. Despite that enormous burden, he remained steadfast to the end to all those causes and people he had worked with for more than 50 years. When I visited him in the Royal Free Hospital recently he told me that he had three ambitions which he hoped he would be spared for. In no particular order they were to see Labour win the next election, to finish a book he was writing and to see the year 2000. I told him to settle for the last and let the others take their course. 'Twas not to be and the very sad news that David passed away peacefully at home with his loved ones still came as something of a shock, and the cause of grief around the Palace of Westminster.

In other obituaries you will find lists of his achievements and his successes. They were many and they were great. When I entered the Commons in 1974 he was already on the 'up' escalator, having entered the

Commons himself in 1964 where he quickly earned the confidence of Harold Wilson who promoted him up to the rank of Minister of State. When James Callaghan became Prime Minister in 1976 he gave David the post for which he will be most remembered – Secretary of State for both Health and Social Security. He loved that responsibility and brought his special brand of compassion and caring to a post which required both – and a great deal more.

Not unexpectedly from a man who had filled the post of Overseas Secretary of the Labour Party with distinction, his energy knew no bounds in his later years as he responded to calls for his attendance at international seminars in every conceivable corner of the world. That he did it and yet never let his party down in the Lords is one of life's unexplained mysteries. The United Nations and the Anti-Apartheid Movement were just two who benefited enormously from his deep commitment, as well as all of the trials and tribulations of that far away country Tibet.

When Fred Mulley died he had attended the House the night before and voted in a defeat for the Government. When I spoke to David's son Paul less than 48 hours before David died, I asked him to tell David that on that Thursday night we would be springing what is euphemistically called 'an ambush' which we would win – and that we would be voting for David. When he was told by his family the next day that we had indeed beaten the Government, his nurses said that they detected an immediate improve-ment in his condition, and that David gave a great big grin and the thumbs up sign. He died the next day.

As Captain Ennals he landed on the Normandy beaches not on D-Day but 12 hours earlier. He was in charge of a group who had the task of radioing intelligence from the sand dunes back to the warships. Two weeks later he was badly wounded, captured and then released by advancing Americans. His limp and awkwardly held arm remained a constant reminder of those painful experiences.

David never pulled rank. There can have been few ex-Cabinet ministers who more cheerfully accepted the burden of that high office and who wanted to play their full part for their party in the Lords. Labour colleagues have lost a good comrade. Parliament and the country have lost a great servant, and the human race has lost one of its best and a lovely man.

The House Magazine, 26 June 1995

Lord Gormley 1917–1993

Although those of us who are fortunate enough to be offered and accept a peerage get used to the 'm'lord' style of address, often from our friends who enjoy the honour as much as we do, I just cannot recall anyone in these later years who did not call Lord Gormley 'Joe'. His life and his work as well as his achievements came before he entered the Lords in 1982, sadly to coincide with a stroke which denied him the platform I know he looked forward to using from the red leather benches in the House. I had the great – yes the great – thrill of sitting there with him in 1983/84 before he accepted that his opportunities to continue to defend the miners and mining communities he loved would become increasingly rare. As I would come through the swing doors of Peers' Entrance, Joe was often sitting there, squeezing a rubber ball in his hand, and to the enquiry of 'How are you Joe?' came the regular reply 'I'm all right. I'm getting better. I'm glad to be here'.

Joe and his life long mate, Nellie, were Lancashire through and through, as well as of mining stock. His autobiography *Battered Cherub* is one of the easiest reads there is, especially for someone like me who comes from Northumbrian mining stock and lived for a time in a pit village. If you want to catch the flavour of both his book and his life just look at the title of the first chapter – 'Clogs and Ferrets'. It tells it all. It is clear that Joe was one of nature's natural leaders, for from his early life at Bold colliery (St Helens) until his retirement from the presidency of the National Union of Mineworkers he displayed the cunning and the courage which, in the proper proportions, is transparent and acclaimed by those who are looking for leadership. His base was Lancashire – just as that of Arthur Scargill's was Yorkshire.

Arising from his joint lifelong rise up the ladder towards the top within the Labour Party he served for many years on the National Executive Committee and rubbed shoulders with Harold Wilson, Jim Callaghan and Barbara Castle. Unlike some who served at the top, without very much evidence of an apprenticeship, Joe had worked within the Labour Party at ward and constituency level long before he represented his miners at the top. He also found time to serve on the magisterial bench.

All this made him a powerful advocate for his people, be they miners or Labour voters and their families. He was not only successful but popular within his union. But his bluff no-nonsense style was a winner with the public too, by comparison with the reign of his successor. It is true to say that Joe was the acceptable face of trade union moderation, a first class ambassador for all he represented and a wonderful man with his lovely wife Nellie whenever there was time for social events such as at the conferences. He was a pint of beer man and his table was never quiet, for it was a mecca for the host within the Labour Movement for whom Joe was a great and popular man.

Joe brought added dignity to the miners, for they had long earned and enjoyed a high place in the league of Britain's industrial workers. Joe was fiercely jealous of the struggle that, not only he, those he had worked with had fought and overcome. The concluding works of *Battered Cherub* are a testament and a valediction to his life and his work.

'During my presidency almost exactly 600 men were killed in the pits. Coal is not cheap. But if during that same period I succeeded in making the miners feel proud to be miners again, and in making the country realize the value of the industry again, I will be able to look back and feel I have achieved something worthwhile. Above all else, I was proud to be the President of the National Union of Mineworkers.'

The House Magazine, 14 June 1993

Lord Hirshfield 1913–1993

Desmond Barel Hirshfield was one of Harold Wilson's Life Peers who was elevated in 1967 at the age of 55 after a then lifetime of support for the Labour Party behind the scenes. Not a backroom boy but one who had not sought service to the party by seeking elected office, but one who gave his talent and expertise to the party in the form of advice based on his professional judgements and experience. Thus Desmond Hirshfield, who was a chartered accountant by profession, came to the attention of Harold Wilson when his accounting firm acted as the accountant to the Labour Party and when Harold Wilson was the supreme manager and organizer of all things Labour. There is little doubt that this 'hands on' experience will have impressed Harold Wilson with his business acumen and shrewdness and he marked him down for service to the Labour Party from the red benches of the Lords. He was one of the earliest members of the Jewish community to be so chosen.

Desmond Hirshfield was the son of Leopold and his family was a traditional Jewish one, and throughout his life he gave generously of his time and talent to Jewish good causes, following the family tradition. For instance his 30 years devoted service to the Norwood Child Care Project brought him tributes from a wide circle of friends.

He was highly respected within the accounting profession and he and his firm became acknowledged experts in trade union finance and practice. This led to his appointment and creation of the Trade Union Trust Managers Ltd in 1961 where he served as chairman until 1983. During this period he served on the Top Salaries Review Body from 1976 to 1984 as well as being a member of the Committee on Consumer Credit (1968–71) and of the Central Advisory Water Committee (1969–70). He was a member of the Court of Governors of the London School of Economics, and served as deputy chairman of the Northampton Development Corporation (1968–1976).

In his private life he was a charming and much loved figure who had risen in life from the humble beginnings. Born in Birmingham he spent much of his childhood in Merthyr Tydfil, South Wales, (his father, a dentist, practised in Aberfan) and then on to the City of London School.

In 1934, at the age of 21, he captained the British team at the World Maccibi Games in Prague. Speaking to his wife Bronia (who had a son from her first marriage) she conveyed to me something of the rich political and social life they both enjoyed in the immediate post-war years and on into the present day. Desmond Hirshfield was a shrewd and successful accountant with political leanings to the Left, but genuinely motivated in his desire to give the workers – especially trade unions – a slice of the action as well as a slice of the profits of their labours.

As he talked about his ideas and produced his schemes designed to ensure fair reward and protection he met and was a friend of the leaders of the Labour movement and party during those years – 'Clement Attlee and Hugh Gaitskell and their wives were our friends, and we spent many a happy weekend in each others homes putting the flesh on the bones of Desmond's ideas. Harold Lever, Tony Greenwood and Ray Gunter were others we were closely involved with,' she told me. His painting skills were such that he was able to stage more than one exhibition of his work. Desmond Hirshfield will be remembered with affection and respect.

The House Magazine, 20 December 1993

Rt Hon Lord Houghton of Sowerby 1898–1996

Douglas Houghton was born in Long Eaton, Derbyshire, in 1898, where the headmaster of the school he attended was the father of Richard, now Lord Attenborough. By the time the First World War began in 1914, he had commenced work as a civil servant in the Inland Revenue Branch. He told me that every one of more than 100 entrants with him joined up and served in the forces. Douglas had a hard war, serving in the Civil Service Rifle Corps and seeing action in more than one battle but especially at that horror of carnage – Paschendaele. I once asked him to describe it to me and he said mud – nothing but mud, dodging into shell holes and being filled with terror, was how he recalled this awful experience which stayed with him for the rest of his life.

Leaving the Army, he rose up the ladder of the Trade Union Movement, for he became the General Secretary of the Inland Revenue Staff Association where, for a time his assistant was one James Callaghan.

Harold Wilson made him Minister without Portfolio, and later, in 1967, he took on a veritable bed of nails when he became the Chairman of the Parliamentary Labour Party. He told me 'Wilson who had, as Leader, been the Chairman of the PLP, wanted me in his place, not just to relieve him of the burden, but also to deal with a difficult situation. All too often, as soon as the PLP meeting ended Members would leak selectively to the press who waited outside. I decided to spike their guns by calling an immediate press conference after each meeting. Thus, leaks ceased and we all got a fair press.'

All his life, Douglas had been a supporter of animal welfare causes, serving for many years as President of the League Against Cruel Sports and in Parliament on the All-Party Group for Animal Welfare. He never settled merely for a place on a committee, he was a crusader, his piercing voice ringing round the Chamber. Standing not taller than five feet he adopted a pugnacious challenging stance and was as passionate an advocate as one could wish. When Kenneth Baker, as Home Secretary, brought in the Dangerous Dogs Bill in 1991, as a result of some horrendous incidents when pit bull terriers caused dreadful injuries to children, it was strenuously condemned by Douglas as far too draconian and left far too much power in the hands of the police and the magistrates. 'Buster' and 'Dempsey' were dogs achieving national fame as a result of the fight put up for their lives by Douglas and others. His final parliamentary battle was to introduce his Dangerous Dogs (Amendment) Bill and from a wheelchair, on April 2, he defiantly shouted 'I move' when his Bill was read – unchallenged – for the third time. A well attended House growled its approval not only for the passing of the Bill, but in tribute to the spirit of this indefatigable parliamentary battler. We all sensed that this could well be the last time we would see and hear this deeply committed human being.

And so it proved to be. A journey from the hell of Paschendaele, to the pinnacle of the Trades Union Movement, into the Cabinet and thence onto the national stage as a defender of animals, propelled him into the hearts of millions, but especially into the affection of parliamentarians over the past 50 years.

The House Magazine

Rt Hon Lord Howell of Aston Manor

As the news of the death of Dennis Howell circulated around Westminster there was a true sense of sadness that we had all lost a dear friend and that the world was the poorer for his passing. He laughed at himself. He came to Edmonton to speak at our constituency dinner some years ago, and noting that we were cheek by jowl with Tottenham regaled us with tales of his exploits as a referee at White Hart Lane. 'One day when I was under stress I refused to give a free kick for an infringement. A Spurs player said out loud that I must have been blind not to see the foul. I said aggressively "what did you say?" only for him to tell all and sundry that the ref was not only blind but deaf as well!'

Like me he started his political journey from within the council chamber and also like me he fought one Tory seat before reaching Westminster representing Birmingham All Saints. My unsuccessful fight was against Iain MacLeod in Enfield West. He too lost that first seat but was to come to represent Small Heath for more than 30 years during which he blossomed into one of the most likeable parliamentarians of his or many other generations.

Whilst some say that he was not an orator they surely had not heard him orate on matters affecting Birmingham. One of my abiding memories is of Dennis becoming almost incoherent with rage when he was describing the state of the National Health Service in Birmingham, and especially when he was on his feet complaining about the lot of those in mental hospitals. Other speeches I can recall without effort were his speeches on the Football Spectators Bill which the then government sought to make a statute to ban spectators from football grounds if they did not carry an identity card.

Whilst he proudly carried his title of Lord Howell of Aston Manor he had at first tried to persuade the Garter King of Arms to allow him the title of 'Lord Howell of Aston Villa'. Garter won.

Like many, many other members of your Lordships House, Dennis did a virtual full time job for his favourite charities and sporting events, being in constant demand to open, close and wish well for many a good cause. It was while performing at such an event that he collapsed and subsequently died. For some time we knew that the Dennis of old was slowly fading before our eyes, him having suffered earlier heart attacks, and I suspect never fully getting over the tragic loss of his son David some 12 years ago, and of his wife Brenda and David having a miraculous escape from an IRA car bomb attack in 1974.

I will remember him as a shrewd political operator, with great deeds to his credit as he planned and plotted for the Labour Party he loved. When he had determined what was right – usually himself – he fought his corner until the cause was lost. To have him on your side was a head start – to have him as an opponent gave you that sinking feeling that this battle would be hard fought. We have lost a Westminster character who will be missed, none more so than in his native city, but especially by Brenda and his remaining children.

The House Magazine, 27 April 1998

Rt Hon Lord Jay of Battersea 1907–1996

Douglas was educated at Winchester and New College Oxford and at the age of 23 became a fellow of All Souls. Before the war he was an economic journalist, serving on the staff of *The Times* from 1929–33, then *The Economist* 1933–1937 before going on to the *Daily Herald* 1937–1940. It was in 1940 that he entered the ranks of civil servants when he became an Assistant Secretary at the Ministry of Supply and in 1943 he became Principal Assistant Secretary at the Board of Trade. Some 20 years later he was to return to this department, but as President of the Board in Harold Wilson's first administration.

As would be expected of a parliamentarian of his stature, Douglas gave us an insight into his world when he wrote his autobiography in 1980 – *Change and Fortune – a Political Record.* It is a record of work rather than private or family life. A glance at the index shows the breadth of his experience and of those he met and worked with over 50 years in public life; Konrad Adenauer; Stanley Baldwin; Lord Beaverbrook; Isaiah Berlin; William Beveridge; Chou-En-Lai; Winston Churchill; De Gaulle; Eisenhower; Gandhi.

In such a pivotal role as President of the Board of Trade allied to his profound knowledge of economic affairs, he was deeply involved in 1966/67 as Harold Wilson sought to change Labour policy. Then resting on the opposition to entry into the Commons Market, postulated by Hugh Gaitskell in the early sixties. As Wilson and his Foreign Secretary, George Brown, changed Labour's policy to that of seeking membership, Douglas was heavily involved, with others, in arguing the case for EFTA (European Free Trade Area) allied to a passionate advocacy for retaining viable trade arrangements with the Commonwealth countries.

It was in August 1967 that Douglas records in his book – *Change and Fortune* – 'To find oneself suddenly bereft without warning, as I did on Sunday 27 August 1967, of one's current job and cherished projects, one's office and one's trusted colleagues, is a strange experience.' Earlier he told us of the manner in which he was sacked. 'On 25 August I had a phone call to meet Wilson in Plymouth the next day. He then told me he was dropping me from the Government, because he was instituting an unwritten principle that all Ministers should retire at 60, and I had passed this watershed by six months. I asked if he had any complaint about my record at the Board of Trade and he said "None", adding that it all had nothing to do with the Common Market or what he called "The Press Campaigns" against me. This I no more believed than did anyone else.'

Douglas married first Peggy, who in her own right was a prominent figure in London County Council circles, especially in the realm of education and the welfare of children. They had two sons, Martin and Peter, and two daughters, Catherine and Helen (twins). The marriage came to an end in 1972 whereafter he was married, for the second time, to Mary who was at his side at their home in Minister Lovell, Oxfordshire when he died. Let his epitaph come from the closing words of *Change and Fortune*. After parading the qualities and character of Athens and Sparta – Left and Right – he proclaimed his love of Britain and the British people thus; 'What other country after all, has preserved an unbroken record of constitutional Government for nearly 300 years, and fought right through the two great wars, without attacking anyone else, or being attacked themselves, to eventual Victory? In a morass of transient controversies let us not forget that. It is one reason why I can conceive of no better fortune when the time comes to cultivate private rather than public aspirations, than to live, love, garden and die deep in the English Country.' Labour colleagues have lost a dear friend, and Parliament mourns the passing of a statesman of the first rank.

The House Magazine, 18 March 1996

Lord Jacques of Portsea Island 1905–1995

Lord John Jacques was a unique and distinct character in at least five separate spheres of activity and he left his mark wherever he went. A Co-operative official serving at the highest level; as a leader in education and accountancy; in the City of Portsmouth where he lived for more than 50 years serving on the Magisterial Bench; in the world of retailing where his talents were recognized by the giants of that industry; and in the House of Lords where his tenacity in defending the Labour Governments of Harold Wilson and James Callaghan earned him the deep affection of Michael Foot who was the Secretary of State for Employment.

John Jacques, born in Ashington in the heart of the Northumbrian coalfields, stood less than five feet in height, an attribute which stood him in good stead when he started work in 1918 – where else but down the pit. Not for long, for his mother was a great Co-operator, and it was with the Ashington Co-operative Society in his teens that he began that remarkable journey. He quickly developed a keen interest in the philosophy of Cooperation as well as mastering the intricacies of taxation and accountancy. This took him to the Co-operative College then based in Manchester where he obtained a BA Degree in Commerce at Manchester University. It also led to him writing the definitive works for Co-operative students in Co-operative Law and Taxation.

It was from that base in Portsmouth that John Jacques went forth as the representative of the Portsea Island Mutual Co-operative Society (PIMCO) and rose up the Co-operative ladder. There were perhaps two especial periods. In 1956 the Co-operative Movement recognized that after being in the market place for more than 100 years it was time to reassess the direction in which it was to go. An Independent Commission was formed with Hugh Gaitskell as Chairman, and Tony Crosland as Secretary, its main recommendation being to drastically reduce the number of separate independent societies.

From 700 then, by voluntary amalgamation, they were reduced to less than 50. At that time John received the accolade given to few – the Presidency of the annual parliament of the Co-operative Movement – Co-operative Congress. In 1961, the Labour Party sent as its fraternal delegate, Harold Wilson, who sat on the platform and heard John deliver what was acknowledged as an outstanding Presidential Address. Harold told me later that it was that speech which caused him to make a note of John Jacques as a candidate for the House of Lords and in 1968, John became Lord Jacques of Portsea Island. He started yet another career.

He quickly entered the Whips Office, and with his background in wages negotiations (on the employers' side) his appointment as the Employment Whip was a natural. At the Despatch Box he was concise, lucid and disarmingly simple – but when he was in a fight he gave more than he got. His Minister was Michael Foot, and Michael never stops telling of how dependable John was as his representative in the Lords. In Opposition during the next 15 years, he was Mr Dependable himself, never ever missing an important vote and never leaving the House until he had cleared himself with the Whips.

The Labour ranks in both Houses proudly registered the fact that there are still those who began their working life as miners and who rose to the top – in John's case to the very top. He married first Constance and had two sons and a daughter. When she died he was fortunate to find further happiness with Violet who had been made a widow when her husband, John's younger brother Billy, died. We mourn the passing of a great Co-operator, a good comrade and a lovely man.

The House Magazine, 15 January 1996

Lord John-Mackie 1909–1994

The sad news that John Mackie had died reached us in the House of Lords on the morning the House rose for the Whitsun Recess. Although not normally able to intervene in debate or Questions it so happened that there was a question involving 'the usual channels' that morning, and so I took the opportunity to pay tribute to John in the Chamber he so loved and had enlivened for many years. That it was in the presence of his brother George was fitting, and as Viscount Ullswater, the Government Chief Whip, was able to share our expressions of sympathy it made the shock of our loss a little more bearable.

When he came before the selection conference for the safe Labour seat of Enfield East in 1958 he could claim the unusual local connection for a

Labour selection conference of being a farmer at nearby Nazeing. Prior to arriving successfully on the Enfield scene, John had stood up to be shot at in earlier elections at North Angus and Mearns in 1951 and at Lanark in 1955. I can truly say that John Mackie was taken to the hearts of the hard working North London constituency, not least because I lived and worked there but also because I was the Leader of the Enfield Council for much of his 15 years. We developed a good working relationship in which I supplied him with intelligence on the manner in which his constituents were living so that he articulated on their behalf on the Floor of the Commons. In turn, he provided me with valuable information. When I was faced with the knowledge that a petition containing thousands of signatures against comprehensive education had been presented (by Iain Macleod) to Parliament I asked John to examine it and he was able to give me scores of addresses from all round the country which had been pleaded in aid as local interests. Incidentally Ralph Harris (now Lord Harris of High Cross) played a part in those controversies some 30 years ago as a local resident legitimately affected.

Always a firm supporter of the Common Market, he never hid this from his constituency party. In 1971 he was due to be endorsed for the new shaped Enfield North constituency, normally a formality, but he allowed this to be delayed beyond October 1971, when he was one of the 69 who voted against Labour's three line whip on entry. (Incidentally – along with John Smith and Ivor Richard). As a result John had to go through a second selection after a tied vote at first bite. He decided to retire in 1973 when he became disenchanted with the party policy to be succeeded by Bryan Davies. It was wholly fitting that he was appointed Chairman of the Forestry Commission by Harold Wilson and he used most effectively this experience many times in subsequent years in debates in the Lords.

John was one of the six children of an illustrious father, Maitland Mackie, and his brother George, who sat with him in the Lords for many years, also saw service in the Commons but adorning a different party – the Liberals and now the Liberal Democrats. They often spoke in the same debates in the Lords and although they jousted in jest, they never openly quarrelled.

I would now wish to speak as John's Chief Whip, for whatever other interests or activities engaged his time and mind, John was always a political animal. I well recall how desolate John was at the death of his great friend, Aneurin Bevan, when he returned from his funeral on that bleak Welsh mountainside. John had prepared himself for the day that he was to be laid to rest. Forty years ago he stored fine English oak grown on his own farm which was made into his coffin. On June 1st, just four days short of his diamond wedding anniversary, he made a farewell tour of his farm in the company of all his family on a farm tractor, which then proceeded to convey him to Nazeing parish church. The Co-op made all other arrangements. John would have liked that, as we all did, when we sang the final hymn at the service – 'We plough the fields and scatter the good seeds on the land.'

Lord Kagan 1915–1995

The House of Lords counts amongst its members a number with an incredible story to tell. Prisoners of war – and those escaped. Those who landed on the beaches on D-Day. Those who flew with incredible bravery. Joe Kagan was a Jew who survived living under the Nazis during the war. By any accounts, he had a story to tell. He was a textile manufacturer's son, educated at Leeds University where he took a degree in commerce. When he spoke in debates in the Lords, his speeches were enriched by references to his earlier life and his continuing association with Lithuania. The popular prints have had a field day in retelling – some of it was accurate – the purple passage in his stormy life during the 1960s and 70s when he shot to national prominence as the inventor of the Gannex raincoat, his fall from grace and then silence.

Rabbi Hugo Gryn said at his funeral that Joe had asked him to tell those who attended to rejoice. It was not a sad day but a day to be thankful. Gilbert Gray QC said that for many years they had both agreed to speak at the other's funeral and that just before Christmas, Joe had asked to be released from that commitment. The well filled Golders Green Crematorium looked on, content that Joe had kept his humour and his peace of mind right to the end. When I visited him in the Brompton Heart Hospital in December, I found him still full of ideas and political talk. He had a good record for attendance and voting and had many friends all round the House. With the death of Joe Kagan, we have lost someone with a unique experience of terrible times and have lost a good comrade who will be missed by many. He leaves a wife, Margaret, two sons and a daughter.

The House Magazine, 13 February 1995

Lord Leatherland 1898–1992

'Old soldiers never die, they only fade away' could well be an epitaph which rested on the wiry frame of Charlie Leatherland with both dignity and comfort, for he was one of that fast diminishing band of those who served in the trenches of the First World War from the outset and through to its bloody end. Understating his age, he enrolled in the Royal Warwickshire Regiment in 1914 and at the age of 18 was a Company Sergeant Major in a machine gun regiment. Mentioned in despatches and earning the Military Service Medal, he saw action on many fronts, and often managed to make reference to this episode in his life of which he and his many friends were justifiably proud. On one such occasion, amongst his Labour Peers, he reminded them that he was speaking as an old soldier, one who saw action on the Somme. All who heard him knew they were listening to a real old soldier, only to have another First War veteran Lord Houghton of Sowerby, who is just four months younger, tell us that he fought at Paschendaele – another bloody and horrific battlefield. They don't make them like that any more!

He was an alderman on Essex County Council from 1946 to 1968 and was Chairman of the Council in 1960–61. He was closely involved in the creation of the University of Essex and besides being a member of the University Council for many years, he was also, for a time, the Treasurer of the University. Not unexpectedly the University awarded him an Honorary Doctorate and he was made a Life Member of the University Court. He had been a Deputy Lieutenant of Essex and a member of Basildon Development Corporation during its formative years. His daughter Irene reckoned his part in creating the University was the most satisfying of his whole life.

Lord Leatherland was, by profession, a journalist and he rose to become the Assistant Editor of the *Daily Herald,* albeit towards the twilight of that great paper of the Labour Movement.

Incidentally, his editor at the time was John Beavan, the paper's last editor, and now a colleague on the Labour benches in the Lords, sitting as Lord Ardwick of Barnes. Because of his newspaper experience, he was a member of the Monopolies and Mergers inquiry into newspaper mergers. He was intensely proud of the fact that he had been awarded four Prince of Wales Gold Medals for social and economic essays in 1923 and 1924, and of his membership of the Royal Economic Society.

Those who grow old in a service they adore are fortunate indeed. Despite the fact that injuries sustained on war service (a bullet wound in his left knee) dogged him to the end, he remained cheerful and generous, a good companion and a remarkable man. He was one of those venerable socialists who burnished their own reputation and that of the Labour Party in service to the end. Along with such as Manny Shinwell, Hervey Rhodes, Fenner Brockway, Gerald Gardiner and Michael Stewart – all of whom sat on Labour's benches in the Lords with him, and in my time there since 1983 – Charlie Leatherland was a noble old soldier in the service of his beloved Labour Party. His many friends, all around the House, mourn the passing of a great man.

Baroness Lestor of Eccles 1932–1998

During the count at the General Election of 1983, my wife Margaret whispered that Labour had lost Harlow, and I knew that my good friend Stan Newens had lost a seat for the second time. Later she told me that we had lost Eton and Slough and my heart sank. Not only was my friend Joan Lestor to leave the Commons, but if they had lost their seats with majorities of three thousand and more, my majority in Edmonton of a bare 2000 would not survive. And so it proved to be. To me, to lose Joan from Labour's fighting force in the Commons was akin to the shock of the loss of Shirley Williams at the 1979 Election. And while Shirley came back into the Commons for a different seat – and a different party – Joan was to return in triumph succeeding her good friend Lewis Carter-Jones at Eccles for the same party she had loved for so long.

It was from the local government school of apprenticeship that she made it there in 1966 first on the Wandsworth Council and then that school for budding parliamentarians – the LCC. She had been brought up by a father who was prominent in the Socialist Party of Great Britain, a party Joan subsequently joined before joining the Labour Party in 1955. Perhaps it was her studentship at the London School of Economics which provided her with a Diploma in Sociology that set her on a lifetime of interest and commitment to the welfare of children. I think not, for anyone who had talked with Joan for any length of time immediately knew that those commitments were lifelong. They found expression too in the way she devoted herself to bringing up her two children and the delight and joy she found when she became a grandmother, telling the Commons with a big grin on her face: 'We too became a grandmother.'

Joan had the distinction of serving twice as a Junior Minister at the Department of Education, firstly under Harold Wilson in 1969 and then again in 1975. It was from that post that she resigned as a protest at what she saw would be the effect of cuts in expenditure. Not many ministers resign on matters of principle, but in the Labour Party such actions do no harm to the esteem in which you are held.

Undoubtedly of the Left rather than the Right in Labour terms she was seen as one of the acceptable faces of the Left by those on the Right – like me. Thus, when she was elected to the Shadow Cabinet time after time it was with the votes of such as me who voted the slate of the Right – with minor exceptions for Joan and Neil Kinnock. Her refusal to back Tony Benn for the Deputy Leadership of the Party in 1981, together with Neil Kinnock, will be seen in history to have been one of the defining abstentions which altered the course of Party history – even history itself.

She will be remembered as a politician of high principle and steadfast loyalties, no better seen than in her work in the field of Overseas Aid, the portfolio she held in the Shadow Cabinet when she retired in 1996. She numbered many leaders from the Third World amongst her friends, and she was enraptured when one of them – Nelson Mandela – paid his State Visit to Britain in 1996. Parliament and the people of Britain have lost a dedicated public servant and those who knew her best have lost a lovely companion and a beautiful friend.

The House Magazine, 6 April 1998

Rt Hon Earl of Listowel GCMG 1906–1997

There can be few who enjoyed life so much as Billy, and to the end he retained an infectious interest in the workings of Parliament. The Leader of the House, Lord Cranborne, led tributes to him the day after he died, and he reminded us that he had been a member of the House of Lords since 1931, taking his seat in 1932. Thus, as he was proud to say, Billy had been a member for more than 65 years, and at his death he was the oldest active member of the Lords. Even though I had marvelled at the length and breadth of his service, I learned with many others the true extent of that outstanding contribution only when he had gone. Each compartment of that busy life is full of incident and for the greater recording of some of the outstanding achievements, I list them.

Before he came onto the parliamentary scene in 1932 he had nailed his colours to the mast in his university years at both Oxford and Cambridge. It is recorded that at the Union he had spoken in support of the Miners' Leader, A.J. Cook, and that he had worked at Toynbee Hall in the East End as Clem Attlee had done before him. Whilst his brother John Hare was later to become Lord Blakenham and Chairman of the Conservative Party, his other brother Alan became an officer in MI6 and subsequently became Chairman of the Financial Times. Bill plunged into Westminster affairs with great effect. In time he became the Deputy Leader of the Lords due to there being so few Labour Peers and before that, due to his recognized expertise on Far Eastern affairs, he was made Under Secretary to the India Office in Churchill's war time coalition government. Lord Hailsham is the only other surviving member of that administration. He had also been Labour's Chief Whip during the war years, so that when Labour came to power in 1945 he was well equipped to serve at the highest levels. First he was Paymaster General, then Secretary of State for India, then Secretary of State for Burma and the Minister of State for Colonial Affairs.

Until the fall of the Attlee Government he served as Parliamentary Secretary at the Ministry of Agriculture and Fisheries. His experience and sympathy for their cause eventually led to his appointment during the Macmillan Government, as Governor General of Ghana at the direct request of the new independent country's first Prime Minister, Kwame Nkruma.

In 1994 he made his last speech on the Report to the House by a Committee chaired by Lord Walton of Detchant on 'Medical Ethics' in which he said 'I cannot agree with the first of the summary of conclusions which says "We recommend that there be no change in the law to permit euthanasia". Since 1935 when the Voluntary Euthanasia Society was first formed by two doctors who asked me to join them I have been advocating a change in the law which would allow a doctor to terminate, with the patient's consent, the life of a terminally ill or incurable patient but that could only take place after the patient submitted a document called an "advance directive" informing his doctor what sort of treatment, if any he wished to be given in the event of contracting an incurable or terminal illness.'

His last letter was sent a week before he died on receipt of flowers and best wishes from his colleagues. It concluded by saying 'I am sad to be missing the build up to the General Election and look forward to catching up on Hansard and the news generally' and then he penned in his own writing 'and victory!' He will be missed by many throughout the world, none more so than on the Labour Benches, and our deepest sympathy is extended to his wife Pamela, Countess of Listowel and members of his family.

The House Magazine, 13 March 1997

Rt Hon Baroness Llewelyn-Davies of Hastoe 1915–1997

Bertie Denham was a legend in his own lifetime and made his performance as Captain of her Majesty's Bodyguard of the Honourable Corps of Gentlemen-at-Arms a fitting one to disguise the fact that he was the Government Chief Whip in the House of Lords – and a very good one too. From time to time those same Gentlemen invited their Captain to join them for dinner when the principal guests were Her Majesty and Prince Philip. He had the opportunity to invite two personal guests and one year he invited Black Rod and me when I served as his 'Shadow'. It was a great privilege, which I appreciated very much. It was then in St James' Palace as I sat amongst the Queen's Bodyguard that they regaled me with their memories of the first and only woman to occupy that position as their Captain. Pat Llewelyn-Davies made a great impression. They proudly displayed a unique photograph of Pat standing at their head dressed in an outstandingly smart uniform and carrying a stave of authority – every inch a Captain and every inch a lady. They told me they all loved her – and I knew that they meant it.

There are those in the Lords today who knew Pat long before she made it to the national political scene – from her days in Cambridge and as a young civil servant where she had as a friend Victor Rothschild (later Lord) and Anthony Blunt. As Patricia Parry, together with her friend Tess Mayor, Rothschild was to let his London flat to them and when they subsequently sublet part to Blunt – and Guy Burgess – it gained them some notoriety years later when they both were central to the spy scandals which rocked Britain during the 1950s.

Whilst it will be as an outstanding Chief Whip in both Opposition and in Government that Pat will be most remembered, she also built up a record of achievement and involvement in the affairs of the House of Lords, which will long be remembered and talked about with much laughter and love. She laughed easily, and her face would often crease up into what I can only describe as a beautiful smile. She bustled rather than walked our corridors of power and stood no nonsense from those who came to the Lords from Cabinet and other high places. All were the same, no one was spared and she got the maximum out of her troops. One such possible malcontent was Manny Shinwell, causing her to say on one exasperating occasion 'I am about to propose a motion for the abolition of everybody over the age of 90!' She was in her place on the Privy Council bench, however, when Manny rose on his 100th birthday to regale the House with his own special brand of humour and wisdom.

Until towards the end she insisted on serving on important House Committees and sitting on the Woolsack. She encouraged many younger and new members. She was a formidable member of that group in the Lords who came there from Cambridge and Cambridgeshire political life – by no means all of them on the Labour benches.

My memory of her is my door as the Opposition Chief Whip being slowly opened and the puckish face of Pat coming into view and then having a serious discussion on a matter of the day, which had exercised her mind. She never ever rose to cause trouble, for she had by then become mistress of the art of making friends and influencing events, which she did to the end. Her last years were made easier by the love and affection shown to her by Lord Cub Alport, who provided a warm place of comfort and protection, which we all appreciated. The Labour Group of Peers, the House of Lords and the nation are the poorer for her passing and our love and thoughts are extended to her three daughters Melissa, Harriet Rose and Rebecca.

The House Magazine, 1 December 1997

Rt Hon Earl of Longford KG 1905–2001

'An aristocrat who embraced public life and campaigned for prisoners and against pornography,' So ran one of the fulsome tributes made to Lord Longford when the news of his death was brought to us in early August. The fact that it was on the anniversary of the day Britain went to war with Germany in 1914 had a certain ring about it – and him. He leaves behind a wonderful record of having been there, done that, and enjoyed himself at most stages of his life. Those of us who witnessed the swift decline in his physical wellbeing during his last weeks, when he had to have recourse to a wheelchair, will put that image to one side, for he was someone who stood up, spoke up and was proud to be counted on the issues in which he believed passionately. Our abiding memory is of a quite unique participant in our affairs.

If reference needs be made to his ministerial and other posts we have to refer back to the Attlee government of 1945–50. I remember Tony Blair coming to address Labour Peers when he had first become Leader of the Labour Party in 1994, and hearing him say afterwards that 'When I thought I was quoting a bit of history by referring with gratitude to those who had served in the Attlee Government, I came face to face with some who had indeed been in Attlee's first administration, such as Frank Longford, Arthur Bottomley and Billy Listowel – who had also been in the Churchill coalition government!'

He started off as an Under Secretary in the War Office then moved on to the Duchy of Lancaster with special responsibility for Germany before going on to be the Minister for Aviation. In the dying days of Attlee's government in May 1951 he was promoted to become the First Lord of the Admiralty. Harold Wilson made him Lord Privy Seal and Leader of the House of Lords in 1964, whilst at the same time he was also Secretary of State for the Colonies. But he resigned his official posts in 1968 over disputes concerning Labour's inability to raise the school-leaving age.

When he reached his 90th birthday he held a great party in the home of his daughter Antonia and her husband Harold Pinter. It was an event to treasure and when he invited me to join him to celebrate his 95th birthday in December 2001 I gladly accepted, only to find that my good fortune had led to an invitation that same evening to Number 10 Downing Street where, as the Proposer of the Welcome to the Address from the Throne, I would be let into the secrets of the Queen's Speech the next day. When I explained this to Frank he said 'You must attend Number 10. I will have other birthdays but you will not get another opportunity to welcome the Gracious Speech'. Alas, it was not to be. I once asked him if he had led a happy life. He replied: 'Ted, I have led more than one happy life, but that

of being married to Elizabeth and having such a wonderful family is the
greatest of many happinesses.'

The House Magazine, 1 October 2001

Rt Hon Lord Mellish of Bermondsey 1913–1998 Protector of the Docklands

Bob Mellish was a great Chief Whip during a period when he had the
difficult job of delivering majorities for a Labour Government when he did
not have the troops. His period from 1969 to 1976 saw the tail end of
Harold Wilson's last period. Backing the wrong man for his successor
between Jim Callaghan and Michael Foot cost him his job. He did not
complain for he had enjoyed the confidence and goodwill not only of the
Parliamentary Labour Party but had served at the highest level coming from
lowly beginnings.

No one knew or could understand the character of London Docklands,
nor the people who worked and lived there, better than Bob Mellish. He
had represented them as the Member of Parliament for Bermondsey for 36
years. He was ferocious in defence of their interests, fearless in advocating
their needs and loud in his condemnation of those who sneered at their
rough and ready style. If ever anyone earned the title of 'Dockers' MP' it
was Bob. He had been an official of the Transport and General Workers
Union at the age of 25 and returned from war service in 1945 having
reached the rank of Captain in the Royal Engineers and served in the South
East Asia Command. In the last period of the Attlee Government he began
to climb the ministerial ladder when he became the PPS at the Ministry of
Supply and then Pensions.

Bob was very proud of his roots, and immensely proud to be a Londoner.
I first met him when he came to Enfield in the mid sixties wearing his hat
as the Parliamentary Secretary at the Ministry of Housing, and was
accompanied by Evelyn Dennington, then Chairman of the GLC Housing
Committee. His impassioned plea to us to build more homes to house
Londoners was impressive, and was repeated inside every London Council
Chamber at that time.

It inspired Enfield to pledge to build 1000 new homes a year – a task we
delivered before losing office in that catastrophic year of 1968 when Labour
lost power throughout the land. Bob was inspirational – even evangelical
with his cockney humour and impassioned style. He was a leader in every
sense of the word.

Peter Shore had tried to get what were called 'The riparian boroughs' –
those with Thames frontage – to combine and develop London Docklands.
In the late seventies the area was crying out for new life after centuries of

making London the greatest port in the world. Twas not to be. Local petty jealousies and pride stopped any progress towards a plan to rescue that part of London. Along came Michael Heseltine in 1980 and produced legislation for the creation of Urban Development Corporations. Less democratic but driven by the colossal scale of opportunity and backed by the resources of government. He wanted Bob Mellish to become the Deputy Chairman of the London Docklands Development Corporation. If ever a man was made for that job it was Bob, but he had a dreadful time within the Labour Party for accepting this opportunity – nowhere more so than within his own constituency party, then veering strongly to the Left as most were in the early eighties. He resigned from the Labour Party with a broken heart, and when he came to the Lords he sat on the Crossbenches.

An exception was when the Government tried to legislate for the crowd problems in football by producing the Football Spectators Bill requiring identity cards for football fans. Bob revealed himself as the President of the Millwall Supporters Club and relished this opportunity to turn his special brand of good sense on the Tory benches for a change.

The House Magazine, 25 May 1998

Rt Hon Lord Mulley 1918–1995

In the session ending November 1993, the House of Lords sat on 194 days. Fred Mulley attended on 192 of them. In the session ending November 1994, the House of Lords sat on 142 days, and Fred Mulley attended the House on 138 of them. The night before be died, he attended despite being far from well because I mounted the strongest possible whip in order to secure a better deal for the wife in a divorce and for her to obtain access to the man's pensions to which, as married partners, they had both contributed. The Government was defeated by five votes in a division in excess of 350. The last parliamentary action of Fred was to help to inflict that defeat. His heart too must have been in a second defeat inflicted on the Government, which was to lead to a better deal for war widows. His long and distinguished service as a defence minister during the sixties and seventies gave him added impetus to come to the aid of those whose lives he had held in his capable hands for so long.

Unassuming, sometimes to a painful degree, Fred went about his tasks with both dedication and determination. That he survived more than five years as a prisoner of war is tribute to his spirit, and as I have learned with both awe and pride, there are within the ranks of those who are Members of the House of Lords, on all party benches, those who offered their lives to defend the nation and lived to make that awful experience a springboard for a life of service to others.

His eminence within the hierarchy of the Labour Party stemmed from his solid base within the trade union, but he earned the approval of both Harold Wilson and James Callaghan, who between them saw him appointed to a wide range of ministerial positions, which included Defence (under Denis Healey), Aviation, Foreign Office, Disarmament, Transport and Education. Fred proved to possess one of the safest pair of hands in the business; his dogged defence of any brief was legendary, while he was Mr Courtesy himself to both opponent and supporters alike.

Few can tell of the toll taken out of parliamentarians better than those who served in the Whips Office. Standing by the Tellers' Box as weary colleagues dragged themselves past like zombies at 4.00 a.m. in the morning was a depressing experience. In that period of 1976 to 1979 Fred carried the burden of ministerial responsibilities whilst Labour had no majority in the lobbies. Like all other ministers, he could not be spared the added burden of trudging through the lobbies after a full ministerial day, which frequently included visits to Brussels and Strasbourg.

The House Magazine, 27 March 1995

Lord Pitt of Hampstead 1913–1994

The fact that his family and his host of friends at Westminster and beyond had been expecting the sad news of his death for some time did not diminish or ease the pain felt so keenly when the fear became a reality. No one knew better than he that he had entered the last year of his life in 1993, but until the return of Parliament in October he did not let that prospect affect his cheerful repartee to his many colleagues in the House of Lords. To give you some idea of his diligence, on every single sitting day in that long parliamentary session from May 1992 to November 1993 – 194 days – he attended every one. How's that for a man in his eighties and still burdened with other people's cares?

He had come amongst us here in Britain from his Caribbean island of Grenada more than 60 years ago when he studied medicine at Edinburgh University, and it was there that he began to develop a taste for political life – agitation – that never left him all his life. He told me 'Life was tough for black students in Edinburgh in the thirties. Many devised ways of overcoming discrimination. We developed a network of sympathetic landladies who could be relied on to give rooms to black students. When it came to entertainment we were equally resourceful, avoiding Edinburgh nightspots which excluded blacks, preferring to spend our time together or at student organized events'.

He was an outstanding member of the old LCC and then the Greater London Council. One of my abiding memories is attending his Chairman's

Reception, and standing in line at the bottom of the stairs leading up to the Great Hall. At the top, faces aglow with pleasure and pride, stood David and Dorothy, greeting everyone as if they were the most important guests of the evening, and making it plain beyond doubt that he was proud to be receiving us in the place where his fellow councillors had honoured him.

David was an international statesman; of that there is no doubt. For long years he was the bridge here in Britain and a port of call for leaders of emerging countries throughout the Commonwealth, Kwame Nkrumah, Jomo Kenyatta, Julius Nyerere, Hastings Banda, Kenneth Kaunda, Martin Luther King and of course the man he idolized, Nelson Mandela, recognized his stature and his importance to black people. What a pantheon of black activists who had struggled and won! David could stand tall amongst them all.

His years as a Labour Peer were full of work well done. Undoubtedly becoming the first black man and GP to become the President of the BMA brought great joy and satisfaction to him, his family and his ever widening circle of friends. He showed his great interest in two other fields. He was an outstanding chairman of the housing charity Shelter for many years, and he elevated the importance and value of tourism to London when he served with distinction as the deputy chairman of the London Tourist Board for a long spell.

When he spoke in debates in the House of Lords he was always listened to – quite frankly it was difficult not to listen to him if you were within earshot of the Chamber! He tried to persuade and cajole rather than browbeat; his last words were always a plea and not a threat. When I last enjoyed his always good company and saw him in hospital at the end I knew that he felt he had accomplished much, if not all, of what he could. 'The art of the possible' and the acceptance that there are limits to what can be achieved were ever present in the mind and on the face of David Pitt. From Hampstead, Grenada to Lord Pitt of Hampstead – not bad. Walk tall David.

The House Magazine, 9 January 1995

Lord Ponsonby of Shulbrede

Lord Ponsonby of Shulbrede was Tom to everyone. In the world of Westminster he fitted his role of Labour's Chief Whip in the Lords like a glove. His was a hereditary title. His grandfather was Arthur Ponsonby, Private Secretary to Campbell-Bannerman, who served under Ramsay MacDonald and who was sent to the Lords as Labour's Leader.

I first met Tom when he was Shirley Williams's deputy at the Fabian Society and I was leader of the Enfield Council. His leadership of the Labour Group on the Kensington and Chelsea Council cemented our friendship along with deep involvement in Local Government, especially in

London. When we both began to work together in the Lords we sat on benches stiff with friends we had made over 30 years and who had been leaders of large councils throughout the land. Tom had been Chairman of the GLC, demonstrating his flair for solution making in the interests of Londoners. This feel for finding ways of making local government work brought him the Chairmanship of the Local Government Training Board, which he held until his death. His work for and in the tourist industry was a legend.

Another endearing partnership was with Cledwyn Hughes, Labour's Leader in the Lords. They were a genuine team, and whilst there are democratic groupings and Labour has an impressive Front Bench team, Cledwyn and Tom carried the burden of leadership along corridors and into offices and committee rooms of both Government and Opposition alike. Sometimes they won, sometimes they lost, but always with panache and Labour's best interests at heart.

One of my abiding memories of Tom at work was his unfailing accessibility to his colleagues. As Chief Whip he rarely made it from the Chamber to his room without at least one and often more of his colleagues wanting a word with him. Without fail he would grasp them firmly by the arm and lead them straight to his room. He knew the value of dealing with colleagues as if the issue of the moment was as important to him as it was to them.

Shirley Sheppard and her colleagues served Tom, making the Opposition Whips' office a warm, friendly, efficient place, giving Tom complete confidence and peace of mind that 'back at the ranch' all was well. They mourn the passing of their 'chief'.

Ah those tributes. A stunned and unbelieving House of Lords listened to one poignant speech after another. Every word was exquisitely apposite, delivered with heart stopping sincerity. Lords Belstead, Cledwyn and Jenkins, Baroness Llewelyn-Davies and others deeply moved the whole House. Tom's family and friends listened to this unique Parliamentary occasion from the Distinguished Visitors Gallery. Tom was so lucky in his family who were with his wife Maureen at the end. Maureen was central to Tom's happiness, often with him at events but a stranger to the Palace where Tom was a master. She will have the love of her family to sustain her, but she will know that her family consists of thousands who mourn the passing of a man who earned their love as well as their respect. Many of us noted that Tom's son Fred, now 4th Baron Ponsonby of Shulbrede, was present at that deeply moving moment. He will get more than the traditional growl of 'Hear Hear' when he takes his place on the Labour Benches.

The House Magazine 25 June 1990

Baroness Serota DBE 1919–2002

Bea was one of that impressive list of Labour ladies in local government, sadly now greatly diminished from their heyday of the first 30 years after the end of the war. They had collectively toiled in the vineyards tirelessly to bring about not just Labour local government but a national Labour government. The sixties and seventies were to see them step out of the shadows and into the limelight and to perform brilliantly with their newly acquired powers. Bea was a star.

By the time she entered the House of Lords in 1967 she had behind her a record of service of which anyone could be proud and all the while bringing up a family and being devoted to her husband and to making a loving home for them all.

She was the President of the National Council for the Unmarried Mother and Her Child. To top all that she also found time to chair the Advisory Council on the Penal System.

These are worthy jobs in which Bea was to demonstrate her greatest strengths, common sense and a deep conviction that it was the role of those with advantage to help those who were disadvantaged. But she would tell you that her time as a health minister from 1969 to 1970 brought her great joy. As I enter my local hospital in Epping I am met by a plaque on the wall, which reads, 'This extension was opened by Baroness Serota, Minister for Health, May 14th 1969'.

She was the principal Deputy Chairman of Committees and Chairman of the European Select Committee from 1986 to 1992 and served as a Deputy Chairman until her death. I venture to suggest that there are few – if anyone – who can have had such a long and distinguished record of service at every level. But it may not be for that that she will be remembered. Not only was she a font of all knowledge governmental but she was always, always ready to exchange views with the newest members of your Lordships' House, be it mundane things or matters of high policy.

Bea will not only be missed, she is irreplaceable. There is no one else on the Labour Benches or in the House who carried the same aura of deep, deep respect for the quality and length of service and success.

She was the embodiment of wisdom. The best epitaph to dear Bea is to try to follow her example, and be grateful for having had the privilege of knowing, and loving such a remarkable woman. She is survived by her husband Stanley and a son and a daughter.

The House Magazine, 4 November 2002

Rt Hon Lord Shackleton KG QBE FRS 1911–1994

Eddie Shackleton was born in 1911 and educated at Radley and Magdalen College, Oxford. The explorer instinct, which he must have inherited from his father, led him to become a member of expeditions to Borneo and Greenland in 1932 and 1934. He became the Labour Member of Parliament for Preston in 1946, having tried to turn Epsom to Labour in 1945, and in that first period he was the PPS to Herbert Morrison. He subsequently went on to represent Preston (South Division) from 1950 to 1955, and when he was elevated to the peerage in 1958 he was in a position, with the return of a Labour Government, to become the Minister of Defence for the Royal Air Force in October 1964.

His service in the House of Lords began auspiciously with that appointment but he went on to greater things. He became the Deputy Leader of the House of Lords between January 1967 and 1968, and then from 1968 until the defeat of Harold Wilson's Government in 1970, he was the Leader of the House of Lords, during which service he was the Lord Privy Seal.

Undoubtedly Lord Shackleton's name will be forever commemorated with that of the Falkland Islands. He undertook a survey of the Islands in 1976 and produced an economic study for the Islands in 1982. The past 10 years had seen a staunch parliamentary battle with the Ministry of Defence in respect of the future of HMS *Endurance*. The original *Endurance* was the ship that his father used all those years ago, and it was the 1981 decision to withdraw the previous *Endurance* which was held by many to have sent the wrong message to Argentina about Britain's resolve over the Falklands. In May 1991, the Government announced that the Navy's Antarctic patrol ship *Polar Circle* was to be renamed *Endurance*, and this brought great satisfaction to Lord Shackleton and his many friends for a famous parliamentary victory. It was a campaign he enjoyed, one which enhanced his reputation as a great parliamentarian.

Honours poured onto the shoulders of Eddie Shackleton. He received a Doctorate in Law from the University of Newfoundland and an Honorary DSC from Warwick in 1978. He was awarded the Royal Scottish Geographical Society Medal in 1989 and the Royal Geographical Society Special Gold Medal in 1990. He became an Honorary Companion of the Order of Australia in 1990.

He was passionate in his interest in the protection of and the development of the Antarctic. He occupied a respected place on the Privy Councillor bench in the House of Lords, next to Jim Callaghan, and was a frequent questioner of ministers and in other ways. He was deeply respected and loved by his Labour colleagues and this love and affection was shared all around the House.

The House Magazine, 17 October 1994

Rt Hon Lord Shepherd 1918–2001

The House of Lords suffered the latest hammer blow when it learned of the sudden death of Malcolm Shepherd, formerly the holder of many high offices. Labour Peers were in the middle of their regular Thursday afternoon party meetings when their leader, Margaret Jay, was handed a piece of paper containing the awful news that Malcolm had collapsed and died that very morning whilst on holiday in Lanzarote. Malcolm made up a sad quartet of deaths notified to the House within the past six weeks. First there had been Lord Cledwyn of Penrhos, followed by Lord Mackay of Ardbrecknish who had just assumed the office of Chairman of Committees. This was followed by only two weeks with the death of Michael Cocks and then dear Malcolm. Never short of either wisdom or ability, to lose such able members was a savage blow to the whole House.

If ever there was a man made for the job it must have been Lord Shepherd of Spalding, who at the time of the 1999 reform of the House of Lords Act was one of 18 Labour hereditary Peers. Subsequently, as one of four living ex-leaders of the Lords he was made a Life Peer, thus retaining his right to speak and vote, a right he treasured. He had inherited his title from his father who had played a great part in securing the Labour victory of 1945 when he was the National Labour Party agent. He had been the Labour agent in Blackburn when the Member of Parliament had been the nationally known Philip Snowden. This led to Malcolm's father going on to higher things. When Churchill sent for Attlee in 1940 to consider forming the wartime coalition, Labour was at conference, and Attlee took George Shepherd with him to negotiate the terms of the coalition.

When he died Malcolm succeeded to the title and after some years began to be active in the Lords. In those days there were few Labour Peers, and Malcolm climbed swiftly up the greasy pole, becoming Deputy Opposition Chief Whip, then Opposition Chief Whip, and Government Chief Whip when Wilson came to power in 1964.

He had served in the Royal Army Service Corps and ended the war with the rank of Captain, having seen active service in North Africa where he was in action at El Alamein, then Sicily and Italy. He had become a member of what was called 'Special Services' whose activities were always shrouded in mystery. He would not be drawn on the details of that service, save to say that it had been real – very real – cloak and dagger stuff.

His service at the Foreign Office gave him some anxious moments. It was during the unhappy time of the Biafra turmoil that one of the leading protagonists said: 'This Lord is not our Shepherd' but it was a different reception that he got when he was in charge of giving Gibraltar a new constitution in 1969. This was clear and unambiguous: 'Her Majesty's

Government will never enter into arrangements under which the people of Gibraltar will pass under the sovereignty of another state against their wishes,' Against a background of the then state of relations with Spain, this was met with immense gratitude. Sadly, when Malcolm was due to conclude his holiday in Lanzarote he was to go on to Gibraltar to attend a dinner in his honour, one of many given whenever he visited.

Having endeavoured – not without success – to play a leading part in the affairs of the House of Lords for more than 40 years, it was with a sense of completeness that during the great debates on the reform of the House of Lords Bill he told the House: 'We have talked about change now for many, many years, and it is now time to vote on it.' He did, and voted himself out of a place, only to be brought back as one of a handful of special exceptions. The whole House was glad, as we were saddened by losing such a good man and a good friend.

The House Magazine, 16 April 2001

Rt Hon Lord Shore of Stepney 1924–2001

I was proud to have known and worked with Peter Shore. He was the kindest of men, and the most courteous – both in private conversation and 'on the stump'. Add to that the fact that he was able and articulate and a political pragmatist and you have a picture of a man of considerable stature in the Labour Party, Parliament and the affairs of the nation.

During his high tide in government in 1969 I was one of three speakers invited by the Colchester Labour Party to speak at a rally. The other two were David Basnett and Peter Shore. It was not a good time for the Labour government and Peter had one of the tricky ministerial roles in economic affairs, but he revealed to me at any rate a patience with a sullen audience that I recall with affection. He not only answered the questions but gave a lesson in comradely wisdom that turned potential hostility into warm approval – if not understanding. Again, when I was a Member of Parliament and we approached a general election, he came out to Edmonton in a very busy schedule and charmed my party and many others who needed an uplift in our morale.

When he decided to become a Member of Parliament – for Stepney – it took him some time to attune to the needs of one of the poorest parts of Britain with its even then rich ethnic mix. Together with his neighbour, Ian Mikardo, he forged a partnership on behalf of his constituents, which to this day is proving a lifeline for many. When I paid a visit to a refuge for victims of alcohol and drug abuse on Mile End Road, in my capacity as trustee of a charity, the warden and many workers and residents spoke of all that Peter had done for them including helping to raise £2 million for a new building.

As someone who was on the campaign team which saw James Callaghan victorious and become Prime Minister in 1976, and as a member of the campaign team for Denis Healey which saw him defeated by Michael Foot when Jim resigned, I saw the efforts of Peter to rise to the very top of the slippery pole as courageous attempts by a sincere politician, and the fact that he was rejected more than once as the cruel strokes of political life.

When he came to the Lords in 1997 he joined a veritable band of ex-cabinet colleagues who had made it before him. By then he was suffering failing health, but he was a colleague with a high attendance record. He fought for the things he had believed in for a very long time, and if that meant that he ran counter to the policy of his own frontbench team, then so be it. Especially on all matters relating to the European Community he fought his corner and although what he said was often contrary to my own beliefs, I feel he did so in a voice and with a passion that was both distinctive and arousing. He remained till the end a name on the Annunciator that drew people into the Chamber rather than in the other direction. His contribution to British political life is profound, and all colleagues – on all benches – in the Lords will miss this honest politician.

The House Magazine, 15 October 2001

Lord Soper of Kingsway 1903–1998

Donald Soper was a hero to millions of people. He was to me, for living on Tyneside it was during the war and post-war period that his name, his voice and his beliefs first captivated and then motivated young men and women. When I entered the House of Lords in 1983 I was to meet him, and marvel that a boy from Scotswood Road, Newcastle, could sit on a bench and be the equal of such as Donald Soper. Charisma is not an inappropriate word for Donald, and he was the easiest of companions to talk with. I recall clearly a train journey from Euston of about two hours all of which seemed to evaporate into thin air as we chewed over the matter of the day. That day was the day John Profumo resigned.

In 1983 when I joined the House of Lords there were giants still striding the world of Westminster, household names with resonances much more widely. I sat in thrall as Manny Shinwell spoke with passion on his 100th birthday. Fenner Brockway still able and eloquent. Douglas Houghton still stirred the pews with his staccato delivery. Barbara Wootton was then in her prime, and dear Donald could charm the birds off the trees when he spoke. His was always – to me – the voice of sweet reason. He never preached to us, he argued with us, and convinced many with his rational and compelling delivery.

His forte was the campaign. He was a campaigner par excellence, be it poverty, nuclear disarmament, blood sports, child prostitution, or any manifestation of injustice. He was a socialist and proud to call himself so – a badge he wore with pride but even though we knew where his political beliefs were founded, they never intruded.

When I worked in Leman Street, E1, I counted it as a bonus that I could walk to Tower Hill in five minutes and enjoy the best – free – entertainment and inspiration going. His was a wonderful demonstration to any young aspiring politician of how to deal with a fractious audience or heckler. He never seemed to me to lose his temper, although when he was in full flow it was one of the wonders of the civilized world. Once I saw and heard him in Hyde Park, it was the time of the Soviet march into Prague. I was on the back of a Co-op coal lorry with Alice Bacon, George Brown and Eirene White – surrounded by an estimated 10,000, many of them supporters of Biafra who were demented at the political situation in Nigeria at that time. After 'our show' I hastened to hear Donald speaking to a smaller audience – but better!

Donald was forever grateful for the act of Harold Wilson which sent him there in 1965 – one of Harold's first lists – and as his Chief Whip for seven years in the nineties I can affirm that until his last period he wanted to play a full part in divisions and the life of Parliament.

The House Magazine, 16 January 1999

Lord Underhill 1914–1993

A sense of real and personal loss pervaded the House of Lords when the sad news of the death of Reg Underhill was received. There can be few Peers who made such a mark within a few years, especially as he came to the House without having had the benefit of a period of service in the Commons. Yet his was a name not unknown either at Westminster or, indeed, wherever the 'corridors of power' are alleged to rest. And while far too many Peers who come to the Lords at which is euphemistically called 'the end of a working life' or on retirement, Reg Underhill seized the opportunity given to him by Prime Minister Jim Callaghan with both hands.

For 40 years Reg lived and worked at the very heart of Labour politics. In his early days at Transport House he was the personal assistant to Morgan Phillips, then he filled a series of administrative roles until he arrived at the apex of that line of promotion when he was appointed National Agent in 1972. With Ron Hayward he represented the senior civil servants of the Labour Party, at a time when the Labour Government was going through great difficulties, not all stemming from its legislative programme. A strand of political philosophy calling itself the Militant Tendency took advantage of such situations and Reg was in no doubt that – unchecked –

it would be enormously damaging to the Labour Party. He presented his evidence and his analysis – as well as his solutions to the National Executive Committee, only to have his report 'lie on the table' – Labour-speak for 'take no action'. It was at his own expense that he circulated what became known as the Underhill Report to every Constituency Labour Party. The devastating consequences of ignoring that report haunt the Labour Party to this day.

He had a long spell as Labour's Northern Ireland spokesman. His life experience of seeking conciliation and unity rather than conflict and disharmony was invaluable, and he made a host of friends amongst the wide spectrum, which covers life in Northern Ireland. However, it was in the realm of local government that he became pre-eminent. Shortly after reaching the Lords he became the President of the Association of Municipal Authorities and played a prominent and effective part in the many battles of the 1980s, which circulated around the local government plane. In the legislation, which abolished the GLC, he marshalled the great swathe of affected bodies efficiently and effectively. Truly, his style, at once unassuming and authoritative, beguiled the House. His sincerity was without question and I cannot recall a single debate in which he participated when he caused either anger or resentment. His fairness was transparent to his political foes as much as to his political friends. With his long time friend Lord Stanley Clinton-Davis, they elevated Labour's stance in transport matters to one which not only earned Labour brownie points, but drew from their opposition unstinted praise for their political nous.

When I visited Flora on the day Reg died I took some red carnations, which she put in a vase alongside daffodils from their garden. We both smiled, red and yellow being Labour's colours. Reg would have liked that. The nation has lost a valuable parliamentarian, the Labour Party has lost an accomplished advocate, and many of us have lost a dear friend. Out thoughts are with Flora, her two sons and daughter at this time.

The House Magazine, 22 March 1993

Lord Willis 1918–1992

The last of six Labour Peers to die in 1992 was Ted Willis, of Sevenoaks according to the record, but for me, of Tottenham and his beloved White Hart Lane. Like millions of others I had heard of and yearned to meet the Ted Willis of screen, television and stage fame. Other tributes have leaned heavily on his outstanding talents of writing and imagination sufficiently for me to go easy on that part of his life, but what a life!

Representing Edmonton, which shares a common boundary with Tottenham, I first knew of his 'other life' through mutual friends who knew

Ted in the twenties and thirties. His was a reputation of hard political activity, which led to positives – no negatives. Charismatic as those of us who came later learned to know him; he must have been a human dynamo to those who first knew him through the struggles within the then Labour League of Youth. That he finally went off to join the Young Communist League, only to return to the Labour fold years later, is part of his turbulent youth. I have little doubt that the hard facts of life as lived in the Willis household (and many others) in those depression years helped shape his political philosophy, and certainly gave him an insight into how 'the other half lived' which made him such an outstanding advocate for Socialism.

Ted was a lovely man, most warm, open and generous. Within weeks of my entering the Lords in 1983 he had invited my wife Margaret and me to an award ceremony as his guest at one of the top tables. The Turkish Ambassador was a fellow guest, for Ted was a stout supporter of the Turkish cause, and I remember that one of the highlights of that day was to meet the actresses who received one of the top awards, from the cast of 'Widows'. A great memory, thanks to Ted. I first met Inspector Wexford through Ted. George Baker was but one of the television friends he entertained at the Lords. It was great.

I will remember Ted – and Audrey who was his lovely life partner – with great affection. His was not the delivery of an Olivier, but that of a man who knew what he was talking about. Having stood on the terraces at White Hart Lane as a boy and then graduating into the boardroom where we both were privileged to be guests of the Chairman on many occasions, he not only knew his football, he was passionate about it. Thus, when the Government tried to bring in the Football Spectators Bill to make it compulsory for fans to carry an identity card he went potty. He did more than that. He brought Irving Scholar, the then Chairman of Spurs, to address a packed meeting in the Lords. The Bill was sunk, but I like to think that it was the common sense and wisdom of Ted Willis that helped to do it. It was the same when he spoke on broadcasting and film industry matters. We all knew that he knew more about those things than anyone else, certainly more than the ministers!

If he had been spared but one more month Ted would have spoken on a topic of his own choosing: 'To call attention to the life and work of James Keir Hardie and in particular to his political philosophy and its advantages.' He had won a ballot and would have introduced it. Ted, it was a great speech. You would have been content and we would have been proud. Amen.

The House Magazine, 11 January 1993

Baroness White of Rhymney 1909–1999

Eirene White leaves an impression of orderliness and quiet authority, of decisiveness in public speaking and of kindliness towards both her friends and her political opponents in equal portions. She was one of the earlier batch of Labour Peers when she was ennobled in 1970, and by then she had lived a full life in every way, tasting high office in her chosen profession of journalism, in serving her political ambitions within her chosen party – the Labour Party – and in high offices of state, going on to fulfil her public service career when she became the Deputy Chairman of Committees in the House of Lords.

Welsh in every way and proud of it besides, she was the daughter of the famous and much respected Tom Jones who was deputy secretary to the Cabinet under four Prime Ministers: Lloyd George, Bonar Law, Ramsay MacDonald and Stanley Baldwin. He was not only a great influence on Wales. He was especially close to Lloyd George. Unlike Eirene, they were both Welsh speaking and conversed in that language often as an aid to secrecy. With such a background it is no wonder that the political influence of the time rubbed off on her, and must have accounted for her shrewdness in later life.

She made her first attempt to enter Parliament in 1945 where she failed bravely in Flint, a seat she was to capture in 1950. One of her neighbours was Cledwyn Hughes in Anglesey and from then on they formed a friendship, which was to last to this day. Cledwyn saw her appointed as his deputy at the Welsh Office in 1966 and said of her 'Eirene made a splendid deputy, not least because she was so familiar with all things appertaining to Wales. She won the respect of the whole of Wales, which does not always happen with ministers in the Welsh Office, and it was fitting that she went on to higher office. She was a true friend and will be missed.'

Eirene White gained a place on the National Executive of the Labour Party in the Women's Section without the support of the big trade unions, this marking her out as an independent spirit which she displayed throughout her membership of the National Executive, although she usually could be found amongst right wingers as opposed to those on the left. In time she was to be elected Chairman of the Party.

In 1968 we found ourselves on the back of a Co-op coal lorry in Hyde Park during a protest rally against the invasion of Prague by the Russians – she speaking for the Labour Party and I for the Co-operative Movement. Our rally was almost taken over by demented Biafrans protesting at the Civil War in their country at that time, but Eirene handled a potential crisis with a firmness and fairness, which won the day.

The House Magazine, 10 January 2000

CHAPTER 13

Reflections of Labour Peers group 1979–1997

I HAVE MORE THAN ONCE referred to 'The Great Picture' taken in 1994 showing most of the then Labour Peers who had served in a Labour Administration. I have invited some of those who are still with us to convey their views of how they found life in the Lords, and I am grateful to them all for that – and the comradeship we shared. Keep up the good fight!

Lord Merlyn-Rees of Morley and South Leeds

Merlyn Rees is one of a select group of Life Peers who retained their 'maiden name' by the simple device of hyphenating it – thus retaining the distinctive same style and custom by which he has been known at Westminster now for 45 years.

He was President of the Students' Union at the London School of Economics in 1940 where he graduated with the degree of LL.D before going into the RAF and reaching the rank of Squadron Leader. He went on into a career of teaching before he fought his first parliamentary election at Harrow East in 1955, winning Leeds and Morley in 1959 and held it until he went to the Lords in 1992. He held a series of junior posts before reaching Cabinet rank in 1974, first as Secretary of State for Northern Ireland and then Home Secretary. He was the organizer of the campaign which successfully led to Jim Callaghan following Harold Wilson as Prime Minister in 1976.

'The continuity of the composition of the House of Lords is a remarkable feature. In the Commons there is a palpable change after each General Election. A new House is formed, whereas that of the Lords seems to go on without hesitation or pause. A delight in coming here was to see and find so many of your friends from the Commons already sitting on the red benches. In the Commons all knew exactly where the enemy was – it was in front of you and across the Chamber, whereas in the Lords it is often difficult to find out where the Opposition is coming from.

'In the Commons one had a pretty good idea why we were there – the job was known and we went at it with gusto, but in the Lords I often wonder what exactly it is for. Bearing in mind that most Lords' Ministers have had little Ministerial experience, on both sides of the House Ministers perform well but in the more abrasive nature of the Commons, many of them would have been in difficulties.

'One cannot but be affected by the sense of history in the Lords. Perhaps it has something to do with the fact that the Chamber of the Lords is now 150 years old, and that of the Commons barely 50, but it is also affected by the fact that families are there who go back hundreds of years. I found that being able to serve on Cross Party Committees with very experienced Peers from industry, commerce and the armed services impressed me with the collective wisdom in this place. Something of the excitement from the Commons was created whenever we staged a successful ambush and this was needed, for it gave the less active Labour Lord a sense that he or she was part of the team, and that there was still life in us left!'

Lord Mason of Barnsley

'Coming to the Lords was like arriving on an escalator and landing on a lilo' was how Roy Mason described the difference between the two Houses. Roy had gone down the mines when was 14 years of age and he celebrated 50 years in Parliament in 2003. His Ministerial career included spells as Postmaster General, Minister of Power, President of the Board of Trade, Minister for Defence and Secretary of State for Northern Ireland. In the Commons he was perpetually in office and in Opposition – saddled with departmental briefs, but once in the Lords he had space to pursue personal interests. 'I found the atmosphere relaxing, and whilst always supporting the Labour Benches I could form alliances across the Chamber. One of the most satisfactory was with Admiral of the Fleet, Lord Lewin of Falklands fame (on the Crossbenches). We successfully finally convinced the powers that be that Bevin Boys should form part of the parade at The Cenotaph on Memorial Sunday'. He was able to enjoy such interests as designing ties, which he explains is called Cravetology, and his designs have been in demand for groups at Westminster now for many years. He is proud of that which he designed for George Thomas when Speaker, which features a Daffodil – and the Mace! He developed his interest in First Day covers and has a unique collection of them sufficient to have become a philatelist of distinction. He is especially proud of the First Day cover which bears the signatures of no less than eight Prime Ministers.

He found the opportunity to participate in Question Time enjoyable, and is always involved when issues such as mining, Yorkshire or smoking are raised. He is an active member of many Parliamentary Groups such as the Lords and Commons Pipe and Cigar Club and the Angling Club. Undoubtedly his activity as the Chair of the Yorkshire section of the Princes's Trust, which he was for 15 years, has been good work done by stealth. 'It is greatly satisfying to know that during the period we were able to start more than 2,000 young people on the road towards starting their own business; and to see years later that most of them had succeeded'.

One of his most successful campaigns in the Lords led to a change in the law. A great devotee of Working Men's Clubs, he was dismayed to find that buying wine there 'by the glass' was not the practice elsewhere. ('It was rip off waiting to be rectified') and he promoted and finally secured legislative change whereby restaurants and clubs have to offer 'Wine by the Glass' as well as by the bottle.

He was made a Deputy Lieutenant for South Yorkshire in 1992 and a Member of the Privy Council in 1967. There are few with a better attendance record in the House of Lords.

Lord McIntosh of Haringey

Andrew McIntosh was educated at the Royal Grammar School, High Wycombe, Jesus College Oxford and the Ohio State University. He served as a Councillor, first on the Hornsey Council, and then on the London Borough of Haringey Council and the Greater London Council from 1973 to 1983, where he was the Leader from 1980–81. He entered the Lords in 1983. Prior to that, he had run his own Market Research Company. He became the Deputy Leader of the Opposition in 1992 during that time he spoke from the Frontbench on Education and Science, the Environment and Home Affairs. He was the Chairman of the Fabian Society in 1985–86. When Labour came to power in 1997 he became the Government Deputy Chief Whip.

'I served under a great Leader of the Labour Peers in Cledwyn Hughes. He brought to his position that sense of having been in power, as indeed he had, with his illustrious Ministerial record in the Commons, but he had also been a distinguished Chairman of the Parliamentary Labour Party. In that role he had to apply the wisdom – even cunning – that he had developed in North Wales, and he was able to synthesize the varying strands of Labour politicians making up the Labour Peers Group. It was a privilege.

'One thing the Labour Group didn't have which I regretted – and still do – is a 'tearoom or dining place' we could call our own. Yes, we have facilities, but they are shared, and what we need is a place where we can gossip and discuss things partywise.

'One of my roles for the then Opposition was to cultivate the friendship and eventual support of some on other benches. When, as we were in such a minority, we had to appreciate help from a handful, for often they made the difference.

'Looking across the Chamber I found that the Conservative Frontbench suffered – to our delight – from having at times almost every post filled with

Hereditary Peers. That is the way it was – but they failed to utilize many from the Commons with Ministerial experience who were left to languish on the Backbenches. Now they have rectified that error – and we are the losers now that we are in Government.

'My stint with the Home Office brief brought aggravations and anxieties from the changes wrought in the Commons by both Tory Home Secretaries changing Ministerial styles and policies – and equally from changes made by Labour Shadow Ministers in Opposition. All in all, the Labour Peers Group in Opposition was a great bench and a privilege to be part of.'

Lord Judd of Portsea

Frank Judd entered the Commons in 1966 as the Member of Parliament for Portsmouth West, having first contested Sutton and Cheam in 1959. He quickly made his mark as Parliamentary Private Secretary to Tony Greenwood at the Ministry of Housing. Later he was Parliamentary Under Secretary of State for the Navy, then Minister of State at the Department for Overseas Development, followed by being the Minister of State at the Foreign and Commonwealth Office. Out of office until returned to the Lords in 1991 he became the Director of Voluntary Services Overseas (VSO) and then Director of Oxfam. In Opposition in the Lords, he was on the frontbench leading on Overseas Aid, Foreign Affairs and Education. He was educated at the City of London School and the London School of Economics.

'When I met the likes of Cledwyn Hughes in the Lords I knew I was home, for he represented the kind of Labour politician I admired. It was fun to be amongst some of the giants I had grown up with. There was a sense of comradeship which was palpable. We all knew why we had been sent to the House of Lords, what was required of us and how to go about achieving it. The small teams of colleagues who met with few support staff to work out tactics all had a sense of literally being in the frontline. The odds against us ever defeating the Government were huge, yet we managed to do that often, and when we did it was a great boost to our morale.

'I would say that the great difference between being in the Commons and the Lords was the recognition that in the Commons it was all about political power, whereas in the Lords it was all about political influence. It seems to me that we had an Education Bill almost every year and so I was involved almost constantly in fighting the good fight against the kind of policies I found detestable. There was one advantage. Whenever I had to listen to the kind of prejudice and narrow-minded policies from the opposite frontbench I had my faith in my philosophy strengthened. I listened to them and I knew why I was a socialist.'

Rt Hon Lord Healey of Riddlesden

'In 1952, during the election campaign which brought me into the Commons as MP for South East Leeds, I spent a pleasant Saturday afternoon adjudicating a public speaking contest for the Labour League of Youth and gave the first prize to a young Yorkshire lass called Betty Boothroyd'. (It was the same Betty Boothroyd who had brought the fraternal greetings from Labour to the Co-op Youth the previous year when I was their National President, at Wortley Hall, Sheffield).

Denis Healey had come to the Commons after seven years as the International Secretary of the Labour Party, during which he had built up many contacts with the emerging Socialist Groups in the world, but especially in Europe. 'They all thought highly of Labour and Clement Attlee, for it was we who had been the first country after the war to bring in a Labour Government and had set them on the same road'. He had been a student at Balliol College Oxford, and before that he had attended Bradford Grammar School at the same time as Barbara Castle was a pupil at Bradford Grammar School for Girls. During the war he saw service in North Africa and Italy and reached the rank of Major, being mentioned in Despatches. Altogether, in Opposition, and in Government, he served in either Cabinet or Shadow Cabinet from 1954 to 1992; when he went into the Lords. 'I came from a Commons which when I entered it could be easily identified, for most Labour Members really wore cloth caps, and most Tories wore top hats. There was then a real class atmosphere, and partisanship was the order of the day.

'In the Commons one of the most dramatic episodes was that during the Suez Crisis, and one of the most dramatic speeches made was that of Enoch Powell during the debates on the Hola Camp scandal. I always enjoyed the cut and thrust of debate and appreciated the wit of Geoffrey Howe whom I had ridiculed by describing one of his attempts to criticize me as being savaged by a dead sheep – only for him later to categorize a speech by me as feeling like being nuzzled by a friendly ram. I had to assert that that remark was close to accusing me of necrophilia!

'Equally, when my very good Yorkshire friend Alice Bacon came to the Lords I enjoyed her telling me that after she had completed the ritual and went to have her hand shaken by the Lord Chancellor, sitting upon the Woolsack, it was Quinton Hogg who greeted her by saying 'Bacon – meet Hogg!

'I found the flummery and ancient rituals and procedures of the Lords ludicrous and well worth being swept away, but I valued highly meeting again many with whom I had served in my Cabinet posts, such as Lords Craig, Guthrie, Carver and Bramall, and Lords Carrington and Howe. I came to like the style in the Lords where you could say what you thought and make friends across the Chamber easily. Nowadays, there are few if any in the Commons who fought in the Second World War, whilst in the Lords there are still many. I would say that Labour has a good frontbench with some who would easily reach Cabinet rank if in the Commons and I think especially of the likes of Patricia Hollis who is by any ranking – a star'.

Lord Haskel of Higher Broughton

Simon Haskel came into the Lords in 1993 with a record as an industrialist, especially as the Chairman of the Perrots Group and associated companies operating in Yorkshire. He was the Co-Chairman of the All Party Group for Manufacturing and Industry and of the Labour Finance and Industry Group. He served in the Opposition Whips Office in the House of Lords from 1994 to 1997 and served as a Government Whip when Labour gained power in 1997.

'My memory of those days in Opposition are of the spirit and camaraderie amongst Labour colleagues. I quickly saw that we had many amongst us who had come from the Commons, and they were always looked up to and respected for their service there. In fact, many of them were household names. But we also had non-Commons members such as Victor Mishcon who dazzled not only us but the House, and especially the Government whenever he performed at "the box"!

'I found my feet in the Lords mainly through my service as a Whip. Meeting every week to contemplate the week's business, we were able to get an over view of what to do and how to do it. With my own portion of Labour Peers to look after, we had to become knowledgeable as to their needs, weaknesses and strengths. Never a week went by without my making sure that I knew what was happening to them, and that they knew where to find me if they were in trouble. We had little power as Whips, so we had to rely on "friendly persuasion" to convince them with argument and, as a last resort, to appeal to their sense of loyalty to the Party. We had no power or goodies to dispense but we achieved remarkably high levels of support in divisions.

'One of the things I learned was to make friends with the Opposition – especially their frontbench. We had the power to make their jobs difficult if they did not help us to do our job. In return we could understand and appreciate the Government point of view. It now works when Labour is the Government. Friendships forged when roles were reversed give former Ministers access to Civil Servants, just as we had with their departments when in Opposition.

'Relying on lobby organizations and interest groups for briefings was very helpful but I always regretted the fact that they assumed that, by giving them to us, we could affect miracles. We had to be careful and not build up their hopes too high. The highlight of many a week was to bring off an ambush against the odds. Yes, it was a bit of a game, but it was fun!'

Lord Clinton-Davis of Hackney

After three unsuccessful attempts to be elected to the Commons, Stanley Clinton-Davis became the Member of Parliament for Hackney in 1970 and served there until 1983. He was educated at the Hackney Downs School, and went on after service on the Borough of Hackney Council, to become the Mayor of Hackney. In the Labour Government of 1974 to 1979 he served as a Parliamentary Under-Secretary at the Department of Trade, where he specialized in Prices and Consumer Protection, Shipping and Aviation matters. Later he became a Commissioner to the European Community from 1985 to 1989; serving as Environment Commissioner and entered the Lords in 1990, where he filled a number of posts for the Opposition.

'My overwhelming memory of our period in Opposition in the Lords is that the talent resting on the Labour benches was under-used. By comparison with the experience available in the Commons, we had every rank of Ministerial responsibility waiting to be used, and it rarely was. I blame a culture for this neglect on the fact that, coming from the Commons, I plead guilty to knowing next to nothing of what went on in the Lords. There was not enough collaboration or co-ordination between Labour in both Houses. Despite this we had some notable successes, modestly in the field of Transport where I performed. Dear Reg Underhill, although without Commons experience, amply demonstrated his political nous, and we were able to forge alliances with Liberals and Conservatives and Crossbenchers which caused the Government much trouble. Of course, we all enjoyed tweaking the nose of the Government by staging successful surprise votes but, we could have made a great mark if we had developed a better use of the talents we had and by a more structured approach to using Labour's strengths in both Commons and Lords. There were too few meetings between Labour colleagues in both Houses and I believe that made us less effective than we might otherwise have been.

'Although we did not do if often, when we did beat the Tories it brought huge delight. The excitement amongst Labour Peers – elderly Labour Peers – in the hours leading up to "ambush time" was palpable, and to see Ted picking up the Vote Result and marching towards the Woolsack was great. It was a great morale booster and made the inconvenience of staying late worthwhile. It was good for morale at the other end of the Palace, for with hardly any successes there, Labour MPs shared in our satisfaction. I also thought that the quality of our Front bench was good, and that of the Tories not so good.'

Lord Carter of Devizes

Denis Carter came into the Lords in 1985 having fought the seat of Basingstoke in 1970. He is one of a rare Labour breed – he has a background in agriculture. Before entering the Lords he had been in great demand on all things agricultural, serving on Labour Party Policy forums for many years, being in close touch with all the Labour Party agricultural spokespersons and helping to shape policy. When he entered the Lords he became a spokesman on Agriculture, Social Services and Health, taking a special interest in disabled issues. He served in the Labour Whips Office and for a time was the Deputy Chief Whip, and became the Government Chief Whip when Labour won the 1997 General Election.

'My over-riding memory is how congenial it was to work in a small group with like minded convinced colleagues. We knew the limitations of what we could do, but I quickly found that there was often a spirit, like being holed up in The Alamo. We enjoyed showing and sometimes shouting our defiance at the Government benches in the confident and certain belief that one day we would be on the Government benches – and so it proved.

'I speak of the days when all that Labour Peers had was the help of one Research Assistant – before the Cranborne Money came on stream – and thus our research and support help was severely limited. We relied on the good will of lobby groups and they were very good. We achieved very little without the help and votes from other parts of the House. We were respected and I know that Willie Whitelaw recognized the farce, which was the disparity in numbers, and personally recommended that Labour be given more Life Peers.

'I learned that in the Lords there are many Peers who, from family links, know a lot about the needs of the disabled and the severely handicapped and with the looser whipping system in the Lords it was often possible to forge an all-party alliance which helped to change legislation.

'I thoroughly enjoyed my time in the Whips Office, and took great pleasure in creating the right circumstances for "the ambush". Whilst there were many on the Tory benches who had political skills, many of us on the Labour benches had been active more at a grass roots level than most. The sheer joy of defeating the Government was reward enough for the hard work it entailed, if only to watch the faces of Labour's great and good break out in smiles as I carried the result paper up to the Chairman on the Woolsack. They were great days and helped to forge that feeling of comradeship which sometimes is missing these days.'

Lord Bruce of Donington

'Before the war I was a Tory and when the war started I was in the Territorial Army. I enlisted as a private and finished as a major. I ended my war on the Staff of the Supreme Headquarters of the Allied Expeditionary Force – SHAEF – under the direct control of Ike Eisenhower. I fought the 1945 General Election in Portsmouth North and won. During the campaign we discovered that our Tory opponent was putting out a poster with a huge photograph of himself and the words 'Vote for Captain Grey – Churchill's Man', so we put out one with my photograph which said 'Vote for Major Bruce – the People's Man'. It was a stimulating contest but I lost it at the next election. During the war I had been in correspondence with Aneurin Bevan and within a short while of us both meeting up when I reached the Commons, he invited me to be his PPS – Parliamentary Private Secretary. It brought me on the inside in the creation of the National Health Service and his brand of socialism has never left me'.

Trained as a Chartered Accountant, he found this training stood him in good stead, especially later when he served in the European Parliament at the time when Westminster sent the British delegates 'from the centre' and not by direct election. He became an acknowledged authority on budgetary matters and brought this specialized skill into the Chamber of the House of Lords, which he entered on the recommendation of Harold Wilson in 1974.

'When Harold sent for me I feared it may have been for a job which took me away from earning my living, so I was glad that I went to the Lords which allowed me to do just that. People have yet to realize that to go the Lords during the period when you have to earn a living can be a mixed blessing'.

Donald Bruce fought his Portsmouth seat once more (before making way for Alma Birk, who subsequently joined him in the Lords) and also fought the seat of The Wrekin – twice. He quickly made his mark when he accepted the Treasury and Economic brief and spoke from Labour's front bench for more than ten years.

He earned the reputation of always speaking his mind, and always meaning what he said. 'I found in the Lords that I could influence Party policy on the margin, due to the more relaxed regime of discipline, and was able to pursue my interests; especially on the European issue alongside a notable band of others who shared my deep scepticism of the Community. It got away with far too much, and from the backbenches I was able to warn the Party of the folly of its ways. Having reached the grand old age of 90 I still value the opportunities membership provides. My political enemies were not always across the Chamber, but I was always conscious of the danger of Labour being divided.'

Baroness (Patricia) Hollis of Heigham

Patricia Hollis came to the Lords with one of the most impressive records of service and achievement there is. Born in Plymouth, she went on to an academic record of some brilliance: Cambridge University (BA, MA); University of California; Columbia University, New York; Nuffield College, Oxford (MA, DPhil, Hon DLitt); Anglia Polytechnic University. Having gained honours with her work on 'Labour Women', she went on to produce 'The Pauper Press'; 'Class and Class Conflict 1815–50'; 'Women in Public 1850–1900'; 'Ladies Elect: Women in English Local Government 1850–1900'; and she was the author of *The Life of Jennie Lee*.

She became a Lecturer, then Reader and, finally Dean of the Arts Faculty at the University of Norwich, and is a Fellow of the Royal Historical Society. She was a member of Norwich City Council from 1968 to 1991, latterly as Leader, and fought three General Elections for Yarmouth, twice in 1974 and in 1979. When she came to the Lords, she served in the Labour Whips Office for five years and became the principal spokesperson for Social Security from 1990 to 1997. When Labour came to office in 1997 she became the Minister in the Lords responsible for Social Security and Pensions. She was made a member of the Privy Council in 2002.

'It was fun in opposition, for although we knew the arithmetic was against us, it did not stop us fighting the good fights. From my experience elsewhere, I had learned the value of forming alliances across the Chamber, and especially of likeminded women on other benches. I also learned to form alliances with sympathetic colleagues from other parties who could – and would – be prepared on special issues to come into the Labour lobby. When these accounted for, say, five or six votes, they made the difference. I also appreciated that whilst it was fun to tweak the Government's nose, if the issue we won on was small beer then it would be overturned in the Commons. So I concentrated on achieving victories on matters of substance, and if this had been achieved with all-party support, the likelihood of making it stick was much better. Votes from the Crossbenches and the Bishops often helped!

'It was a tragedy for all of us when John MacKay died. He had been my principal opponent and I respected his skills – and he mine. Some of our greatest battles centred around the issues of family law, divorce and pensions – especially for women after divorce. John MacKay once told me that as a Minister, he had more than nine hundred civil servants to back him up, but over a period, I had the backing of a handful – but what a handful! On one Bill, I had the invaluable support of Andrew McIntosh, Brenda Dean (trade union leader), Bill McCarthy (industrial relations guru), John Eatwell (Neil Kinnock's economic advisor), Betty Lockwood (ex-Chair of Equal

Opportunities Commission), Simon Haskel (industrial chief) and Muriel Turner (Occupational Pensions Board). What a team! I was proud to lead them – more than once – to victory!'

Lord Archer of Sandwell QC

Peter Archer hails from the Black Country, and entered the Commons to represent Rowley Regis and Tipton in 1966 before representing Warley West from 1974 until he went to the Lords in 1992. He was called to the Bar more than 50 years ago, in 1952, and became Solicitor General from 1974 to 1979. He served in the Shadow Cabinet from 1981 to 1987 and filled a host of shadow posts in both Commons and Lords. He took a keen interest in Human Rights and was the Chair of the British Section of Amnesy from 1971 to 1974. Currently he is the Chairman of the Council of Tribunals.

'I suppose that one of the striking features of the Lords, by comparison with the Commons, must be the less partisan atmosphere, although it would be a mistake to misjudge that for the absence of political atmosphere. It is less political in many ways, but when the chips are down one can see – on all benches, including the Crossbenches – a real reflection of the Party battles being fought down the Corridor. The whipping system in the Lords is much less rigid, but having served under the more harsh regime in the Commons I was always happy to conform in the Lords. Like many others coming from the Commons, I confess that I ought to have known more about how the Lords works, and I take my hat off to those many ex-Commons colleagues and others who came in from outside straight onto Labour's front bench and performed magnificently.

'I am immensely proud of the fact that I was responsible in the Lords for removing the last vestige of Capital Punishment from the Statute Book. After the great reforms of the 1960s and 70s there still remained subject to Capital Punishment such crimes as that of setting fire to Her Majesty's Shipyards, and the deflowering of the King's Daughters. I helped to get rid of that threat. Equally, together with Greville Janner, I have been responsible for managing the funds available to repay to the rightful owners the appropriated assets taken by the Nazis, mainly from Jews. That work goes on.'

First Day in the House of Lords by Richard Acton

'I took my seat in the House of Lords on Wednesday 13 December 1989. For a Hereditary Peer, the procedure was simple. Having decided to sit as a Crossbencher, a space was left for me at the right end of the front crossbench. I duly sat there, and indeed knelt there during prayers. Then I took the oath, signed the roll, and shook hands with the Lord Chairman of Committees, who was sitting on the woolsack. He apologized and explained that the Lord Chancellor was away. There seemed to be a lot of cries of "Hear! Hear!", but I later discovered that the House greeting for a Hereditary Peer was very muted compared to the roar for a Life Peer.

'After leaving the Chamber, I walked back to the Peers Lobby, re-entered, and now formally took my seat in the selfsame place at the front of the Crossbenches. From my immediate right came a friendly voice: "You will need an Order Paper." I looked up, and on the Labour Privy Council Bench at right angles to me sat Lord Callaghan with a twinkle in his eye. Next to him sat Lord Wilson. Lord Callaghan handed me an Order Paper. I glanced at it, and then emboldened by the occasion, said: "Would you sign it for me?" He beamed and took the paper. On it he wrote: "Jim Callaghan with best wishes to Richard Acton on the first day he arrived!" He handed the paper to Lord Wilson, who in turn wrote: "And from Wilson of Rievaulx".

'That Order Paper, with the signatures of two former Prime Ministers, takes pride of place in a scrapbook my wife made for me a unique souvenir of my first day in the House of Lords.

Lord Williams of Elvel

Charles Williams is the son of a Professor of Divinity at Oxford and is married to Jane Portal, who was one of Winston Churchill's secretaries in the post-war period. Whilst at Oxford he was Captain of the University Cricket team, preceded by Colin Cowdrey and followed by Mike Smith who both went on to captain England. He went on to play for Essex. Following a career as a banker he became the Chairman of the Prices Commission in 1977. He entered the Lords in 1985, where he subsequently became the Deputy Leader to Cledwyn Hughes, during which he spoke from the Frontbench on Trade and Industry, Defence and Environment. He led on the exhaustingly complex and detailed Financial Services Bill, the Companies Bill and the Copyright Bill. He has written highly acclaimed books on the lives of General de Gaulle, Don Bradman, Conrad Adenauer and Marshall Petain.

'I was never a great fan of the staged "ambush", although I appreciate that they served a purpose in the great tapestry of Opposition. I enjoyed tweaking the nose of the Government, and having learned the procedures of conduct and debate from a study of what is called "The Red Book", I used this knowledge to the advantage of Labour Peers. Slackness on the part of Government Whips could open up such possibilities as "Counting Out" the House if Government Whips failed to keep sufficient troops to head off a late vote. I also enjoyed being entrusted by my colleagues with the task of leading on Labour Debates where I could deploy Labour policy at some length.'

Lord Richard of Ammanford

Ivor Richard was born and educated in Llanelly before going on to Cheltenham College and to Pembroke College, Oxford, where he was made an Honorary Fellow in 1981. He was called to the Bar in the Inner Temple and became a Bencher in 1985, having become a Queen's Counsel in 1971. In the Commons, he represented Barons Court from 1964 to 1974, having contested South Kensington in 1959. He served as PPS (Parliamentary Private Secretary) to the Secretary of State for Defence from 1966–67 and became Parliamentary Under-Secretary for the Army at the Ministry of Defence from 1969–70. He was appointed the UK's Permanent Representative at the United Nations from 1974 to 1979 and an EEC Commissioner, for Social Affairs, from 1981 to 1984. He was elected Leader of the Opposition in the Lords in 1992 and when Labour came to power in 1977 became the Leader of the Lords.

Ivor tells of the time he was invited by the then Leader of the Labour Party, Neil Kinnock, to consider going to the Lords. He was suitably flattered and said that this would give him a new lease of life; to which Neil replied 'Boyo, this is not a lease it is a freehold.'

His first day in the Lords took him to the Long Table in the Peers Dining Room, where, by convention, Peers sit next to whoever is sitting there. He tells that this man was a complete stranger who, after a few minutes, looked up and said: 'I see they have changed the pictures'. When Ivor had to say that he did not know this, the Peer said: 'My grandfather's picture has been hanging here for many years – and now he has gone.' Ivor never saw him again.

'One of the problems with the Lords is that everyone is so polite. Peers actually listen to what you have to say, unlike in the Commons. You have actually got to have something to say, and it is not always easy. Manner and courtesy are the order of the day, and this is to the benefit of the Lords over the Commons. My recollections from time to time in Opposition are of having listened to, and made friends with some great people. To look around and recall seeing such luminaries as ex-Prime Ministers Jim Callaghan, Harold Wilson, Alex Douglas-Home and Margaret Thatcher – and such Foreign Secretaries as Peter Carrington, with Home Secretaries Merlyn Rees, Douglas Hurd, Willie Whitelaw and Secretaries of State for Northern Ireland such as Roy Mason, Merlyn Rees again, Peter Brooke and Patrick Mayhew, makes the Lords a special place.

'The Crossbenches house many of the great military men of the recent years and on the Liberal Democrat benches there have been such characters as Nancy Seear, Roy Jenkins, David Steel and a special friend, John Harris. And I have not failed to note that the original "Gang of Four" – Shirley Williams, Roy Jenkins, Bill Rodgers and David Owen, all came eventually to the Lords. Truly, life takes many twists and turns!'

Lord Barnett of Heywood and Royton

Joel Barnett first attempted to enter the House of Commons in 1959 when he contested the seat of Runcorn. He then served as the Member of Parliament for Heywood and Royton from 1964 to 1983. An accountant, he quickly made his mark in the Commons and was the official Opposition Spokesman on Financial and Economic Affairs from 1970 to 1974. On Labour forming the Government in 1974 he was appointed Chief Secretary to the Treasury and was a member of that impressive team of Treasury Ministers under the guidance of the Chancellor of the Exchequer, Denis Healey. Another who served there with distinction, and now sits alongside him in the Lords, is Robert Sheldon. Joel Barnett was the Treasury Spokesman in the Lords before leaving the frontbench on becoming the Deputy Chairman of the BBC. He is a product of the Manchester Central High School and a lifetime supporter of Manchester United.

'As a Treasury Spokesman in the Commons, I had more than my fair share of winding up economic debates late at night, after many members had what is euphemistically called "dined well". It made for a boisterous time, which I always enjoyed, and the difference here in the Lords is quite remarkable. Here you are actually allowed to not only make your own speech but to listen to those of other Peers, and to be allowed to reply to the points made – without interruption – a treat rarely extended by anyone to anyone in the Commons.

'The other great change and difference from my Commons days and now, is that then, proceedings in either House were not televised. The Lords led the way in the 1980s and the Commons followed. However it is described, it changed the atmosphere in both Houses, and I am not sure that it is for the better'.

Lord Gladwin of Clee

Derek Gladwin entered the Lords with a considerable record of service to trade unionism and to the Labour Party. He served as the Chairman of the Standing Orders Committee at the Labour Party Conference from 1974 to 1990, after many years working his way through the ranks of the General and Municipal Workers Union. He reached the high position of National Industrial Officer, and went on to become the Southern Regional Secretary. He is a graduate of the London School of Economics and of Ruskin College and was a Visiting Fellow at Nuffield College, Oxford from 1978 to 1986. He was a Board Member of the Post Office from 1972 to 1994. He then entered the Lords in 1994 where he served in the Opposition Whips Office from 1994 to 1997. Sadly he died in 2002.

'Working in the Whips Office taught me to focus on those members for which I carried some responsibility. You learned to know those of your flock you could rely on, and those you could not. For instance, although Marcia Williams was very ill, whenever we needed her she would tell me that she would be there – and she was. A great trooper.

'Having come into the Lords with a strong experience in trade unions, it was a great pleasure to find that from differing strands of the Party there was a definite group feeling. No one tried to pull rank. One of my strongest memories is that the leadership, frontbenchers and backbenchers all felt that they were part of a team. That is something that is missing now that we are in Government. It is inevitable that when Ministers and Whips are so very busy there is a tendency for them to 'pop in and pop out'; and present day backbenchers notice this and are somewhat sad. When in Opposition they were constantly around, all over the place, using their contacts with backbenchers and being available to guide and encourage.

Although mounting and steering the ambush to a successful conclusion caused much organization, and not a few heart-stopping moments, they were all worthwhile. We all knew that any victory could, and often was, turned over in the Commons, but the feeling that every now and again this disparate group of Labour Peers could inflict humiliation on such serried ranks of mainly hereditary Peers brought great joy and satisfaction to comrades, young and not so young. All told I look back on my time in the Whips Office as part of my learning curve in many things, not least in man management which built upon my time as a trade union organizer – and I am grateful for that experience'.

Index